SIMON NGUBENI

Communion
WITH
CHRIST

A HANDBOOK ON HOW TO ABIDE IN HIM

PUBLICATION DETAILS

Title: *Communion with Christ: A Handbook on How to Abide in Him*

© 2016 Simon Ngubeni

Website: www.simonngubeni.co.za

All rights reserved

ISBN: 978-0-620-71500-3 (print)

ISBN: 978-0-620-71501-3 (kindle)

Published September 2016

Johannesburg, South Africa

Dedication & Acknowledgments

To my father, mother, younger sister and best friend; your love and support have made life a joy. You are a constant source of inspiration.

I dedicate this book to the friends and individuals who have been honest enough to share their spiritual experiences and challenges with me. Your testimonies and victories have driven me to get this book out. God bless you.

Authors Preface

Every Christian has the privilege of abiding in Christ, and a constant communion with God is the only right experience for the Christian to have. While many may see this as an unreachable aspiration, it has never been God's intention for His followers to have an unstable experience in their walk with Him.

Two years before publishing this book, I was requested to present a series of presentations for a seminar on how professed Christians may have an intimate and consistent walk with Jesus. This was for a mission conference attended by a predominantly youthful group, eager to be equipped to be of better service. The request for the presentations came at a time when I was going through an intense personal study on the subject; I was not content with the idea of an inconsistent Christian walk. That season of study resulted in a series of presentations under the theme *"Communion with Christ."*

After the conference, I continued to receive requests for the material and notes from the seminar. From the testimonies received at the end of that conference, as well as through various other encounters afterwards, it became increasingly evident that an experience of abiding in Christ is foreign to many professed Christians--even among some who may be actively engaged in religious service. The need for a clear, simple and practical outline on how to have an intimate and consistent devotional walk with Christ became strikingly apparent. To give such guidance is what this material aims to do; hence the idea of a "handbook".

The chapters that make up the book are mostly drawn from a series of Bible study handouts. In compiling this material, these chapters have since been adapted and edited to follow a reader-friendly format. The ideas and points shared throughout the book are all primarily Biblical, while various other authors and passages are cited for their simple and illustrative expressions of the points made. A majority of these citations are gathered from the vast collection of writings from bestselling author, Ellen White. Where this is the case, the author is often not mentioned in the references in order to avoid repetition.

It may be important to note that the most fruitful reading of the book may be gained by going through it slowly. Even to a generally fast reader who may wish to go through a quick initial reading, I would encourage a slower second reading through the book.

At the end of each chapter is a series of questions related to the overall subject of that chapter. These include questions received while presenting the material in various places, as well as questions that relate to general experiences that a believer may face. The hope is that the content of each chapter will give substantial answers to the questions listed.

It can be said that *Communion with Christ* is most beneficial to a Christian who seeks to know how they may have a richer and more sustained walk with Jesus. Throughout each chapter we consider both foundational principles as well as practical points for having a meaningful devotional life. I write with the confidence that those new and "old" in their Christian experience will find value therein.

It is my hope that the content of this book will have the same (if not greater) impact on the reader as it has had on myself as the writer. In writing as a layperson, the weighty themes of the plan of salvation & the Christian experience are shared in their simplicity and practical application to everyday life. My wish is that through this book every reader may be able to grab hold of the blessing that it is our right and privilegeto have: a real and constant communion with Christ.

-- Simon M. Ngubeni

Walking With God

O let me walk with Thee, my God,
As Enoch walked in days of old;
Place Thou my trembling hand in Thine,
And sweet communion with me hold;
Even though the path I may not see,
Yet, Jesus, let me walk with Thee.

I cannot, dare not, walk alone;
The tempest rages in the sky,
A thousand snares beset my feet,
A thousand foes are lurking nigh.
Still Thou the raging of the sea,
O Master! Let me walk with Thee.

If I may rest my hand in Thine,
I'll count the joys of earth but loss,
And firmly, bravely journey on;
I'll bear the banner of the cross
Till Zion's glorious gates I see;
Yet, Savior, let me walk with Thee.

-- L. D. Avery-Stuttle

Contents:

I

Introduction | Consecration

The Call to Abide

Picture the scene; it's the last supper and Jesus has just given His disciples a demonstration of true humility in washing their feet. In the cool of evening, Jesus lets the disciples know that they will not be seeing Him for some time. Leaving them with the promise of the Holy Spirit, Jesus encourages His disciples with words which apply just as directly to His followers today:

> "Abide in Me, and I in you. As the branch cannot bear fruit of it-self, unless it abides in the vine, neither can you, unless you abide in Me. "I am the vine, you are the branches. He who abides in Me, and I in him, bears much fruit; for without Me you can do noth-ing" John 15:4-5 NKJV

Christ's call to His followers to "abide" in Him, and how that can take place, is the overall weight and substance of this book. To begin with, let us consider the crucial points in Jesus' words that will serve as the foundation of the various thoughts throughout the book.

The first point to consider is that Christ's call and intention for those who follow Him has always been for them to have an intimate and continual relationship with Him. This intimate relationship is seen in the illustration of a vine and a branch. It was never Jesus' intention that His followers should have an unstable (sometimes in and sometimes out) Christian experience. Rather, Jesus' call to those who follow Him is that they may likewise *abide* in Him. Such an ex-perience is what is meant by the title *Communion with Christ*.

The second thing to note is that the same way a branch cannot bear any fruit unless it is abiding in the vine, neither can we make any step of advance in the Christian life apart from being intimately connected to Christ. The experience of abiding in Christ is the only true way to bear fruit in the Christian life. What this means is that the reason behind not bearing fruit in the Christian life is primar-ily due to not abiding in Christ; not having a vital connection with Him.

The third, and perhaps most crucial, thing to consider through-out the chapters that follow is contained in the words "without Me you can do nothing." All that Jesus ever asks us to do can be done only through His aid. Even so, the very act of abiding in Christ--and maintaining an intimate communion with Him--can be carried out only through the aid received from Christ Himself.

In this relationship, Christ is the supporting vine and we are the dependent branches. The roles are thus distinguished and the branch cannot hope to bear fruit of itself without abiding in the vine.

With these points in mind, our first priority must be to obtain a knowledge of, and a vital connection with, Jesus Himself.

"Acquaint now thyself with Him, and be at peace: thereby good shall come unto thee." Job 22:21

The Challenge to Abiding

By definition, the word "abide" means to remain, to continue and to dwell. In order to thus "abide in Christ", one needs to first be *in* Christ. This is why the first and greatest question with regards to abiding is the question of whether one is in fact "in Christ."

There are two main hindrances to abiding in Christ: The first is the condition of not being in Christ. The second hindrance is that of not being in Him *entirely*. This is the thought behind the words:

"You have no communion with God because you are not united to Christ." Testimonies for the Church, vol.5 p.49

I have come to learn, over the short years of my experience, that this challenge is common among many. The idea of a roller-coaster comes to mind, where the experience is sometimes a steady progression upwards and, at other times, a speedy ride down.

What we must consider is that this is not what Jesus desires for us. When He called us, He called us to abide, and it is a part of His work to free us from this experience.

Walking with God

The Bible and history give numerous examples of men and women who had the experience that we are describing. Enoch is described as a man who, having walked with God, had the experience of abiding in Christ.

"Enoch walked with God: and he was not; for God took him." Genesis 5:24

Enoch is described as being a man who walked with God. This is because his experience was one of an intimate and continued communion with God.

"By faith Enoch was translated… for before his translation he had this testimony, that he pleased God. But without faith it is impossible to please him: for he that cometh to God must believe that he is, and that He is a rewarder of them that diligently seek Him." Hebrews 11:5-6

Notice how Enoch's attitude is described. As one who walked with God, he had the mind-set of seeking God diligently. He had it in his mind that God not only exists, but that He is the kind of God who rewards those who diligently seek after Him. This is a wholehearted ambition:

"And you will seek Me and find Me, when you search for Me with all your heart." Jeremiah 29:13 NKJV

If we are to walk with God as Enoch did, it will be the result of a wholehearted desire to unite with Him.

To hold communion with God is not a casual, shallow experience; but we have the opportunity of being intimately united with Him, as closely as a branch is to a vine. This must be what we seek with the whole heart.

The Most Essential Element

With the above points in mind, the first and most essential aspect to communion with Christ is for one to make a complete surrender of themselves to Jesus and be willing to also remain surrendered.

"We may leave off many bad habits, for the time we may part company with Satan; but without a vital connection with God, through the surrender of ourselves to Him moment by moment, we shall be overcome. Without a personal acquaintance with Christ, and a continual communion, we are at the mercy of the enemy, and shall do his bidding in the end." The Desire of Ages p.324

4

What Seeking God Involves

1. Bible Study

"And you will seek Me and find Me, when you search for Me with all your heart." Jeremiah 29:13 NKJV

Seeking God involves searching for Him. But where should this search take place? Jesus answers this for us:

"You search the Scriptures, for in them you think you have eternal life; and these are they which testify of Me." John 5:39 NKJV

Thus, Bible study is a means by which we are to seek after God.

2. Prayer

In his efforts to seek for God, the prophet Daniel sought for Him through prayer, supplication and fasting. He writes:

"I set my face unto the Lord God, to seek by prayer and supplications, with fasting, and sackcloth, and ashes." Daniel 9:3

3. Meditation

"Blessed is the man who walks not in the counsel of the wicked, nor stands in the way of sinners, nor sits in the seat of scoffers; but his delight is in the law of the Lord, and on His law he meditates day and night. He is like a tree planted by streams of water that yields its fruit in its season, and its leaf does not wither. In all that he does, he prospers" Psalms 1:1-3 ESV

Meditation results in being rooted & planted like a tree by rivers of water, it plays a part in the experience of abiding in Christ.

Christ's Devotional Life

All the points listed above (*Bible Study, Prayer* and *Meditation*) were an active part of Jesus' devotional life.

"He studied the word of God, and His hours of greatest happiness were found when He could turn aside from the scene of His labors to go into the fields, to meditate in the quiet valleys, to hold com-

munion with God on the mountainside or amid the trees of the forest. The early morning often found Him in some secluded place, meditating, searching the Scriptures, or in prayer. With the voice of singing He welcomed the morning light. With songs of thanksgiving He cheered His hours of labor and brought heaven's gladness to the toilworn and disheartened." The Ministry of Healing p.52

"Satan well knows that all whom he can lead to neglect prayer and the searching of the Scriptures, will be overcome by his attacks." The Great Controversy p.519

These three elements--prayer, Bible study and meditation--will be looked into throughout the series of chapters that make up *Communion with Christ*. We want to consider these not in the generic sense, in merely describing what they are, but in a manner that will leave us with a vital connection with Christ.

An All-Important Point

It is essential to think about the fact that both coming to Jesus, and remaining in Jesus, may be done only through and by Jesus. He says "without Me, you can do nothing" (John 15:5), and this statement is no less true when it comes to us abiding in Him. Thus, we are to receive His aid in order for us to abide and remain in Him. It is His power that is to work in us.

"When the soul surrenders itself to Christ, a new power takes possession of the new heart. A change is wrought which man can never accomplish for himself. It is a supernatural work, bringing a supernatural element into human nature. The soul that is yielded to Christ becomes His own fortress, which He holds in a revolted world, and He intends that no authority shall be known in it but His own. A soul thus kept in possession by the heavenly agencies is impregnable to the assaults of Satan." The Desire of Ages, p.324

This point is important to consider. Many are discouraged when considering the exalted principles of the Christian life because they see their weaknesses and inability to keep themselves upright. But Jesus wants to remind us that He is the vine, it is His role to hold us up as the branches. Without Christ, and separated from Him, our

6

very best efforts at fruit bearing will always fall short.

Jesus would have us realise that every step upwards on the ladder of Christian life is made through Him, for He Himself is the ladder. Without Jesus, nothing can be done in the path of salvation. For this reason, we must seek nothing short of being vitally connected with Jesus. To abide in Him, we must have a constant communion with Christ.

How Christ Comes into the Heart

We have noted the point that we must be in Christ. The question that may be asked is "how do we get to be in Christ?" Notice the idea in Jesus' words:

"Abide in Me and I in you." John 14:4

The experience of abiding is mutual. That is to say that while an individual is to abide in Christ, Jesus is to also abide in the individual. The one cannot happen without the other.

But how do we give Christ the entrance? Consider Paul, the apostle's, testimony:

"I am crucified with Christ: nevertheless I live; yet not I, but Christ liveth in me: and the life which I now live in the flesh I live by the faith of the Son of God, who loved me, and gave Himself for me." Galatians 2:20

Paul tells of the experience that he is having; he testifies of the fact that Jesus lives in him. Paul is having an abiding experience of Christ being in him and thus, him in Christ. More than that, Paul is also *aware* of that fact.

One wonders what would give the apostle such confidence to make the bold statement that "Christ lives in me." Paul leaves us little room for guessing as to that answer; he says "I am crucified with Christ." This is what gave Paul the confidence that Christ dwelt in him.

Here we find instruction of how it is that Jesus may gain entrance into our hearts to abide in us, and we in Him. Like Paul, we too must be "crucified with Christ." When that is our experience, we need never wallow in doubt as to our standing with the Saviour.

Being Crucified with Christ

Writing as a living man, Paul's reference to being crucified with Christ is not to be taken literally; but there was something that took place in Jesus' experience on the cross which Paul went through as well. When we undergo the same, like Paul, we too may testify of Christ living in us.

On the eve of His crucifixion, Jesus had an interaction with God the Father which gives us insight as to what being "crucified" with Him entails. That evening, Jesus went to the Mount of Olives as He usually did. With His disciples following Him, He then asked them to "pray that [they] may not enter into temptation." (Luke 22:39). Soon after this, Jesus Himself prayed a very significant prayer:

"He was withdrawn from them about a stone's throw, and He knelt down and prayed, saying, Father, if it is Your will, take this cup away from Me; nevertheless not My will, but Yours be done." Luke 22:41-42 NKJV

In Jesus' prayer at Gethsemane, He prayed to do the will of His Father above His own will. While He was struggling with the temptation to withdraw from His mission of facing the cross, Jesus submitted Himself entirely to the will of God the Father.

It was not the first time that Jesus made such a surrender. Christ's act of full submission to the will of His Father was the daily experience of His life. He had mentioned to the disciples that "My meat ([the thing that keeps Me going]) is to do the will of Him that sent Me" (John 4:34), and this was the case in Gethsemane as well.

When Christ was crucified He surrendered His will entirely to the will of His Father once again. Jesus had made the conscious decision to choose God's way as supreme. To be crucified with Christ means that we are to have the same experience: to choose the will of God and to submit wholeheartedly to it.

Very often, being crucified with Christ comes at the denial of our own selfish wants, so that we, like Jesus, would have to say: "not my will, but your will be done." This principle is the very thought behind Jesus' words to His would-be followers when He says:

"If any man will come after me, let him deny himself, and take up his cross daily, and follow Me." Luke 9:23

When Jesus was on the cross, He had denied Himself for the sake of humanity. On the cross, He was carrying out what He had chosen in the garden of Gethsemane, when He chose to surrender His will to the will of His Father.

Immediately after Jesus had made this surrender, Luke continues to describe a very significant point:

"Then an angel appeared to Him from heaven, strengthening Him." Luke 22:43 NKJV

When Jesus had surrendered Himself to the Father He then received all the strength He needed to carry out what He was appointed to do. It was from the strength that He received, upon surrendering, that Jesus then "became obedient unto death, even the death of the cross." (Philippians 2:8).

Here is the secret of receiving strength and grace from heaven in order to obey; it is in making a total surrender of oneself to the will of God. The needed power comes from choosing His way above our own and being willing to say, "not my will, but Yours be done."

Paul's expression, "I am crucified with Christ," is the expression of his personal, total submission to the will of God. When Paul reviewed his life, he was confident that it was fully surrendered to God's will. He was aware that he had chosen to follow God's will above his own. This was the reason behind Paul's confidence that Christ lived in him.

The First Essential

This is the first and central point throughout the discussion of this book, as we consider how we can abide in Christ. To abide in Christ is the experience of those who are, firstly, *in* Christ. This experience comes through making a conscious decision of full surrender to Christ and His will. This is how Jesus gains permission to enter ones heart.

"Many are inquiring, "How am I to make the surrender of myself to God?" You desire to give yourself to Him, but you are weak in moral power, in slavery to doubt, and controlled by the habits of your life of sin. Your promises and resolutions are like ropes of sand. You cannot control your thoughts, your impulses, [and] your affections. The knowledge of your broken promises and forfeited pledges weakens your confidence in your own sincerity, and causes you to feel that God cannot accept you; but you need not despair. What you need to understand is the true force of the will. This is the governing power in the nature of man, the power of decision, or of choice. Everything depends on the right action of the will. The power of choice God has given to men; it is theirs to exercise. You cannot change your heart, you cannot of yourself give to God its affections; but you can choose to serve Him. You can give Him your will; He will then work in you to will and to do according to His good pleasure. Thus your whole nature will be brought under the control of the Spirit of Christ; your affections will be centered upon Him, your thoughts will be in harmony with Him." Steps to Christ p.47

Jesus longs to enter our hearts, our most intimate experiences; He longs to have a vital connection with us. He offers us a change from a life controlled by sinful habits to one where He lives out His life in us. He can accomplish this in us when we give Him the permission to do so, remembering that "without Me, you can do nothing."

"No man can empty himself of self. We can only consent for Christ to accomplish the work. Then the language of the soul will be, Lord, take my heart; for I cannot give it. It is Thy property. Keep it pure, for I cannot keep it for Thee. Save me in spite of myself, my weak, unchristlike self. Mold me, fashion me, raise me into a pure and holy atmosphere, where the rich current of Thy love can flow through my soul." Christ's Object Lessons p.159

Here is the first step to abiding in Christ: choosing to wholly accept the will of God and wholeheartedly submitting our lives to His will. Thus Christ will find entrance into the heart and we, like Paul, can believe that this is so. Here begins the experience of communion with, and abiding in, Christ.

God's Motivating Force

The book of Hebrews gives an account of various characters that had powerful experiences because of their faith. Among these are individuals such as Enoch, who walked with God (Hebrews 11:5-6). After going through the list of these men and women of faith, the writer then notes the following:

> *"Since we are surrounded by so great a cloud of witnesses, let us also lay aside every weight, and sin which clings so closely, and let us run with endurance the race that is set before us..." Hebrews 12:1 ESV*

The writer encourages us to lay aside, to surrender, every hindrance and sin in order to successfully run the Christian race. He invites us to wholeheartedly submit ourselves to God's will.

In the letter to the Romans, Paul also describes this act of laying aside sin. He notes it as "our old sinful selves [being] crucified with Christ so that sin might lose its power in our lives." (Romans 6:6 NLT).

Notice here the relationship between "laying aside sin" and "our old sinful selves being crucified with Christ." By calling us to lay aside the sins and weights that slow us down spiritually, the writer of Hebrews invites us to be crucified with Christ. The appeal to lay aside sin is, simply put, a request to surrender our lives to the will of God. When we do this, sin will lose its power in our lives.

It may be noted, however, that making such surrender is not always easy. Those who are honest enough will note that at times there is reluctance and unwillingness to surrender oneself to God's will. Sometimes it is difficult to wholeheartedly pray the prayer: "not my will but Yours be done."

In view of this difficulty, God has provided a strong motivation to meet our unwillingness. Immediately after the appeal to lay aside every sin, and to surrender ourselves to God, we read these words:

> *"We do this ([we submit to God]) by keeping our eyes on Jesus, the champion who initiates and perfects our faith. Because of the*

joy awaiting Him, He endured the cross, disregarding its shame... Think of all the hostility He endured from sinful people; then you won't become weary and give up." Hebrews 12:1-2 NLT

Jesus went through the experience of the cross in order to save humanity; saving sinners is the joy that was awaiting Him. We are called to think about this reality in order for us to be encouraged to lay aside every weight.

In giving His life on the cross, Jesus gives us the example of true surrender. He understands how it feels to surrender one's life. As the Creator of the universe, Christ gave all of Himself in order to save undeserving sinners, in order to save us. Christ's death on the cross is God's highest motivation for us to wholeheartedly submit to Him. God calls us to meditate on Jesus' sacrifice so that we may be motivated to choose His will.

The reason God does this is because God influences us by His love; it is "the love of Christ [that must] compel us." (2 Corinthians 5:14). God does not force anyone to submit to Him. He invites us to contemplate on Christ's death on the cross; that is the highest expression of love that God could give:

"Greater love has no one than this, than to lay down one's life for his friends. You are My friends if you do whatever I command you." John 15:13-14 NKJV

When we get a sense of how much Jesus has put on the line to save us, individually, we will be moved to give ourselves to God's will also. Pay close attention to the following statement:

"Never can the cost of our redemption be realised until the redeemed shall stand with the Redeemer before the throne of God. Then as the glories of the eternal home burst upon our enraptured senses we shall remember that Jesus left all this for us, that He not only became an exile from the heavenly courts, but for us took the risk of failure and eternal loss. Then we shall cast our crowns at His feet, and raise the song, "Worthy is the Lamb that was slain to receive power, and riches, and wisdom, and strength, and honour, and glory, and blessing." Revelation 5:12." The Desire of Ages, p.131

When we reach heaven we will then realise, with renewed eyes and ears, just how much Jesus has put at stake for the sake of our redemption. This realisation will lead us to throw our crowns at His feet in gratitude; understanding how much God has given us in the death of Christ will lead us to give all that we have to Him.

This is to be the case even on Earth also. Contemplating how much God has given us in the gift of His Son is what drives us to choose His will. Thus, whenever one is reluctant to make a wholehearted submission of their lives to God, they may be encouraged by considering Jesus and His death on the cross. Think of just how far Jesus was willing to go to save you, personally.

God the Son humbled Himself to become a human. More than that, we see Him in the garden of Gethsemane, facing the guilt of the world's sins. In this encounter, He literally sweats blood from the stress of what He was to suffer at the cross that night. The burden was so heavy that, in His anguish, He was tempted to withdraw and to leave humanity to perish in their sins. This is why He prayed for the possibility of not going through with the experience. While going through this anguish, such as has never been felt by anyone else, Jesus still submitted to doing the will of His Father. In His great love for humanity, Jesus chose to take the risk of losing the entire universe.

It was love for us, as individuals, that moved Jesus to still go through with the cross. In His time of extreme suffering, His unwillingness to see humanity lost led Jesus to submit Himself completely to the will of God. It was love for humanity that drove His prayer: "Father, if it is Your will, take this cup away from Me; nevertheless not My will, but Yours, be done." (Luke 22:42)

When we are hesitant to submit ourselves to God, He calls us to consider the sacrifice He made to save us. Through that, we may be confident that He has our best interests at heart. Seeing that Jesus was willing to take the risk of eternal loss to save us, we may be encouraged that we can confidently dedicate ourselves to Him. As we thus submit ourselves to God's will, together with every weight and sin, we will experience Christ abiding in us. Self-surrender is the doorway to an intimate communion with Christ.

From the assurances of God's word, as well as by my own personal experience, one can confidently say that surrendering one's life to God's will comes with no regrets. Even today, God invites us to submit ourselves wholly to Him, so that we may experience what it means to abide in Him. Today, we may sincerely pray the prayer, "not my will but Yours be done."

> *"What do we give up, when we give all? A sin-polluted heart, for Jesus to purify, to cleanse by His own blood, and to save by His matchless love... God does not require us to give up anything that it is for our best interest to retain. In all that He does, He has the well-being of His children in view. Would that all who have not chosen Christ might realise that He has something vastly better to offer them than they are seeking for themselves. Man is doing the greatest injury and injustice to his own soul when he thinks and acts contrary to the will of God. No real joy can be found in the path forbidden by Him who knows what is best and who plans for the good of His creatures. The path of transgression is the path of misery and destruction." Steps to Christ p.46*

Necessities for Abiding

The chapters that follow discuss how we may better know and understand God's will in order to submit to it (*Ch.2-3: Search the Scriptures*). We also take a look at how we can trust God enough to make a wholehearted surrender to Him, especially when it is difficult to do so (*Ch.4: Biblical Meditation & Ch.7: Abiding Faith*). Among other vital things, we also consider how we may remain surrendered (*Ch.5: Scripture Memorisation & Ch.6: Relentless Prayer*) as well as how to face things that work to separate us from Christ (*Ch.8: Triumph over Temptation & Ch.9: What If I Fall*).

Abiding in Christ, and Christ in you, is the experience that all may have today. We conclude the book by considering how we may have this experience continually (*Ch.10: The Experience You May Have*). In order to abide in Him, Christ invites us to make the wholehearted submission of our lives to Him. Like Paul, we may have a confidence that Christ lives in us, when we pray the prayer "not my will but

14

yours be done." This is the doorway to the experience of abiding and having an intimate communion with Christ.

Questions on Chapter 1

What kind of experience does Christ invite His disciples to have?
(p.2)

What hinders a person from abiding in Christ? (p.3)

What does it mean to abide in Christ? (p.3)

What is required for abiding in Christ? (p.4)

How do I know if I am abiding in Christ? (p.4-5)

What is one of the most important points for abiding in Christ?
(p.5)

How do I enter into the experience of abiding in Christ? (p.7)

What does it mean to be "crucified with Christ"? (p.8)

How do I surrender my heart to Christ? (p.9)

What do I do if I know I don't want to surrender to Him? (p.11)

Have I submitted myself wholeheartedly to God's will?

2

Search the Scriptures | Heart Preparation

❧

The Fundamental Principle

Why to Search the Scriptures

Heart Preparation

The Fundamental Principle

I'm quite interested in science; by science I generally mean any field of knowledge or study of the behaviours, structures, laws etc. of the physical and natural world. Consider this thought:

"The science of redemption is the science of all sciences; the science that is the study of the angels and of all the intelligences of the unfallen worlds; the science that engages the attention of our Lord and Saviour; the science that enters into the purpose brooded in the mind of the Infinite--"kept in silence through times eternal" (Romans 16:25, R.V.); the science that will be the study of God's redeemed throughout endless ages. This is the highest study in which it is possible for man to engage. As no other study can, it will quicken the mind and uplift the soul." Education p.126

God's plan of redemption can also be looked at as a science. The work of restoring the image of God in fallen humanity is even referred to as "the science of all sciences."

In every branch of science or knowledge there are various laws, formulas or principles that govern and explain how things behave. Examples of these scientific principles include the law of gravity, that: "what goes up, must come down;" or the law of motion, the reality that: "every action has an equal and opposite reaction."

Unchanging principles and formulas are found in the plan of redemption also. The reason this is important to note is because when we rightly grasp the basic principles of "how things work", it is then that we are better enabled to benefit from them. This is true in the natural and the spiritual world. Misunderstanding the principles of how things work, on the other hand, can lead to unfavorable results.

With that being said, we can consider that in the plan of redemption there are certain "formulas," so to say, that also give specific results. There are various principles which, when followed, will ensure that we experience God's intention for us.

Note Jesus' words to His disciples, and consider the principle that we find there:

"Abide in Me, and I in you. As the branch cannot bear fruit of itself, unless it abides in the vine, neither can you, unless you abide

in Me. "I am the vine, you are the branches. He who abides in Me, and I in him, bears much fruit; for without Me you can do nothing" John 15:4-5 NKJV

Jesus outlines what we may call the principle of fruit-bearing, which is essential for us to consider. This is the foundational idea that the only way to bear fruit, in the Christian journey, is through having a vital connection with Him. Without this experience, we can do nothing in and of ourselves.

Throughout this chapter, (as well as throughout the remainder of the book), we will be considering the principles behind having this vital connection with Christ. What we will find is that communion with Jesus, abiding in Him, is an experience that every sincere child of God may joyfully experience.

Why to Search the Scriptures

To restate Jesus' point: unless we abide in Him, we can do nothing to advance in the Christian life. The most essential component that we need, therefore, is to have is an intimate knowledge of Jesus. And this we may have. Due to how easy it is to browse over something when reading, and not catch the thought behind the words, the point will occasionally be re-emphasised, that: every step on the Christian walk, every act required of us in order to obtain salvation, can be done through and by Jesus; and without Him, not a single step of advance can be made.

The reason why many fail in their Christian walk is because of misunderstanding the vital point that without Jesus we can do nothing.

Where Jesus May be Found

"You search the scriptures, for in them you think you have eternal life: and these are they which testify of Me." John 5:39 NKJV

"If you would become acquainted with the Saviour, study the Holy Scriptures. Fill the whole heart with the words of God. They are the living water, quenching your burning thirst. They are the living bread from heaven." God's Amazing Grace p.228

The entire Bible has been given in order to reveal Jesus to us, thus we may find Christ throughout the entire Bible if we search for Him. The scriptures testify of Jesus. To obtain and keep an open line of communion with Him, we must search the scriptures.

"Beginning at Moses and all the prophets, ([Jesus]) expounded unto them in all the scriptures the things concerning Himself." Luke 24:27

While walking with two of His disciples after His resurrection, Jesus referred to the Old Testament writings to show the necessity of His life and crucifixion. All the things contained throughout the Bible are concerning Him. Thus:

"Spiritual life must be sustained by communion with Christ through His Word." God's Amazing Grace p.228

The word of God was given to us to grant us an experience of abiding in Christ. Returning to the idea of a science, we can consider this as a God given formula, that we can hold communion with Christ by taking hold of His word.

"As in the natural [world], so in the spiritual world. The natural life is preserved moment by moment by divine power; yet it is not sustained by a direct miracle, but through the use of blessings placed within our reach. So the spiritual life is sustained by the use of those means that Providence has supplied. If the follower of Christ would grow up "unto a perfect man, unto the measure of the stature of the fullness of Christ" (Ephesians 4:13), he must eat of the bread of life and drink of the water of salvation. He must watch and pray and work, in all things giving heed to the instructions of God in His word." Acts of the Apostle, p.284

Searching the scriptures is essential for abiding in Christ. It is in understanding this point that the question of "how to study the Bible" becomes vital.

"Study to show thyself approved unto God, a workman that needeth not to be ashamed, rightly dividing the word of truth." 2 Timothy 2:15

The fact that there is a right way to divide the truth means that there is also a wrong way. For that reason, we want to learn how to rightly divide the word of truth, in order to arrive at a saving knowledge of Jesus.

Heart Preparation

"And He spake many things unto them in parables, saying, Behold, a sower went forth to sow." Matthew 13:3

Jesus gives a parable which illustrates the different factors that affect how we receive His word and the extent to which that word affects us. In the parable, the sower sows his seeds on four different ground conditions: the way-side, the stony ground, the thorny ground and the "good ground."

While the same kind of seed is dropped in the different ground conditions, no two conditions bring the same result. The condition of the soil where the seed fell had a direct influence on what the outcome of the seed would be, whether it would produce fruit or not.

"Now the parable is this: the seed is the word of God." Luke 8:11

While God's word remains the same, we find that the impact that God's word has on those who interact with it is not always the same. In the parable, only one of the four ground conditions had fruitful and lasting results. Jesus explains why:

"...the ones that fell on the good ground are those who, having heard the word with a noble and good heart, keep it and bear fruit with patience." Luke 8:15

The same way the growth of a seed has much to do with the condition of the ground on which it falls, likewise the result of studying God's word has much to do with the manner with which it is received and the conditions of our hearts when receiving it.

Therefore, through considering how we can prepare our hearts to search the scriptures, we want to ensure that the soil is rightly prepared to receive the seed. How to gain such a preparation is discussed in the thoughts that follow. With the heart rightly prepared for the seed of God's word, we can bear the fruit that the word is designed to produce in us.

Realising the Power of the Word

"By the word of the Lord were the heavens made; and all the host of them by the breath of his mouth... For He spake, and it was [done]; He commanded, and it stood fast." Psalm 33:6, 9

When God created, the primary thing that He used to make the entire universe was nothing other than His spoken word. That same power that God used to create the heavens and the earth is found in the Holy Bible. Think on that point for a moment; the pages of scripture that we hold in our hands contain the very word used to create the heavens and the earth.

Understanding this calls us to reverently approach the Bible as the powerful and life-giving word of the Creator of the universe.

"The creative energy that called the worlds into existence is in the word of God. This word imparts power; it begets life. Every command is a promise; accepted by the will, received into the soul, it brings with it the life of the Infinite One. It transforms the nature and re-creates the soul in the image of God.

The life thus imparted is in like manner sustained. "By every word that proceedeth out of the mouth of God" (Matthew 4:4) shall man live." Education p.126

The Bible has in it the very same power and word that God used to create the universe. Its power and effect in creating is exactly same.

"And God said, Let there be light: and there was light." Genesis 1:3

The fact that God's word creates the exact thing which it speaks is an evidence of the fact that all that God speaks is the truth, that His word can be trusted. That is why Jesus could say to the Father: "your word is truth" (John 17:17).

In preparing our hearts to receive God's word, our attitude towards it must be to regard it as a transforming power and the surest source of truth.

Willingness to Obey

After being shown a vision of end time events, the prophet Daniel is told of the time of the end, during which the visions which he has been shown would be unsealed and understood. As it relates to that period, and the events leading up to it, he is told:

> *"Many shall be purified, and made white, and tried; but the wicked shall do wickedly: and none of the wicked shall understand; but the wise shall understand." Daniel 12:10*

From the words spoken to Daniel we can learn a simple, yet essential point as it relates to how to understand the writings of Daniel and scripture in general.

The wicked are those "that forsake the law" (Psalms 119:53). Of these, none will able to rightly understand what the Word of God teaches. The wise, on the other hand, will be given the privilege of understanding. "Whoso keepeth the law is a wise son" (Proverbs 28:7). The wise, according to scripture, are those who are willing to obey whatever God instructs. Thus Jesus counsels:

> *"If any man will do ([the Father's]) will, he shall know of the doctrine, whether it be of God, or whether I speak of myself." John 7:17*

No matter how educated or uneducated one may be, the key to understanding doctrine is a willingness to obey all that God has instructed. None of those who forsake God's law will understand.

> *"A true knowledge of the Bible can be gained only through the aid of that Spirit by whom the word was given. And in order to gain this knowledge we must live by it. All that God's word commands, we are to obey. All that it promises, we may claim. The life which it enjoins is the life that, through its power, we are to live. Only as the Bible is thus held can it be studied effectively." Education p.189*

The Right Attitude

> *"You will show me the path of life; In Your presence is fullness of joy; at your right hand are pleasures forever more." Psalms 16:11 NKJV*

Where God's presence is, there is fullness of joy; and the scriptures, which testify of Jesus, are designed to give us that joyfulness.

"And these things write we unto you, that your joy may be full." 1 John 1:4

Whether we realise it or not, in approaching the word of God, we somewhat enter into the presence of the Creator of the universe, where there is that fullness of joy. This means that we are to come to a study of the Bible with an attitude of humility and reverence, taking note of God's presence.

"We should come with reverence to the study of the Bible, feeling that we are in the presence of God. All lightness and trifling should be laid aside." Gospel Workers, 1892 edition p.127

"The spirit in which you come to the investigation of the Scriptures will determine the character of the assistant at your side. Angels from the world of light will be with those who in humility of heart seek for divine guidance. But if the Bible is opened with irreverence, with a feeling of self-sufficiency, if the heart is filled with prejudice, Satan is beside you, and he will set the plain statements of God's word in a perverted light." Ibid

As mentioned earlier, the condition in which the word of God-- the seed-- is received, directly affects the its results. This is the case even in the attitude one may have in approaching the scriptures.

Realising this truth should dispel the urge to come to the Bible merely a as a tool to proudly sustain our opinions, or as a weapon in arguments. God's word is too precious to open with such a spirit. In His presence we are to be humble, teachable and sincere, with a willingness to lay down our finite human reason to the wisdom of God.

"If we study the word of God with an interest, and pray to understand it, new beauties will be seen in every line. God will reveal precious truth so clearly that the mind will derive sincere pleasure and have a continual feast as its comforting and sublime truths are unfolded." Testimonies for the Church, vol. 2 p.338

Realising that the words of scripture are the very ideas of God, speaking directly to me as an individual, should create a greater interest to learn what God has to say. When approached with such an attitude, every line of scripture can be appreciated.

Many more would find pleasure and benefit from searching the scriptures were there to be a shift in the attitude they have when approaching scripture. The Holy Bible is too lightly regarded; it is not seen to be what it truly is: "The creative energy that called the worlds into existence… it imparts power; it begets life."

Another expresses the thought in this way: that "the paradigm (or outlook) with which we approach a circumstance, drastically affects how we experience it." What is your attitude towards the Bible?

Personal Bible Study Should Take Priority in Christian Life

"I have not departed from the commandment of His lips; I have treasured the words of His mouth more than my necessary food." Job 23:12 NKJV

In defending himself against his friends' accusations, Job presents to them the attitude that he had towards God's word. If Job were to be given a choice between the words of God and his "necessary food", God's word would come out first.

To Job, the word of God took the highest priority. This must be the attitude of those who, like Job, "fear God and shun evil" (Job 2:3).

When we make the word of God a priority, things of lesser importance should not take it's place.

"Guard jealously your hours for prayer, Bible study, and self-examination. Set aside a portion of each day for a study of the Scriptures and communion with God. Thus you will obtain spiritual strength, and will grow in favor with God." Gospel Workers, p.100

The words of scripture were no less of a priority in the life of Christ in His humanity on earth. Throughout His life, the hours for Bible study were preciously guarded as a priority.

"In childhood, youth, and manhood, Jesus studied the Scriptures.

As a little child He was daily at His mother's knee taught from the scrolls of the prophets. In His youth the early morning and the evening twilight often found Him alone on the mountainside or among the trees of the forest, spending a quiet hour in prayer and the study of God's word." Education p.185

As in the life of Jesus, the morning hours after waking up and the moments before retiring in the evening are often the best times for personal Bible study. This was how Christ held communion with His Father.

The Humble, Teachable Spirit of a Learner

"And this is life eternal, that they may know You, the only true God, and Jesus Christ whom You have sent." John 17:3 NKJV

While praying for His followers, Jesus brings out the importance of having a knowledge of God. A correct understanding of God and His character is vital for obtaining eternal life. Peter even goes as far as to note, of God, that "His divine power has given to us all things that pertain to life and godliness, through the knowledge of Him." (2 Peter 1:3)

Thus we find that knowledge, an intimate knowledge of God, is vital for life here and hereafter.

Noting this important point, Paul then counsels us on one of the subtle, but very real, dangers that come with having knowledge.

"Knowledge makes us feel important..." 1 Corinthians 8:2 NLT

There is something about a person realising that they know something, especially something that a majority of others seem to not know or understand, that can cause one to become proud. This is the danger that must be guarded against with knowledge.

The importance of this is seen in the point considered earlier, that "none of the wicked will understand"; and pride is wicked indeed. It is for this reason that cultivating the humble and teachable spirit of a learner is essential in preparing the heart to understand more of God's word.

"If anyone thinks that he knows anything, he knows nothing yet as

he ought to know." 1 Corinthians 8:2 NKJV

When we approach the scriptures with the attitude that we know nothing yet as we ought to, even the passages that we may think we "know" will give fresh revelations of the character of God. I love teaching on John 3:16; this verse is among the most popular texts of scripture. For a long time I thought I "knew" this passage; I would not even turn to it when someone would stand to preach on it, because of how it was a part of my "general knowledge." It was for this reason that the verse did not impact me as God's word should. Having thought I "knew" it, I had nothing more that I could learn from it. I have seen this to be the case with many other individuals as well. But note:

> *"In the most simply stated truths are involved principles that are as high as heaven and that compass eternity." Education p.125*

God's word, even the most apparently simple ideas, contains gems of truth which are of infinite depth. In realising that we know nothing yet as we ought to, we are prepared to benefit much, even from the passages that we may have long been familiar with.

Cultivating a teachable spirit also means never studying the Bible to win arguments or to prove that our opinions and ideas are right. The seed that is God's word will produce the greatest of fruit in our spiritual lives when we come with an unbiased, teachable attitude--seeking to know "what does God have to say, to *me*?"

Accepting All Scripture as Profitable

Every thought of the scriptures is inspired and the Bible contains insights into the mind and heart of God. This is why the Bible can be accepted as profitable and we always stand to benefit from it. Every text of scripture has been put there for a purpose and nothing that is in the Bible is of less value than another.

> *"All scripture is given by inspiration of God, and is profitable for doctrine, for reproof, for correction, for instruction in righteousness: That the man of God may be perfect, thoroughly furnished unto all good works." 2 Timothy 3:16-17*

If all scripture is profitable, then no part of it should be taken for granted. The writings of the Old Testament, as well as those of the New Testament, the writings of the prophets, the psalms, the gospels and epistles, all are designed and adapted to bless the various minds that God has created.

One may safely accept all that God speaks, through His word, as trustworthy and dependable. The same authority behind the writings of Paul and John is the same authority in the writings of Moses; and from each of these we stand to gain a blessing.

One opens their heart to experience the blessings of God's word when approaching it with the attitude that all the thoughts contained in it will be profitable to them.

The Help of the Holy Spirit

The same Holy Spirit that inspired the scriptures is the only means by which the scriptures may be understood. If one is to arrive at a correct understanding of truth, God must be the first teacher.

"Knowing this first, that no prophecy of the scripture is of any private interpretation. For the prophecy came not in old time by the will of man: but holy men of God spake as they were moved by the Holy Ghost." 2 Peter 1:20-21

"But the Comforter, which is the Holy Ghost, whom the Father will send in my name, he shall teach you all things, and bring all things to your remembrance, whatsoever I have said unto you." John 14:26

"Howbeit when He, the Spirit of truth, is come, He will guide you into all truth: for He shall not speak of himself; but whatsoever He shall hear, that shall He speak: and He will show you things to come." John 16:13

The Holy Spirit is the teacher of all the divine truth which He himself has inspired. Who can be a better teacher of the scriptures than Him?

"The Comforter is called "the Spirit of truth." His work is to define and maintain the truth...There is comfort and peace in the

truth, but no real peace or comfort can be found in falsehood. It is through false theories and traditions that Satan gains his power over the mind. By directing men to false standards, he misshapes the character. Through the Scriptures the Holy Spirit speaks to the mind, and impresses truth upon the heart. Thus He exposes error, and expels it from the soul. It is by the Spirit of truth, working through the word of God, that Christ subdues His chosen people to Himself. " The Desire of Ages p.671*

Without the aid and guidance of the Holy Spirit, one cannot arrive at an understanding of the truth. His help is freely given and every sincere child of God has access to the Holy Spirit as a direct and personal teacher of Bible truth. We can depend on Him.

Not Putting Our Dependence on People

"Whom shall He teach knowledge? And whom shall He make to understand doctrine? them that are weaned from the milk, and drawn from the breasts." Isaiah 28:9

The question of who God will teach is important for us in this discussion. If one wants to have God as a teacher, and to obtain an understanding of His doctrine, the condition is that one must be weaned from the milk and, as a maturing child, to no longer be fed from the breast.

When a young child is weaned, she is no longer completely dependent on her mother to feed her. When one is weaned from the milk, they are ready to feed on more solid food and, eventually, to feed themselves. This idea illustrates the experience of a new born Christian and how he is to remove dependence from other people as he grows in his own Christian journey. Such individuals are the ones whom God will teach.

A further description of this point is illustrated to the Hebrews:

"For though by this time you ought to be teachers, you need someone to teach you again the first principles of the oracles of God; and you have come to need milk and not solid food." Hebrews 5:12 NKJV

Those still in need of milk are those who, not being prepared yet for solid food, are described as needing to still be taught. Still needing milk is a reference to having to still understand the first principles, the basic points, of God's word. This is why the thought continues that:

"Everyone who lives on milk is unskilled ([or inexperienced]) in the word of righteousness, since he is a child." Hebrews 5:13 ESV

Those who are weaned from the milk have been taught and they have grasped the basics of the gospel. These do not need to depend too heavily on finite humans for their instruction. This attitude is a part of the preparation needed as we approach studying the Bible.

In order for God to teach you and I knowledge, personally, and enable us to understand doctrine, it is important that one does not depend on others to feed them, as a child depends on her mother for milk.

This is the mindset of those who receive knowledge and understanding from God and we may trust Him to teach us. One's spiritual understanding should not be based on the conclusions of human beings, but on God.

It may be important to note, however, that it is a part of God's will to have teachers among His people. This is essential "for the equipping of the saints, for the work of the ministry, for the edifying of the body of Christ, till we all come to the unity of the faith and the knowledge of the Son of God, to a perfect man, to the measure of the stature of the fullness of Christ; that we should no longer be children…" (Ephesians 4:11-14).

While God places teachers that we may be edified, it is not God's will for us to depend on them for our spiritual food as a suckling child to a mother. Having learnt the way of the gospel by His teachers, God would have us weaned from the milk and to depend on Him as a teacher.

Requires Patience & Persistence

One lesson that I learnt early in life was that the most valuable things in the world do not come easily or freely. With things that people pursue, energy and resources are invested in what is believed to be of value--trusting that the results will be worth it. Such is the case with the treasures found in God's word as well.

"My son, if you receive my words, and treasure my commands within you...Yes, if you cry out for discernment, and lift up your voice for understanding, If you seek her as silver, and search for her as for hidden treasures; then you will understand the fear of the Lord, and find the knowledge of God." Proverbs 2:1-4 NKJV

Solomon, the wise man, likens understanding God's word to valuable silver and hidden treasure. Valuable treasures such as silver, gold and diamonds are searched for patiently and diligently. Miners labour and sweat to discover even a small piece of the treasure, and the joy of the discovery is always worth the effort of the search. This is the case with studying God's also. Bible study requires patience and persistence in searching its pages for truth. This is why we must be prepared to put in effort to search the scriptures diligently, and the rich reward will always be satisfying.

"The most valuable teaching of the Bible is not to be gained by occasional or disconnected study. Its great system of truth is not so presented as to be discerned by the hasty or careless reader. Many of its treasures lie far beneath the surface, and can be obtained only by diligent research and continuous effort. The truths that go to make up the great whole must be searched out and gathered up, 'here a little, and there a little.' Isaiah 28:10." Education p.123

"For whatsoever things were written aforetime were written for our learning, that we through patience and comfort of the scriptures might have hope." Romans 15:4

Such patience and diligence also require consistency. Personal Bible study is not an occasional thing, done once every now and again when the schedule seems fitting. There must be consistency in communing with God and personal devotion is to form a part of the Christians lifestyle.

"As the miner discovers veins of precious metal concealed beneath the surface of the earth, so will he who perseveringly searches the

word of God as for hid treasure find truths of the greatest value, which are concealed from the view of the careless seeker. The words of inspiration, pondered in the heart, will be as streams flowing from the fountain of life." Steps to Christ p.90

An attitude of patience and persistence is an important element in heart preparation for searching the scriptures and abiding in Christ. It is this spirit that will prepare us for discovering truths of the greatest value.

God's Part in Preparing Our Hearts

When Jesus says the words "without me, you can do nothing" He really means it. Having spoken about the importance of having the heart rightly prepared to receive God's word and bare fruit, even this preparation cannot be done without Christ's help. Thus God's word promises us that:

"The preparations of the heart in man... is from the Lord." Proverbs 16:1

"My grace is sufficient for you: for my strength is made perfect in weakness." 2 Corinthians 12:9

Christ longs to abide in us (even more than we do) and when we consent, He will do all in His power to grant us that experience. By asking and allowing Him to prepare our hearts to understand and receive His word, He will be seen throughout all the scriptures.

"I will give you a new heart and put a new spirit within you; I will take the heart of stone out of your flesh and give you a heart of flesh. I will put My Spirit within you and cause you to walk in My statutes, and you will keep My judgments and do them." Ezekiel 26:26-27 NKJV

Questions on Chapter 2

How does reading the Bible relate to communion with Christ? (p.18, 19)

Why is it important to study the Bible personally? (p.19)

How can I prepare myself before reading in the Bible? (p.21)

What attitude should I have when approaching the Bible? (p.22-27, 30)

Do I have time set aside for personal bible study in my schedule? (p.25)

What preparation is necessary in order to gain the most from Bible study? (p.28-29)

What if I do not understand what I read from the Bible? (p.30)

What part does God play in preparing me for studying the Bible? (p.32)

3

Search the Scriptures |
The Method

Rightly Dividing the Word

Practical Points for Considering the Word

What to Study?

Promises Concerning the Word of God

Rightly Dividing the Word

In the earlier years of my childhood, I did not like running much. I was not too good at it and whenever I would run with my peers I would always, if not often, come last. This continued on even until my teenage years. At one time I signed up to join practice sessions for a basketball team and it was through those sessions that I actually learnt how to run properly. Although it was at a relatively late stage in life, after I learnt how to run properly I began to really enjoy it. I still do today.

This experience roughly illustrates an important point: that the reason why we do not enjoy certain things, at times, is not because the things in themselves are not enjoyable, but because we have not been engaging with them the right way. I believe this to be the case in Bible study also.

We have learnt earlier that in order to stand approved before God, we must "rightly divide the word of truth" (2 Timothy 2:15). It is thus that we become workmen and workwomen that need not to be ashamed.

Whether or not we abide in Christ is directly affected by how we study His word. It would be safe to say that understanding how to "rightly divide the word of truth" will contribute much to ones enjoyment of Bible study. For this reason, we will now look at a few practical principles on the *methods* for studying the Bible.

Prayerful Study

Prayer is an active component to abiding in Christ and it is just as essential in Bible study. In searching the pages of scripture, it is our privilege to do so having asked God for divine guidance and wisdom.

> *"Thus says the Lord... Call to Me, and I will answer you, and show you great and mighty things, which you do not know." Jeremiah 33:2-3*

The more I come to search the scriptures, the more I see that there are quite a few things which I do not know; nevertheless, God is able to reveal these things, even great and mighty things, to all who call upon Him.

> *"Never should the Bible be studied without prayer. Before opening its pages we should ask for the enlightenment of the Holy Spirit, and it will be given." Steps to Christ p.91*

God is the ultimate source of wisdom and all He would have us do to receive that wisdom is to ask. It is best to pray for God to reveal His truths when studying, that the Holy Spirit may truly be ones teacher.

> *"The word of God is plain to all who study it with a prayerful heart. Every truly honest soul will come to the light of truth. "Light is sown for the righteous." Psalm 97:11." The Great Controversy p.521*

> *"While some portions of the word are easily understood, the true meaning of other parts is not so readily discerned. There must be patient study and meditation, and earnest prayer. Every student, as he opens the Scriptures, should ask for the enlightenment of the Holy Spirit, and the promise is sure, that it will be given." Messages to Young People p.261*

Comparing Scripture with Scripture

The Bible is tied together as a connected whole and the best place to find answers to Bible questions is to refer to the Bible itself. Note the words spoken to the prophet Isaiah:

> *"Whom shall He teach knowledge? and whom shall He make to understand doctrine? Them that are weaned from the milk, and drawn from the breasts. For precept must be upon precept, precept upon precept; line upon line, line upon line; here a little, and there a little:" Isaiah 28:9-10*

After being weaned from their dependence on other people for spiritual food, those who will understand doctrine are those who read the Word of God, comparing "precept upon precept, and line upon line" (Isaiah 28:13).This is the Bible's model of searching for the scriptures.

> *"Scripture must be compared with scripture. There must be careful*

research and prayerful reflection. And such study will be richly repaid." Steps to Christ p.90

God has inspired His word in such a way that the various writers, from their diverse backgrounds, experiences and manners of expression, share the truth in ways that can appeal to all minds. How the intellectual Paul expresses a thought may differ from the poetic David, but these different, yet harmonious, expressions of the same truth testify to its Divine source.

To understand the fuller meaning of the subjects in God's word requires considering how that idea is expressed in different places throughout the Bible, comparing scripture with scripture.

> *"Each Gospel is a supplement to the others, every prophecy an explanation of another, every truth a development of some other truth. The types of the Jewish economy are made plain by the gospel. Every principle in the word of God has its place, every fact its bearing. And the complete structure, in design and execution, bears testimony to its Author. Such a structure no mind but that of the Infinite could conceive or fashion." Education p.123*

The word "precept" refers to an instruction or a principle. For us to not arrive at erroneous or unbalanced conclusions, God would have us understand the meaning of His instructions, commandments and principles by considering them in their varied expressions. We have an example with the fifth commandment:

> *"Thou shalt not kill." Exodus 20:13*

In Jesus' Sermon on the Mount, He explains the deeper application of the commandment as going beyond the physical act of killing and He applies it to the attitudes we have towards others.

> *"You have heard that it was said to those of old, You shall not murder...But I say to you that whoever is angry with his brother without a cause shall be in danger of the judgment" Matthew 5:21-22*

The apostle, John, in his epistle, expresses the same thought thus:

> *"Whoever hates his brother is a murderer..." 1 John 3:15*

These three expressions of the same thought give a wider understanding of the idea. By thus looking at God's word, precept upon precept, we get to grasp the broader meaning of what He has to say to us. This may be on any precept or teaching, whether it be understanding how to live righteously, the life and ministry of Jesus, the great conflict between good and evil, marriage or even seeking solutions to a life problem one faces. The broad range of themes is endless.

In studying God's word "line upon line", the principle is also very fruitful for understanding particular words or topics of interest. This involves doing a word study on topics such as "love", "faith", or "righteousness", and seeing how the word is used and expressed throughout the scriptures. This may be done with the help of tools such as a concordance (some Bibles have a concordance at the back section), by checking cross references, or doing a word search.

Such a manner of study, digging for the truth as for hidden treasure, will be "richly repaid" to the careful and patient reader. Studying the life and biographies of various Bible characters in such a manner also offers fruitful and practical lessons.

Pay Careful Attention

"The Bible is a book of understatements...;" said a presenter in a devotional message. In this statement, the point being illustrated was the fact that the ideas and themes presented in the Bible are of such depth that language often falls short of rightly representing them. He understood that:

"In the most simply stated truths are involved principles that are as high as heaven and that compass eternity." Education p.125

As seemingly simple as they are, at times, it is easy to overlook the depth of the thoughts presented in scripture. This is why, when reading the Bible, it is important to pause and take a moment to consider and pay careful attention to what the scriptures are actually saying. This is how we gain understanding.

"Consider what I say;" said the apostle Paul to Timothy, "and the

Lord give thee understanding in all things." 2 Timothy 2:7

"We cannot obtain wisdom without earnest attention and prayerful study. Some portions of Scripture are indeed too plain to be misunderstood, but there are others whose meaning does not lie on the surface to be seen at a glance." Steps to Christ p.90

It is interesting to note the fact that, while the Bible is filled with deep in profound ideas, God still gives them in simplicity. The power of God's word does not rely on being complicated.

For us to receive an understanding of the deep things of God's word, He reveals them to us when we give them careful consideration, even in their apparent "simplicity."

Consider this "simply stated truth" as an example:

"God demonstrates His love toward us, in that while we were still sinners, Christ died for us." Romans 5:8 NKJV

The thought that a sin-hating God not only loves fallen humanity, but also goes on to demonstrate that love, is a very profound idea. But the reality of that thought affects and changes us only when we actually pause to think about it. This is the nature of God's word. Searching the scriptures requires more than browsing through it, but also to open one's eyes in paying careful attention to the lessons found in the Word. This is essential for obtaining a deeper knowledge of Christ.

Reflection and Meditating

Searching the scriptures goes beyond the act of reading, alone. It also requires careful meditation and reflection on that which has been read.

"Many attend religious services, and are refreshed and comforted by the word of God; but through neglect of meditation, watchfulness, and prayer, they lose the blessing, and find themselves more destitute than before they received it. Often they feel that God has dealt hardly with them. They do not see that the fault is their own. By separating themselves from Jesus, they have shut away the light of His presence." The Desire of Ages p.83

Having heard or read the word of God, whether or not its effect will be lasting is often influenced by taking the time to meditate on it afterwards. This is how its blessing is retained.

As seen in the parable of the sower, Satan is ever seeking to steal away the words of Christ, in order that the seed may not spring up in the heart and bare fruit. One way in which he does this is by leading one to neglect meditating on the Word. Such is considered to be the case with the seed which fell by the way side.

"The seed sown by the wayside represents the word of God as it falls upon the heart of an inattentive hearer." Christ's Object Lessons p.44

Intentionally taking the time to reflect on God's word, whether heard in a sermon or in one's own personal study, is like letting the word of God "sink in," so to say. This may involve thinking on the choices that God would have you make from what has been read, whether or not there's a particular change God would have me make in the life, and what promises we can claim and take with us from the scripture.

The practice of thus carefully reflecting on the word, and seeing where its application can be made personal in the life, is an effective tool to safeguarding the blessings received from the Bible.

Have you ever had devotion in the morning and found yourself struggling to remember what it was about later in the day? Meditating on the word is also a great help to keeping God's word stored in the mind.

"Keep your Bible with you. As you have opportunity, read it; fix the texts in your memory. Even while you are walking the streets you may read a passage and meditate upon it, thus fixing it in the mind." Steps to Christ p.90

Next time you have devotion, or even after each reading of the pages of this book, spend a moment to reflect on what you have read and the impact it is meant to have on your life, personally.

In the chapters to follow, we will be taking a closer look at the idea of Biblical meditation and memorising scripture.

Slow and Steady Reading

"The reception of the Word, the bread from heaven, is declared to be the reception of Christ himself. As the Word of God is received into the soul, we partake of the flesh and blood of the Son of God." The Review and Herald, November 23, 1897

The best benefit of food is often gained from slowly and thoroughly eating it. This is also the case in ingesting God's word, the bread from heaven. As the nutritional value of food is best received by it being thoroughly chewed, allowing it to mingle with the saliva, a slow and steady reading of scripture is the most beneficial.

"There is but little benefit derived from a hasty reading of the Scriptures. One may read the whole Bible through and yet fail to see its beauty or comprehend its deep and hidden meaning. One passage studied until its significance is clear to the mind and its relation to the plan of salvation is evident, is of more value than the perusal of many chapters with no definite purpose in view and no positive instruction gained." Steps to Christ p.90

In reading passages of scripture, read slowly and distinctly, giving careful consideration to each phrase and thought in the text. In so doing, the meaning and understanding of passages is made clearer.

"So they read in the book in the law of God distinctly, and gave the sense, and caused them to understand the reading." Nehemiah 8:8

With Bible study, the purpose is often about quality more than quantity. The desire to grasp as much of the Bible as possible leads to a hasty reading of scripture, I've gone through the same experience also. But God's word requires patience.

As a principle of Bible study and searching the scriptures, meditation and reading slowly is a helpful way to gain understanding.

Reading Repeatedly

Together with reading slowly and distinctly, reading passages of scripture again and again often helps in seeing the thoughts contained in the text.

This idea is similar to the experience of traveling on the same route--as to school or to work--over and over again. Each day, as one travels on a certain road, the more they become familiar with it. Over time, that route can become so familiar that it is possible to even direct someone else on using it.

This familiarity is similarly the case when studying the Bible. By reading through passages of scripture over and over again, they become more familiar and the thoughts they contain become clearer to understand.

We may make an example with the second half of 1 John 1:7:

*"**The blood** of Jesus Christ His Son cleanses us from all sin."*

*"The blood of **Jesus Christ** His Son cleanses us from all sin."*

*"The blood of Jesus Christ **His Son** cleanses us from all sin."*

*"The blood of Jesus Christ his Son **cleanses us** from all sin."*

*"The blood of Jesus Christ his Son cleanses us from **all sin**."*

As the text is read again and again, placing an emphasis on each phrase, the thoughts contained in the scripture become more deeply impressed.

It is sometimes said that "repetition is the mother of learning." The principle of reading repetitively can be effectively applied when reading single verses, passages, chapters and even books of the Bible. This is not necessarily to aimlessly repeat the words, but it is with the main intention of gaining, with each reading, a clearer comprehension of what God's word is actually saying.

As in the illustration of a person traveling the same route over and over again, it is also the case that a new discovery may be made with each trip that a person makes.

When I started my tertiary (college/university) studies, there was a time when I would travel daily from home to the Johannesburg inner-city. As much as I became very familiar with the directions, there was always something new that I would find along the way, things that I had not seen or noticed from previous trips.

Such is the case with the living word of God also. The more one reads through the Bible, or the portions one seeks to understand, the easier it is to notice the things that may have been missed in previous readings of the same passages.

The Verse-by-verse Method

"In daily study the verse-by-verse method is often most helpful. Let the student take one verse, and concentrate the mind on ascertaining the thought that God has put into that verse for him, and then dwell upon the thought until it becomes his own. One passage thus studied until its significance is clear is of more value than the perusal of many chapters with no definite purpose in view and no positive instruction gained." Education p.189

The verse by verse method of Bible study is a simple, yet very valuable, method of Bible study. The basic idea, as elaborated on through the previous principles discussed, is to see and meditate on the thoughts that God has placed all throughout His word.

A major emphasis of this method is to go through *passages* of scripture (whether it is a parable or a prophecy) verse by verse, one point after another.

Thus, the verse by verse method is simply outlined as:

1. Taking one verse after another from a passage of consideration.

2. Concentrating the mind to find out and understand the thought, or idea, that God has placed for you in that verse.

3. Then, to dwell on that thought, to think on it in relation to yourself, until the thought in the text becomes your own and it becomes a personal thought.

I have personally found this method to be a most helpful method, primarily because the emphasis is not only on grasping what the word of God has to say, but on letting His thoughts become my own.

The same way the energy and nutrients of food, when broken down, become absorbed into ones physical system, so God's thoughts are also intended to become a part of one's whole being. Such will be the case when one meditates and dwells on the thoughts found in God's word.

Practical Points for Considering the Word

Questions that Jesus Asked

In response to the lawyer who asked Him "what must I do to inherit eternal life," Jesus' reply gives some helpful points which also apply in personal Bible study:

> *"[Jesus] said to him, "What is written in the law? What is your reading of it?" So he answered and said, "'You shall love the LORD your God with all your heart, with all your soul, with all your strength, and with all your mind,' and 'your neighbor as yourself.' And He said to him, "You have answered rightly; do this and you will live." Luke 10:26-28 NKJV*

Jesus' response to the lawyer was three simple statements which related to the layers reading and understanding of the scriptures. Note how these three questions can also aid in arriving at a clearer understanding and experience of the word of God.

"What is written in the law?" What is the passage saying?
Before trying to apply meanings to scripture, it is important to ensure one first has a clear understanding of what the text is *actually* saying. The principles outlined in the previous section (*The Method*) seek to answer this question. This may at times be easily done by reading verses immediately before and after a text, in order understand its context.

"What is your reading of it?" What is the passage saying to me?
Having understood what the text is saying, one may then prayerfully consider what point God is seeking to get across to you, personally, through that particular passage. Here we seek to find the personal thought which God has placed in the text. This often requires prayer, careful reflection and the Holy Spirits guidance.

"This do and you will live." How may I apply that to my life?
This point deals primarily with prayerfully considering how to practically and personally apply what God has revealed and impressed from the passage read. This also requires prayer and reflection, as well as an honest heart, willing to receive what God has instructed

and revealed. It is when the word of God is thus received, and faithfully carried out in the life, that its life giving power is received.

Questioning the Text

Another lesson that can be drawn from Jesus' interaction with the lawyer is how helpful it is to ask questions while reading scripture. This may be questions that are answerable by the passage itself, or by other parts of the Bible.

A simple example of questioning the text can be made with what has become a "common", but still profound, passage of scripture:

"For God so loved the world, that He gave His only begotten Son, that whoever believes in Him should not perish, but have everlasting life." John 3:16

Now let us consider some questions which are answerable by the verse itself; note the thoughts that come to mind in thinking on the answers:

Who loved the world?

Who did God love?

How did God show His love?

Why did He give His son?

Which Son did He give?

Did God have any other Sons He could give?

How may someone have everlasting life?

Who may believe in the Son of God?

What kind of life does God offer?

What does having eternal life prevent us from?

What would have happened if God had not given His only begotten son?

What would have happened if God had not loved the world?

Who must the world believe in?

Who makes up the world?

Am I a part of the world? Etc.

These are only a few of many questions which may be asked when considering a verse or passage. With the word of God being of infinite depth, no text of scripture can ever be exhausted of the treasures which it offers.

The answers to the questions asked may be found both in the text itself, the verses around it, or even from other passages of scripture ("precept upon precept"). Asking what, who, when, why and how is a helpful instrument for "digging for truth as for hid treasure."

Keeping a Study Journal

In reading and meditating on God's word, it is also good to keep a journal or a notebook to record the lessons learnt and the thoughts found in the passage.

Often, while prayerfully studying the scriptures, one may be convicted on a particular thing, or have raised other questions which may not necessarily be answered immediately. Jotting down the lessons learnt in personal Bible study makes them easier to remember and share with someone else for encouragement.

It may be interesting to note that the material for this book actually developed out of my own personal study journal. The various points found throughout these pages arose while going through a devotional journey of seeking to personally understand how to have an abiding experience with Jesus. Such is the blessing of taking notes while searching the scriptures.

What to Study?

It goes without saying that the Bible is filled with much that can be studied and learnt. It's large compilation of stories, experiences, genealogies and instructions are manifold and very able to keep one pleasantly occupied for as long as life shall last. But what must one study, or where does one even start?

Many are overwhelmed at the thought of "where to start" with Bible study. Depending on our varied experiences, the answer may vary from person to person. Whether it is with one of the gospels, or with the very first book, Genesis, the important thing is to start.

In the various themes the Bible covers, there are some "major themes" that are perhaps of weightier importance than others. Below we consider a few key themes of emphasis throughout scripture. These set the backdrop of the scriptures, the "big picture" so to say. The idea is not so much to prescribe what specific topics to study, and in what order, but rather to grasp the underlying emphasis in all that God is trying to communicate to us by the scriptures.

The Plan of Salvation and its Various Components

In his epistle to the Romans, Paul expounds much on the plan of salvation. As an introduction, he first notes that the gospel, the good news concerning God's power to save us from sin, was promised in the writings of the Old Testament prophets.

> *"Paul, a bondservant of Jesus Christ, called to be an apostle, separated to the gospel of God which He promised before through His prophets in the Holy Scriptures, concerning His Son Jesus Christ our Lord, who was born of the seed of David according to the flesh"*
> *Romans 1:1-3*

In this declaration, Paul is making clear to us what the major theme of the Holy Scriptures is. From the writings of Moses to Malachi, as well as throughout the New Testament, all the writers are revealing to us something about the gospel.

> *"The central theme of the Bible, the theme about which every other in the whole book clusters, is the redemption plan, the restoration in the human soul of the image of God. From the first intimation of hope in the sentence pronounced in Eden to that last glorious promise of the Revelation, "They shall see His face; and His name shall be in their foreheads" (Revelation 22:4), the burden of every book and every passage of the Bible is the unfolding of this wondrous theme, man's uplifting, the power of God, "which giveth us the victory through our Lord Jesus Christ." (1 Corinthians 15:57)"*
> *Education p.125*

Whether it is reading a whole book, or a single passage, we should always be seeking to understand what God is trying to unfold about His plan to save fallen humanity from sin. This will give the greatest value to Bible study.

> *"He who grasps this thought has before him an infinite field for study. He has the key that will unlock to him the whole treasure house of God's word." Education p.126*

The most fruitful outcome of reading the Bible is getting an increased understanding of the grand theme of the gospel, the plan of salvation. We should ever keep the question in view, when studying the Bible: "how can what I have read help me to better understand God's plan to save humanity?" Or, "how does this all tie into God's plan of redemption?"

> *"One passage studied until its significance is clear to the mind and its relation to the plan of salvation is evident, is of more value than the perusal of many chapters with no definite purpose in view and no positive instruction gained." Steps to Christ p.90*

How to be Saved

In a discussion with a lawyer, Jesus was asked the question "what shall I do to inherit eternal life?" Today, we also need to understand how we are to respond to God's plan of saving humanity, and of saving us as individuals. Jesus' response to the ruler is a guide to us also. He asks:

> *"What is written in the law? What is your reading of it?" Luke 10:25-26 NKJV*

Jesus' reply to the lawyer points him to the law, the Old Testament writings. He is letting the lawyer, and us, know that man's duty and responsibility in the experience of salvation is made plain to us throughout the Bible. This is one of its major themes. Speaking to Timothy, Paul writes:

> *"From childhood you have known the Holy Scriptures, which are able to make you wise for salvation through faith which is in Christ Jesus." 2 Timothy 3:15 NKJV*

The Holy Scriptures are able to give us wisdom concerning how to be saved. The various stories & experiences, commands and parables throughout the Bible illustrate how we are to exercise faith, how to obey, how to experience God working in us; in short, how to inherit eternal life. This is a theme that demands our consideration and it is unfolded in various ways throughout the scriptures.

Jesus as the Central Theme

On the day of His resurrection, Jesus had an encounter with two of his disciples who were still disappointed by His crucifixion, just a few days before. Not knowing that it was Jesus, these disciples share their disappointed hopes, which Jesus sought to dispel.

> *"And beginning at Moses and all the prophets, [Jesus] expounded unto them in all the scriptures the things concerning Himself." Luke 24:27*

Jesus pointed these disciples to the scriptures. The cause of their disappointment was their misunderstanding of the scriptures, there was a point that they had missed. Jesus showed them all that the word of God had spoken concerning His life, death and resurrection. Later on that day, describing this encounter, these disciples had this to say:

> *"And they said one to another, Did not our heart burn within us, while he talked with us by the way, and while he opened to us the scriptures?" Luke 24:32*

When these disciples grasped the central theme of the scriptures -- the life, death, character and ministry of Christ -- their hearts burned within them. They could see the fulfilment of God's plan in Jesus' death and resurrection; and when this was the case, it drastically affected their experience. They understood Jesus' words when He said of the scriptures, "these are they which testify of Me." (John 5:39).

The Bible comes alive to the reader when it is read in view of trying to understand the work and character of God. It was not given merely to satisfy our curiosities, but to ground us in an understanding of the personhood of God, to learn the heart and mind of God.

> *"And Jesus said unto them, These are the words which I spake unto*

you, while I was yet with you, that all things must be fulfilled, which were written in the law of Moses, and in the prophets, and in the psalms, concerning me. Then opened he their understanding, that they might understand the scriptures." Luke 24:44-45

God's love for man, His response to the failures of His people and His feelings towards the sufferings of humanity, these have many lessons for us. How God has led his people throughout time, and His thoughts concerning me and you: these ideas, and more, paint the picture of who God is, throughout the Bible.

From the writings of Moses, all the way to the Revelation, the Bible seeks to present Jesus to us. Studying the Bible with the intent to understand what it has to reveal about God's character will enable us to rightly understand its narratives. When searching, it may rightly be asked: "what does this passage (or chapter, or book) have to say to me about Christ and His character?"

The Great Conflict Between Christ and Satan

From the earliest stages of humanity's history, we have been in the centre of a great conflict between Jesus and Satan, the adversary. All throughout history the controversy which began in heaven has unfolded and played itself out on earth, in the experiences of individuals and of nations.

"So the great dragon was cast out, that serpent of old, called the Devil, and Satan, who deceives the whole world: he was cast to the earth, and his angels were cast out with him." Revelation 12:9 NKJV

The great controversy has lied at the backdrop of history as it advances throughout the scriptures. In this warfare, the issues at stake are God's justice & mercy, the character of His law and the salvation of humankind. When considering the Bible through this lens, the events, histories and prophesies of scripture will be seen in their broader scope--as the outworking of the great conflict here on earth.

"Satan's enmity against Christ has been manifested against His followers. The same hatred of the principles of God's law, the same

policy of deception, by which error is made to appear as truth, by which human laws are substituted for the law of God, and men are led to worship the creature rather than the Creator, may be traced in all the history of the past. Satan's efforts to misrepresent the character of God, to cause men to cherish a false conception of the Creator, and thus to regard Him with fear and hate rather than with love; his endeavours to set aside the divine law, leading the people to think themselves free from its requirements; and his persecution of those who dare to resist his deceptions, have been steadfastly pursued in all ages. They may be traced in the history of "patriarchs, prophets, and apostles, of martyrs and reformers." The Great Controversy p.x (Introduction)

Not just in the Bible, but in all the events of history, we may trace the outworking of this struggle. From the patriarchs to the apostles, the reality of the controversy may be seen. Learning how God's people throughout history have faced the fiery darts of the wicked will give much practical guidance for our everyday life.

The Bible reveals not only how the conflict began and has been unfolding over time, but also gives the assurance of how it will end with Christ being victorious. As we see the characters and purposes of the two sides revealed, we find sufficient motivation to lay our trust confidently on the side of Christ.

The above themes set the backdrop of the various topics and subjects found throughout the Bible. In the next chapter (*Biblical Meditation*), under the section "*What God Would Have Us Meditate On,*" we discuss some of the major subjects which God has given us to contemplate on to ensure that we may abide in Him.

Promises Concerning the Word of God

"If ye abide in Me, and My words abide in you, ye shall ask what ye will, and it shall be done unto you." John 15:7

"My son, if you receive My words, and treasure My commands within you, So that you incline your ear to wisdom, and apply your heart to understanding; yes, if you cry out for discernment, and lift up your voice for understanding, if you seek her as silver,

and search for her as for hidden treasures; then you will under-stand the fear of the Lord, and find the knowledge of God. For the Lord gives wisdom; from His mouth come knowledge and under-standing." Proverbs 2:1-6 NKJV

"Make them holy by your truth; teach them your word, which is truth." John 17:17 NLT

"For you have been born again, but not to a life that will quick-ly end. Your new life will last forever because it comes from the eternal, living word of God. As the Scriptures say, "People are like grass; their beauty is like a flower in the field. The grass withers and the flower fades. But the word of the Lord remains forever." And that word is the Good News that was preached to you." 1 Peter 1:23-25 NLT

Questions on Chapter 3

Is there a wrong and right way to study the Bible? (p.36)

How are we to study the Bible? (p.36)

What do I do to gain understanding of what I read from the Bible? (p.39)

How can I avoid hasty and superficial reading? (p.39)

What do I do after reading the Bible? (p.40)

How can I discover the various ideas that are within a Bible passage? (p.42)

What is the most helpful method in daily Bible Study? (p.44)

What approach did Jesus use to give an understanding of the Bible? (p.45)

What three important questions can we ask when learning from the Bible? (p.45)

What can I do to keep track of what I learn from the Bible? (p.47)

What are some of the major themes to be studied from the Bible? (p.47-51)

What promises has God given concerning the power of His word? (p.52)

4

Biblical Meditation

❧

The Importance of Meditation[1]

One of the best lessons I have come to learn is the fact there is a direct relationship between a person's Christian experience and where they focus their mind. Notice how the author of Hebrews puts it:

"For consider ([or think carefully about)] Him that endured such contradiction of sinners against Himself, lest ye be wearied and faint in your minds." Hebrews 12:3

Here lies the cause for the lack of peace in a Christian's experience. The reason many grow weary and faint in their walk with Christ is because the mind is not steadily fixed on Him, it is not considering Him as He should be considered.

"You will keep him in perfect peace, whose mind is stayed on You, because he trusts in You." Isaiah 26:3 NKJV

When the mind is stayed on Christ, when it is constantly abiding in Him, then one may experience perfect peace. The opposite is also true; when the mind is *not* stayed upon God, then there is no peace at all.

We want to have an experience of abiding in Christ. What we will find throughout this chapter is that by keeping our minds focussed on Christ, we may constantly abide in and with Him. It has always been the will of God that we would have the peace that comes from such an experience.

"Mercy unto you, and peace and love, be multiplied." Jude 1:2

Essential for Abiding in Christ

"Therefore, brethren, be even more diligent to make your call and election sure, for if you do these things you will never stumble; for so an entrance will be supplied to you abundantly into the everlasting kingdom of our Lord and Saviour Jesus Christ." 2 Peter 1:10-11 NKJV

Footnote:
1. The word "meditation" is used as a synonym to the words "consider", "contemplate", "think deeply", "reflect," "to pay careful attention", and to "behold".

In writing to the Christians of the early church (also called the "elect"), Peter encourages them to make their "calling and election sure" so that they may gain entrance into Christ's kingdom. He is telling them to remain in the call that they have accepted in order that they may abide and not stumble. He then continues with the following words:

"For this reason I will not be negligent to remind you always of these things, though you know [them] and are established in the present truth." Verse 12

Because it is possible for those who are already in Christ to stumble back to their old life of sin, and no longer abide in Christ, Peter makes sure to remind the church of the truth that they had already known. Even though they were familiar with that truth, Peter would have the church constantly thinking about it.

Thus we find an essential principle for abiding in Christ; it is the fact that in order to make our calling and election sure--in order to abide in Christ--we must constantly be reminded of the "present truth" (the gospel). This is to be the case even though we may already know that truth and even be established in it.

An Example of the Israelites
Moses, near the close of his life, reminded the Israelites about the goodness and mercy of God towards them--despite their unfaithfulness. He then says these words to them:

"Therefore know this day, and consider it in your heart, that the Lord Himself is God in heaven above and on the earth beneath; there is no other." Deuteronomy 4:39 NKJV

As much as the Israelites were to *know* the things spoken by Moses, they were just as equally meant to *consider* them. The Israelites were charged to think about those things that they had already come to know.

Thus we find that only having a knowledge of the truth (as a collection of information) is not enough. The truth that one knows, especially as it relates to the gospel, needs to have our constant thought and attention in order for it to carry out its work in the heart.

Truth Affects Us When it is Considered

In view of the above, Paul speaks these words to the Corinthian church:

"Moreover, brethren, I declare unto you the gospel which I preached unto you, which also you have received, and wherein you stand; by which also you are saved, if you keep in memory what I preached unto you, unless you have believed in vain." 1 Corinthians 15:1-2

Paul had preached the gospel to the Corinthians before. It was to the Corinthians that he had said: "*I determined not to know anything among you, save Jesus Christ, and Him crucified.*" (1 Corinthians 2:2). They had gladly received the gospel and were even said to "stand" in it. Yet even though that was the case, Paul saw it fit to repeat the gospel to them again; to remind them of what they had already accepted and believed.

In speaking of the gospel, Paul highlights that we are saved by it. The apostle uses the words "are saved" in the present, passive tense; that is because he is referring to a present-day experience of being saved, an experience that is taking place right now. This is the case when the gospel which we have once received still has our focused attention.

We are saved by the gospel, we are sanctified and transformed by it, when we keep the gospel fresh in our minds. Not keeping that gospel in memory would mean that the Corinthians had "believed in vain." Thus it can be said that the truth sanctifies us, it makes us more godly, when it has our attention. In a later epistle, Paul mentions to the church at Corinth that:

"We all, with open face beholding as in a glass the glory of the Lord, are changed into the same image from glory to glory, even as by the Spirit of the Lord." 2 Corinthians 3:18

When we behold the truth of God's word, and as we allow it to have our attention, only then does it have the desired impact of transforming us. It is by beholding and meditating on the truth that we are changed by it. As mentioned before;

"Many attend religious services, and are refreshed and comforted by the word of God; but through neglect of meditation, watchfulness, and prayer, they lose the blessing, and find themselves more destitute than before they received it. Often they feel that God has dealt hardly with them. They do not see that the fault is their own. By separating themselves from Jesus, they have shut away the light of His presence." The Desire of Ages p.83

It is by neglect of meditation and prayer that many separate themselves from Jesus. The point being made is that by lightly regarding the task of keeping the mind on Jesus and His truth, many do not abide in Christ as they have the opportunity to.

Meditating was Jesus' practice

Jesus Himself was in the habit of meditating. This was one of the ways in which He kept an open line of communion with God the Father.

"Working at the carpenter's bench, bearing the burdens of home life, learning the lessons of obedience and toil, [Jesus] found recreation amidst the scenes of nature, gathering knowledge as He sought to understand nature's mysteries. He studied the word of God, and His hours of greatest happiness were found when He could turn aside from the scene of His labors to go into the fields, to meditate in the quiet valleys, to hold communion with God on the mountainside or amid the trees of the forest. The early morning often found Him in some secluded place, meditating, searching the Scriptures, or in prayer. With the voice of singing He welcomed the morning light. With songs of thanksgiving He cheered His hours of labor and brought heaven's gladness to the toil worn and disheartened." Ministry of Healing p.52

In His times of reflection and meditation, Jesus found the greatest happiness. He saw it necessary to spend some time meditating so that He may thus commune with His Father. In holding an open line of communion with God through meditating, we may also enjoy the "perfect peace" which Isaiah speaks of (Isaiah 26:3).

Results in Understanding God's Word

As noted in the previous chapter (*Search the Scriptures*), we gain a better understanding of God's word when we meditate on it.

"Consider what I say; and the Lord [will] give thee understanding in all things" 2 Timothy 2:7

In writing to Timothy, Paul presents the idea that it is when God's word is considered (or meditated on and given careful attention), that God then grants further understanding. That is His formula.

In the very next line of the epistle, Paul then tells Timothy to "remember" what he was taught when Paul preached the gospel. Thus we find that Timothy already knew some of the things which Paul was writing about. Although this was the case, Timothy also needed to be reminded of the those teachings, in order for him to give them careful consideration.

A Way to Strengthen Faith

"Many professed Christians, who have a knowledge of the sacred Word, and believe its truth, fail in the childlike trust that is essential to the religion of Jesus. They do not reach out with that peculiar touch that brings the virtue of healing to the soul." S.D.A. Bible Commentary, vol.6 p.1074

Many who profess Christianity, while they may be familiar with the Bible, still do not have the childlike trust in God that is essential for abiding in Him. This is something I have found it to be true as I get the opportunity to travel and preach; but this lack of trust is very unnecessary. Faith can be strengthened when that truth which we "know" is considered and recalled to mind.

"This I recall to my mind, therefore have I hope. It is of the Lord's mercies that we are not consumed, because His compassions fail not." Lamentations 3:21-22

When Jeremiah wrote these words, he was reflecting on the destruction of Jerusalem that had recently taken place. The city and the temple were in ruins and members of his family were taken captive to the foreign land of Babylon. Although it was an extremely difficult situation, Jeremiah still speaks of a hope that he had. Such a hope stems from recalling and meditating on the fact that, because of God's mercy, he had not been consumed. For Jeremiah, the act of meditating became a means to strengthen his faith, even during a very difficult situation.

The point must be noted that God would have us do more with the truth than to only know it. Its impact on our lives is the result of us giving it thought and attention, and frequently so. This is how we can also be strengthened in hope like Jeremiah.

Song Illustration

I love music. Oftentimes it so happens that there may be a song or two that I really enjoy listening to. It may be because of the catchy chorus, or the way that the voices blend together to make up the harmony.

After some time, it so happens that I have stopped to listen and actually consider the lyrics of the song; to listen to what the song is *actually* saying. For some songs, it was only then that the song had its deepest impact; as though the real message behind the song just clicked in the mind. Although I already knew the songs, their impact was not experienced or felt until I paid careful attention to them.

This is sometimes the case with others also. Unlike it being with a song, however, this also occurs in relation to God's word and the experiences that His providence may allow. There are things in God's word and in our daily experiences that He wants to impact us with. In giving those things careful consideration, as with the lyrics of a good song, we can experience the intended blessing behind God's Word and the acts of His providence.

What God Would Have Us Meditate On

Throughout His inspired word, God has given an outline of things for us to keep our focus on. The Bible shows us what things to consider and meditate on in order for us to abide in Christ. Let us note a few:

61

The Love of God

"Behold what manner of love the Father has bestowed on us, that we should be called children of God! Therefore the world does not know us, because it did not know Him." 1 John 3:1 NKJV

God draws us closer to Himself by His love. It is by considering and beholding that love, and where God has demonstrated it, that we draw closer to Him. This is how the experience of abiding in Christ is strengthened.

"The Lord has appeared of old to me, saying: Yes, I have loved you with an everlasting love; Therefore with lovingkindness I have drawn you." Jeremiah 31:3 NKJV

We are drawn closer to God by His lovingkindness, His mercy. The highest expression of this love was revealed in the death of Christ on the cross. "God showed His great love for us by sending Christ to die for us while we were still sinners." (Romans 5:8). Hence Jesus could say the words:

"And I, if I be lifted up from the earth, will draw all men unto me. This He said, signifying what death He should die." John12:32-33

God's infinite love was revealed in the death of His Son on behalf of sinners. This love demands our attention. When we meditate on the demonstration of God's love--the righteous Son of God dying for sinners--it draws us closer to Christ. It is important to pause and think about what that must mean about how God feels about humanity, and about you as an individual.

"Make it a point in your life never to forget God's love." Manuscript Releases Vol.20 p.232

The Life, Death, and Ministry of Christ

"Therefore we also, since we are surrounded by so great a cloud of witnesses, let us lay aside every weight, and the sin which so easily ensnares us, and let us run with endurance the race that is set before us, looking unto Jesus, the author and finisher of our faith, who for the joy that was set before Him endured the cross, despis-

ing the shame, and has sat down at the right hand of the throne of God. For consider Him who endured such hostility from sinners against Himself, lest you become weary and discouraged in your souls." Hebrews 12:1-3 NKJV

In encouraging believers to run the Christian race with patience (with endurance and staying power), Paul urges us to "look unto Jesus." Jesus is the author and finisher of our faith. It is only by abiding in Him, from start to finish, that we are enabled to run the Christian race. This "looking" is done by "considering Him," by letting the mind dwell on thoughts of Him who endured the cross for us. Hence:

"It would be well for us to spend a thoughtful hour each day in contemplation of the life of Christ. We should take it point by point, and let the imagination grasp each scene, especially the closing ones. As we thus dwell upon His great sacrifice for us, our confidence in Him will be more constant, our love will be quickened, and we shall be more deeply imbued with His Spirit. If we would be saved at last, we must learn the lesson of penitence and humiliation at the foot of the cross." The Desire of Ages p.83

In order to have a living experience of abiding in Christ--behold Him; let the imagination be fixed on His life and death as revealed throughout the scriptures. This is how we may have a more constant confidence in Jesus as a Saviour.

Generally, too little thought is given to the life and death of Jesus. Christ's life, however, must be seen not only as a record of history. The mind is to be directed to contemplating on who He is as a person--as the king of the universe, choosing to live the life, and die the death, that He did.

Christ As Our High Priest in the Heavenly Sanctuary

"Wherefore, holy brethren, partakers of the heavenly calling, consider the Apostle and High Priest of our profession, Christ Jesus." Hebrews 3:1

To those who are already partakers of the heavenly calling, to the

Hebrew Christians, the writer gives the instruction to "consider" Christ Jesus. We are encouraged to view Him as the High Priest of our profession. This request is made in view of what the writer mentions before, in the previous chapters of the book of Hebrews. He notes that:

> *"It was necessary for [Jesus] to be made in every respect like us, His brothers and sisters, so that He could be our merciful and faithful High Priest before God. Then He could offer a sacrifice that would take away the sins of the people. Since He himself has gone through suffering and testing, He is able to help us when we are being tested." Hebrews 2:17-18 NLT*

In the first chapter of Hebrews, the writer depicts Christ as being fully divine and, thus, worthy of as much honour as God the Father. In the second chapter, Jesus is then shown to be as fully human as we are. These two qualities make Jesus the perfect high priest. He relates with our human condition enough to be merciful, while at the same time He is powerful enough as God to help us when we are tempted. We must consider Jesus in this manner, in His work as our High priest.

Before the book of Hebrews begins speaking about the sanctuary (in chapters 8-9), its ornaments and its present application, the first seven chapters are spent discussing the attributes of Jesus as the High Priest. Jesus would have us consider Him as our high priest and what that means to us. How we understand His position and His work as our great High Priest in the heavenly sanctuary directly affects our experience as "partakers of the heavenly calling."

God's Character

> *"But we all, with open face, beholding as in a glass the glory of the Lord, are changed into the same image from glory to glory, even as by the Spirit of the Lord." 2 Corinthians 3:18*

We may abide in Christ, and grow from glory to glory, by being transformed by His Spirit. This comes through intentionally beholding, and giving thought to, the character of God (His glory) as

He has revealed it to us.

"The word of God reveals His character. He Himself has declared His infinite love and pity. When Moses prayed, "Show me Thy glory," the Lord answered, "I will make all My goodness pass before thee." Exodus 33:18, 19. This is His glory. The Lord passed before Moses, and proclaimed, "The Lord, The Lord God, merciful and gracious, long-suffering, and abundant in goodness and truth, keeping mercy for thousands, forgiving iniquity and transgression and sin." Exodus 34:6, 7. He is "slow to anger, and of great kindness," "because He delighteth in mercy." Jonah 4:2; Micah 7:18." Steps to Christ, p.10

The act of considering God's character has a transforming effect on our experience. This is important for those who abide in Christ. By beholding God's character, our own characters develop more and more into being like His. Through constantly meditating on what God is really like, in character, we are thus enabled to go from glory to glory through the power of His Spirit.

The Promises of God's Word and Law

"Blessed is the man who walks not in the counsel of the ungodly, nor stands in the path of sinners, nor sits in the seat of the scornful; But his delight is in the law of the Lord, and in His law he meditates day and night. He shall be like a tree planted by the rivers of water that brings forth its fruit in its season, whose leaf also shall not wither; and whatever he does shall prosper." Psalms 1:1-3 NKJV

In order to be grounded in Christ, to be rooted in Him such that our leaves do not whither, we are to constantly meditate on God's word. The word "law" is translated from the Hebrew word *Torah*, which also refers to the writings of Moses, the first five books of the Bible. The psalmist encourages us to meditate on God's word.

"You need to dwell upon the assurances of God's Word, to hold them before the mind's eye. Point by point, day by day, repeat the lessons there given, over and over, until you learn the bearing and import

of them. We see a little today, and by meditation and prayer, more tomorrow. And thus little by little we take in the gracious promises until we can almost comprehend their full significance.

Oh, how much we lose by not educating the imagination to dwell upon divine things, rather than upon the earthly! We may give fullest scope to the imagination, and yet, "eye hath not seen, nor ear heard, neither have entered into the heart of man, the things which God hath prepared for them that love him." Fresh wonders will be revealed to the mind the more closely we apply it to divine things. We lose much by not talking more of Jesus and of heaven, the saints' inheritance. The more we contemplate heavenly things, the more new delights we shall see, and the more will our hearts be brim-full of thanks to our beneficent Creator." S.D.A Bible Commentary, vol. 6, p.1085

It is when we are constantly meditating on God's word, His law, and the rich promises contained in it, that we may more firmly abide in Christ.

God's Providence and Mercy

During Israel's affliction, the prophet Jeremiah found hope in the memory of God's providence. He was encouraged by remembering that God had preserved him and had still been merciful towards him.

"This I recall to my mind, therefore I have hope. Through the Lord's mercies we are not consumed, because His compassions fail not. They are new every morning; great is Your faithfulness." Lamentations 3:21-23 NKJV

Looking back on one's past, and seeing what Christ has done in keeping us, is a helpful tool to abiding in Him even in times of trial. In the closing years of her ministry, and looking back on the work which God had done to advance the cause of the gospel, Ellen White penned these words:

"In reviewing our past history, having travelled over every step of advance to our present standing, I can say, Praise God! As I see what God has wrought, I am filled with astonishment, and with

confidence in Christ as leader. We have nothing to fear for the future except as we shall forget the way the Lord has led us, and His teaching in our past history." Testimonies to Ministers and Gospel Workers p.31

In contemplation of how God has led us in times past, and His goodness towards us personally, we may have hope for now and for the future. If there is anything we are to fear, it must be to fear forgetting God's goodness towards us in the past.

God's Creative Power

"To whom then will you liken Me, or to whom shall I be equal?" says the Holy One. Lift up your eyes on high, and see who has created these things, who brings out their host by number; He calls them all by name, by the greatness of His might and the strength of His power; not one is missing." Isaiah 40:25-26 NKJV

God's power to create is the same power He uses to sustain us in our walk with Christ. We are *"kept by the power of God through faith for salvation"* (1 Peter 1:5). This power is revealed throughout all nature (Romans 1:20). God calls us to contemplate on His creative power and His ability to sustain what He has created. In so doing, our confidence in God will be more firm. When we realise how powerful God is, we will have little cause for worry or anxiety. Hence God asks:

"Why do you say, O Jacob, and speak, O Israel: "My way is hidden from the Lord, and my just claim is passed over by my God?" Isaiah 40:27 NKJV

As we reflect on God's ability to uphold the universe, our confidence in Him to even sustain us will be strengthened. We are to internalise the fact that God upholds the sun, moon and stars with the same power that He intends to use to support us individually. We do not need to ever worry about whether God is able to help in whatever situation one may be going through.

Heaven and What Awaits us in Eternity

When God called Abraham to leave his homeland (in Genesis 12:1-3), we are told that:

"By faith [Abraham] went to live in the land of promise, as in a foreign land, living in tents with Isaac and Jacob, heirs with him of the same promise. For he was looking forward to the city that has foundations, whose designer and builder is God." Hebrews 11:9-10 ESV

Even while in the earthly land of promise, Abraham expected to receive a heavenly city from God. This is why it is said that he and his household "confessed that they were strangers and pilgrims in the earth." (Verse 13).

Abraham still upheld his faith, even until his death, while not having yet received the promise. He could have turned back after the first years of not receiving the promise, yet Abraham and his family still chose to abide in Christ. This was due to where their minds were focussed:

"If they had been thinking of that land from which they had gone out, they would have had opportunity to return." Hebrews 11:15 ESV

Abraham and His family never drew back because their focus constantly looked forward to what God had promised him. We may also fix our minds on the eternal home that God has prepared for those whom He has called. When our eyes are on what awaits us, and not on the old life, we will not find reason to draw back from walking with God.

As the spiritual seed of Abraham, we too may walk with God by considering and meditating on His promises--especially the promise of a sinless and eternally peaceful home.

"If then you have been raised with Christ, seek the things that are above, where Christ is, seated at the right hand of God. Set your minds on things that are above, not on things that are on earth. For you have died and your life is hidden with Christ in God. When Christ who is your life appears, then you also will appear

with Him in glory." Colossians 3:1-4 ESV

"If we would permit our minds to dwell more upon Christ and the heavenly world, we should find a powerful stimulus and support in fighting the battles of the Lord. Pride and love of the world will lose their power as we contemplate the glories of that better land so soon to be our home. Beside the loveliness of Christ, all earthly attractions will seem of little worth." Messages to Young People p.113

The Second Coming of Christ

"Looking for that blessed hope, and the glorious appearing of the great God and our Saviour Jesus Christ." Titus 2:13

As much as looking back at the past mercies of God inspires hope to keep us abiding in Christ (Lamentations 3:21-22), Christians also have the hope of looking forward to the second coming of Christ and the ultimate end of sin.

"Christ was once offered to bear the sins of many; and unto them that look for Him shall He appear the second time without sin unto salvation" Hebrews 9:28

At His return, Jesus appears with salvation to those who have let Him bear their sins. He will deliver those who "look for Him," those who meditate on His second coming.

While the writer of Hebrews counsels the church to meditate on the second coming in order to be prepared for it, John also counsels the church to "abide in [Christ]; that, when He shall appear, we may have confidence, and not be ashamed before Him at His coming." (1 John 2:28).

These ideas are closely related. In order for us to abide in Christ, and maintain our communion with Him, we are to keep in mind the reality of His second coming.

"The truth that Christ is coming should be kept before every mind." Evangelism p.220

God's Goodness with His Severity

Keeping a steady focus on God and the goodness of His character is essential for our individual Christian experience. It is also just as important to keep God's justness in view also. Notice the apostle's words.

"Consider the goodness and the severity of God: on those who fell, severity; but toward you, goodness, if you continue in His goodness. Otherwise you also will be cut off." Romans 11:22 NKJV

Looking at God's dealings with ancient Israel, after bringing them out of Egypt, we witness God's response to those who disregard His goodness. God showed His mercy on the Jews by bringing them out of Egypt. When the Israelites rejected God's goodness, however, and "in their hearts turned back again into Egypt" (Acts 7:39), God let a majority of them die in the wilderness without entering the Promised Land.

This experience of the Israelites is meant to be a solemn warning to us. When we--like the ancient Israelites--turn away from God's goodness by our unbelief, unfaithfulness and neglect, the same thing that happened to them can happen to us also. The New Testament writers make sure to also remind us of this fact.

Paul recounts how, although ancient Israel all made it out of Egypt and experienced the miracles of in the desert, they did not all make it to Canaan. He continues to make it clear to spiritual Israel that "with many of them ([ancient Israel]) God was not well pleased" (1 Corinthians 10:5). This was seen in how "they were overthrown in the wilderness."

"Now these things occurred as examples to keep us from setting our hearts on evil things as they did." 1 Corinthians 10:6 NIV

Here lies the reason why Paul encourages us to not forget God's severity "on those who fell." This is to keep us from falling into the same rebellious condition as them; it is so that we may maintain our abiding experience.

The experience of the ancient Jews is a caution against lightly regarding our duty to ensure that we are abiding in Him.

"Now all these things happened to them as examples, and they were written for our admonition, upon whom the ends of the ages

have come. Therefore let him who thinks he stands take heed lest he fall." 1 Corinthians 10:11-12 NKJV

More than anything, while we consider God's severity towards "them that fell", we need to also consider God's goodness as being most especially related to ourselves. God is not only good, but He is good to me and to you *personally*. In beholding His goodness and His severity it is our privilege to continue, to abide, in His goodness. (Romans 11:22)

In Summary

One may notice here that all the above points are summed up as the fundamental themes of the gospel, and these are laid out all through the Bible. In holding communion with Christ, abiding in Him moment by moment, our minds may dwell on the great plan of salvation. This is to be the theme that we contemplate on, both now and throughout all eternity. It is the central theme of all scripture.

> *"Moreover, brethren, I declare unto you the gospel... By which also ye are saved, if ye keep in memory what I preached unto you, unless ye have believed in vain." 1 Corinthians 15:1-2*

Constantly letting our minds dwell on the plan of salvation will be what keeps us abiding in Christ. This is true for our lives now and this will also be what keeps us abiding in Christ even throughout eternity.

> *"The central theme of the Bible, the theme about which every other in the whole book clusters, is the redemption plan, the restoration in the human soul of the image of God." Education p.125*

> *"The theme of redemption is one that angels desire to look into; it will be the science and the song of the redeemed throughout the ceaseless ages of eternity. Is it not worthy of careful thought and study now?" Maranatha p.365*

Dangers to Meditation

It is a part of God's plan to keep us abiding in Him by having our minds stayed on Him. As stated previously, we are kept in perfect

71

peace in our experience when our attention is constantly fixed on Jesus (Isaiah 26:3).

Knowing this, it should come as no surprise that Satan's constant effort would be to divert the mind from meditating on Christ. We read:

"Satan invents unnumbered schemes to occupy our minds, that they may not dwell upon the very work with which we ought to be best acquainted. The arch-deceiver hates the great truths that bring to view an atoning sacrifice and an all-powerful mediator. He knows that with him everything depends on his diverting minds from Jesus and His truth." The Great Controversy, p.488

Among the greatest strongholds that Satan can have on an individual is when he can divert ones focus from rightly considering Jesus. His efforts are primarily bent towards achieving this aim.

With this in view, we ought to guard what enters our minds and what has our attention so that our focus is never diverted from Christ. "For without Me", Jesus says, "you can do nothing."

Evaluating What Enters the Mind

Noting the importance of this point, God has not left us to guess when it comes to how we may filter the things that come into our minds. He has given us a very helpful principle for measuring what is fit for our mental diet and what is not. Note Paul's counsel to the Philippians:

"Be anxious for nothing, but in everything by prayer and supplication, with thanksgiving, let your requests be made known to God; and the peace of God, which surpasses all understanding, will guard your hearts and minds through Christ Jesus.

Finally, brethren, whatever things are true, whatever things are noble, whatever things are just, whatever things are pure, whatever things are lovely, whatever things are of good report, if there is any virtue and if there is anything praiseworthy—meditate on these things. The things which you learned and received and heard and saw in me, these do, and the God of peace will be with you." Philippians 4:6-9 NKJV

The peace of God, which surpasses all understanding, may be ours; this peace can guard our minds and hearts. Paul encourages us to meditate only on that which is true and good in order to maintain this experience. The principle which is outlined to the Philippians is a helpful way to deciding on the kinds of entertainment to permit into one's mind. For the sake of continuing to abide in Christ, it is often better to not give attention to those things which do not meet this God-given principle.

We may note the intimate connection between our Christian experience and the things that we watch, listen to and think on. At times, the primary reason behind an unstable spiritual experience may be found in the kinds of entertainment one participates in; and Jesus wants to free us from these.

Things to Avoid Letting the Mind Dwell On

God's word abounds with helpful instruction on things to avoid letting the mind dwell on. These are things which, instead of causing us to abide in Christ, do the harmful work of drawing us away from Him. We will consider a few:

Instructions and Teachings that Draw Away from Obeying God

"Cease, my son, to hear the instruction that causeth to err from the words of knowledge." Proverbs 19:27

Consider the appeals of a caring Father. There are a number of things which, without question, cause one to divert form the path of obedience. When we hear instructions which cause us to stray from God's word, it is for our good to cease hearing that instruction.

"By beholding we become changed. By the indulgence of impure thoughts man can so educate his mind that sin which he once loathed will become pleasant to him." Patriarchs and Prophets p.459

One may ask: "How will I know whether or not something is an erroneous instruction, until I hear it?" The wise man, in his counsel, is careful to use the words "cease." While it is true that we may not know that some things are not praiseworthy, until we hear them, it is within our ability to stop listening.

Imaginations that Seek to Divert the Mind from God

"The weapons of our warfare are not carnal, but mighty through God to the pulling down of strong holds; Casting down imaginations, and every high thing that exalteth itself against the knowledge of God, and bringing into captivity every thought to the obedience of Christ;" 2 Corinthians 10:4-5

The imagination, when left to itself, is counted among the "high things that exalt themselves against the knowledge of God". Our thoughts however, together with everything else that seeks to divert the mind away from abiding in Christ, may be brought into obedience to Christ through the weapons of our warfare. These are described as mighty weapons and powerful through God. God's word among these weapons:

"For the word of God is quick, and powerful, and sharper than any two edged sword, piercing even to the dividing asunder of soul and spirit, and of the joints and marrow, and is a discerner of the thoughts and intents of the heart." Hebrews 4:12

When God created humanity, He intended that we should have a pure imagination. Since the fall, however, our imaginations have been weakened: "the imagination of [humanity's] heart is evil from [their] youth" (Genesis 8:21). Satan can take advantage of this when we give him the right to our imagination.

Solomon, the wise man, counsels us to "keep your heart with all diligence, for out of it spring the issues of life." Proverbs 4:23. The things that we allow into our minds affect our everyday experience. This is why it is crucial to guard what we allow our minds to imagine and meditate on.

Vain and Vulgar Conversation

"Shun profane and idle babblings, for they will increase to more

*ungodliness. And their message will spread like cancer." 2 Timothy
2:16-17 NKJV*

In counseling Timothy, Paul warns about the danger of profane and
idle conversation. Inappropriate and vulgar talk has the power to
make a person become more and more ungodly.

How we evaluate what we watch and listen to (see *Evaluating
What Enters the Mind*, p.80) may be safely applied even to the subjects of our conversations.

Arguments and Debates, Especially Regarding "Spiritual Things"

One of Satan's tricks is to create spiritual pride in an individual by
leading them to debate, especially about spiritual things. Arguments
seldom tend to produce the spirit of a learner, seeking to understand
truth; rather, arguments tend to cause one to proudly feel themselves to be right. Such a spirit is unhealthy, because "God resists the
proud, but gives grace unto the humble" (James 4:6). For this reason, it is always best to avoid unnecessary arguments and whatever
may lead to them.

*"Avoid foolish controversies and genealogies and arguments and
quarrels about the law, because these are unprofitable and useless."
Titus 3:9 NIV*

Sometimes, though not always, questions are asked only to provoke
arguments. Because these do not really benefit a person, it is best to
avoid them.

The Faults of Others

*"And why do you look at the speck in your brother's eye, but do not
consider the plank in your own eye?" Matthew 7:3 NKJV*

*"According to the figure that our Saviour uses, he who indulges
a censorious ([critical or disapproving]) spirit is guilty of greater
sin than is the one he accuses, for he not only commits the same
sin, but adds to it conceit and censoriousness." Thoughts from the
Mount of Blessings p.125*

The faults, sins and shortcomings of those around us must bring grief to one who considers how much pain sin brings to the heart of God; nevertheless, we are not to let the faults of others be the subject of our constant meditation.

What is perhaps most dangerous about this trick of the devil is that it not only causes one to be proud in their idea of themselves (by watching the evident faults of others), but it also results in not "looking diligently" to Christ. The natural result of looking to the faults of others, and not to Christ, leads to bitterness:

"Looking diligently ([unto Jesus]) lest any man fail of the grace of God; lest any root of bitterness springing up trouble you, and thereby many be defiled;" Hebrews 12:15

Bitterness, that may lie rooted in the heart, sometimes springs up as a consequence of ceasing to look diligently on Christ, to behold the unpleasant traits of others. Like most roots, this bitterness may lie hidden for some time, only to spring up later.

In order to abide in Christ, it is important to not make the faults of others the focus of our attention.

The Worries and Cares of Life

"Therefore do not worry about tomorrow, for tomorrow will worry about its own things. Sufficient for the day is its own trouble." Matthew 6:34 NKJV

In order to divert our minds from Jesus and His truth, Satan would have us spend time worrying about the things that are not within our power to change. But this does not need to be the case. In walking with Christ, we may have a living experience of trusting ourselves to Him, for Him to take care of us as His possession.

"But watch yourselves lest your hearts be weighed down with... [the] cares of this life, and that day come upon you suddenly like a trap." Luke 21:34 ESV

We are to guard against letting the worries of life take advantage of our hearts, to the extent that we no longer rest in Jesus. This is important to ensuring that the day of Christ's coming does not find us distracted.

"Worry is blind, and cannot discern the future; but Jesus sees the end from the beginning. In every difficulty He has His way prepared to bring relief. Our heavenly Father has a thousand ways to provide for us, of which we know nothing. Those who accept the one principle of making the service and honor of God supreme will find perplexities vanish, and a plain path before their feet." The Desire of Ages, p330

Those who walk with God have the privilege of knowing that Jesus can bring relief to every challenge that they face. We can have peace from knowing that our Saviour can help us in every difficulty. For this reason,

"Don't worry about anything; instead, pray about everything. Tell God what you need, and thank Him for all He has done. Then you will experience God's peace, which exceeds anything we can understand. His peace will guard your hearts and minds as you live in Christ Jesus." Philippians 4:6-7 ESV

Challenges and Helps to Meditation

In a presentation on the topic of "considering Christ", the question was raised: "but how do I stop my mind from wandering off to some other (questionable) things when I try to meditate on Christ?"

This was a very practical question. This question is answerable in two points. The first is this:

"If Satan seeks to turn [the mind] to low and sensual things, bring it back. When corrupt imaginings seek to gain possession of your mind, flee to the throne of grace, and pray for strength from heaven. By the grace of Christ it is possible for us to reject impure thoughts. Jesus will attract the mind, purify the thoughts, and cleanse the heart from every secret sin. "The weapons of our warfare are not carnal, but mighty through God; . . . casting down imaginations, and every high thing that exalteth itself against the knowledge of God, and bringing into captivity every thought to the obedience of Christ." [2 Corinthians 10:4, 5.] Christian Temperance and Bible Hygiene p.136

As noted earlier, when the imagination is left to itself (or to others), it naturally exalts itself against the knowledge of God. Through the weapons of our warfare (prayer and the scriptures), the imagination can be cast down and ordered in the right direction.

The second point is that sometimes the imagination is handed over to the hands of the enemy through the common forms of entertainment that many indulge nowadays; and the mind follows that which it is accustomed to receiving. Through watching and listening to entertainment that does not draw one to Christ, the imagination gets accustomed to dwelling on Christ-less themes. As it is in the physical world, so it is with the mind: what we feed the mind with will affect its health.

In some instances, it may be for one's benefit to cut down on things which draw the mind away from Christ. This includes things such as some television programs and perhaps a change in music selection. Many will be surprised at the extent to which the things they watch and listen to affect what their imagination naturally dwells on.

"The first work of those who would reform is to purify the imagination. If the mind is led out in a vicious direction, it must be restrained to dwell only upon pure and elevated subjects. When tempted to yield to a corrupt imagination, then flee to the throne of grace and pray for strength from Heaven. In the strength of God the imagination can be disciplined to dwell upon things which are pure and heavenly." Mind, Character, & Personality, book 2, p.595

When one cultivates the habit of disciplining the imagination to dwell on what is pure: the mind becomes familiar with the practice.

I am often fascinated at the power of the mind. Sometimes, at very random times, some of the vulgar hip-hop music that I used to write and listen to pays my mind an uninvited visit. Almost immediately, this comes to my attention and the "weapons of our warfare" have proven themselves to truly be mighty through immediately fleeing to the throne of grace.

Through prayer, and by storing God's word in the mind, these thoughts--together with any other thought that seeks to exalt itself against the knowledge of God--may be successfully resisted.

"There are thoughts and feelings suggested and aroused by Satan that annoy even the best of men; but if they are not cherished, if they are repulsed as hateful, the soul is not contaminated with guilt, and no other is defiled by their influence." That I May Know Him, p.140

In Your Everyday Life

One of the best bits of advice I received was during my first year of studying architecture. A prominent preacher, addressing an audience of university students, said: "You need to find God in what you are studying…"

This idea radically impacted how I viewed my studies and it can be a helpful practice in every one of our daily duties. When I started looking at my studies through that perspective, it affected my performance at school. Schoolwork was no longer a burden that drew the thoughts away from God, but became a means of holding communion with Him. I then started asking questions such as: "If God were an architect, what kind of architect would He be..?" Thus, even in our daily labours, we may constantly be learning of God and holding communion with Him through our own experiences.

Consider the thought as expressed below:

"In every line of useful labor and every association of life, [God] desires us to find a lesson of divine truth. Then our daily toil will no longer absorb our attention and lead us to forget God; it will continually remind us of our Creator and Redeemer. The thought of God will run like a thread of gold through all our homely cares and occupations. For us the glory of His face will again rest upon the face of nature. We shall ever be learning new lessons of heavenly truth, and growing into the image of His purity. Thus shall we "be taught of the Lord"; and in the lot wherein we are called, we shall "abide with God." Isaiah 54:13; 1 Corinthians 7:24." Christ's Object Lessons p.26

A Promise to Hold On to

As in all things that pertain to one's spiritual life, when it comes to receiving the power to constantly fix the mind on Christ, He says "without me, you can do nothing."

Like the psalmist, we too may pray the prayer:

"Open thou mine eyes, that I may behold wondrous things out of thy law." Psalms 119:18

Questions on Chapter 4

How does what I think about affect how I walk with God? (p.56)

What is the relationship between abiding in Christ and meditating upon God's word? (p.56-57)

What does God call us to do with the truth once we know it? (p.57)

What is the effect of not taking time to meditate? (p.58)

What are the things that God's word counsels me to think on? (p.61-69)

In summary, what is the overall theme that God wishes us to meditate on? (p.71)

What is Satan's scheme to get us to lose our experience of abiding in Christ? (p.71)

What are we counselled against allowing our minds to meditate on? (p.73)

Why should I be careful about what I watch or listen to? (p.72)

How does meditating on the faults of others affect my spirituality? (p.75)

How do I stop my mind from wandering off to think about things that I should not be thinking about? (p.77)

How do I channel my mind back to God, when it has turned to questionable things? (p.77)

How can I stay my mind on God in my everyday life? (p.79)

5

Scripture Memorisation

Why to Memorise Scripture

Methods for Memorising

Practical Suggestions

Helpful Tools

Why to Memorise Scripture

One of the main points that have been emphasised throughout the previous chapters is the idea that it is Jesus' intention that His people should abide in Him. Another central point is that we should get more closely acquainted with Christ through His word; Christ may be known by searching the scriptures. With this in mind, notice the psalmist's attitude:

> *"Oh, how I love Your law! It is my meditation all the day." Psalms 119:97 NKJV*

> *"Blessed is the man who walks not in the counsel of the ungodly, nor stands in the path of sinners, nor sits in the seat of the scornful; But his delight is in the law of the Lord, and in His law he meditates day and night. He shall be like a tree planted by the rivers of water that brings forth its fruit in its season, whose leaf also shall not wither; and whatever he does shall prosper." Psalms 1:1-3 NKJV*

We have the privilege of being rooted and abiding in Christ like a tree planted by rivers of water. This comes by meditating on His word "day and night." I would not take this to necessarily mean having one's Bible in hand throughout every moment of the day; rather, as a means of continually abiding in Christ, His word ought to be stored in the mind.

I have personally come to learn that having the words of scripture committed to memory becomes very fruitful to meditating on God's word "all the day." More than this, we shall consider a few more motivations for scripture memorisation. We will find that memorising the words of the Bible is one of heavens methods to keep us in communion with Christ.

An Essential Means for Abiding in Christ

Before Adam and Eve sinned, they held face to face communion with God. Since the entrance of sin, however, humanity has lost that privilege. The effects of sin include causing a separation between us and God.

84

"Behold, the Lord's hand is not shortened, that it cannot save; neither His ear heavy, that it cannot hear: but your iniquities have separated between you and your God, and your sins have hid His face from you, that He will not hear." Isaiah 59:1-2

God still longs to commune with humankind. But, as was the case in Eden, sin continues to separate people from God. Through sin, humanity does not abide in Christ as we may. Keeping God's word in the heart is a helpful means of resisting the temptations to sin and thus maintain the experience of abiding in Christ. As the psalmist writes:

"I have stored up your word in my heart, that I might not sin against you." Psalms 119:11 ESV

This was the experience with Christ while He was in His human form on earth; He held continuous communion with God the Father. He was even able to testify of the constant communion He had with His heavenly Father. Jesus could say:

"He who sent Me is with Me. The Father has not left Me alone, for I always do those things that please Him." John 8:29 NKJV

When faced with temptation, Jesus relied on the word of God to resist sin and maintain a constant connection with God. When Jesus was hungry, and tempted by Satan to rely on His divine power to satisfy His appetite, Jesus replied:

"It is written, Man shall not live by bread alone, but by every word that proceeds out of the mouth of God." Matthew 4:4 NKJV

In all three of His responses to Satan's temptations, Jesus -- as our example -- responded with a plain "it is written..." But Jesus was not carrying the scrolls with Him in the wilderness. When He resisted the enemy's appeals it was because the words of scripture were engraved in His memory.

In order for us to abide in Him, we too may have such an experience, by fixing God's word in our memory as Jesus did.

Not Always Going to Have the Printed Page

"The time will come when many will be deprived of the written Word. But if this Word is printed in the memory, no one can take it from us.

Study the Word of God. Commit its precious promises to memory so that, when we shall be deprived of our Bibles, we may still be in possession of the Word of God." Last Day Events p. 67

While we currently enjoy the liberty of freely having and carrying our Bibles, that freedom will not always be guaranteed to us. When the word of God is stored in the mind, however, we may carry it with us wherever we go; and none will be able to take it away from us.

How Truth Sanctifies

As noted before (in chapter 4, *Biblical Meditation*), God's word impacts us most when it has our attention.

Consider, for a moment, something that is often the case when one reads and thinks on a passage of scripture that they may have thought they knew. It may be, perhaps, while hearing it read in a sermon or even receiving it as a text message from a caring friend. Though one may have known the passage, it is upon thinking about it that its meaning makes an impact and conviction settles in. This is how, I believe, God designed truth to impact our experience: when we contemplate on it.

This is often the case with individuals who may have been Christian for a long time, with Bible passages that they may have first fell in love with in the earlier stage of their Christian journey. It is when we meditate on the word of God, and the thoughts placed in it, that we are affected by it.

Noting that we may not always be sitting down to page through the Bible, through memorising God's word, we are enabled to still consider His promises and assurances wherever we may be. Memorising scripture thus plays a key role in our experience of abiding in Christ.

Methods for Memorising

How, then, can we store God's word in the memory? First off, it may be important to note that there are various ways and methods to memorising scripture. Some methods may be more catered to some minds than others. In spite of how one's mind works, however, God's word is still designed to be stored in that very mind.

We start by considering a few general, but important, principles on how to memorise scripture:

Meditating on the Texts

"I will meditate on Your precepts, and contemplate Your ways. I will delight myself in Your statutes; I will not forget Your word." Psalms 119:15-16 NKJV

This is among the most important of all the principles when it comes to memorising God's word. When we meditate on the God's word, when we intentionally contemplate on it and let it have our attention, we will then not forget that word. When you meditate on the words of scripture, with a heartfelt desire to know and follow God's will, the passages of scripture will become as familiar to us as the way around one's home.

When reading a text or passage of scripture, it is important to grasp the thought that is placed in that verse, the main idea within the text. Then we are to contemplate, to think carefully about, the thought that God has put into that text. In so meditating on God's word, together with delighting in it, the result will be to not forget it.

Thus, memorising is more than just storing up the *words*, but it is about retaining the very *ideas* of God in the heart, and letting that transform our thoughts to become more like His. Every other method discussed from here is really a means to meditate on God's word so that it is not forgotten.

Reading and Meditating While Walking

"Keep your Bible with you. As you have opportunity, read it; fix the texts in your memory. Even while you are walking the streets you may read a passage and meditate upon it, thus fixing it in the

mind." Steps to Christ p.90

When meditating on God's word, we fix it in the mind. This can be done whenever the chance avails itself. In our modern age of technology, with Bibles on smart-phones and gadgets, this may be done with ease. Wherever you are, you can read and meditate on a passage of scripture and thus fix it in the memory.

I once used this approach to memorise a short chapter in one of my favourite books. While staying on campus, I would walk for about 15 minutes from where I stayed to my faculty. Before starting out on each day's journey, I would read a single verse from the chapter off my cell phone, and think about it while walking. This was also done when walking back at the end of the day, meditating on the same text.

I would do this each day of the week, a single verse a day. Where I had a hard time remembering a particular text, or if it was too long, I would spend a few more days on it to make sure that it sticks. After a while, having taken the chapter bit by bit, the whole chapter became part of my mind. Because I was meditating on the *thought* behind each passage, I remembered not only the words of the chapter, but grasped the overall *idea* of it. Like the psalmist I could say, "I will not forget Your words."

"Keep a pocket Bible with you as you work, and improve every opportunity to commit to memory its precious promises." Last Day Events p.67

For many, the experience may likely differ from my own, but the principle remains: to make the most of the opportunities God has provided you with. The moments when the mind is inactive, and seemingly on autopilot, use those opportunities to memorise.

While waiting at a bus stop, standing in a queue at the bank, when having "nothing to do" or during the free moments of the day available every now and then; these opportunities may be used to commit the promises of God's word to the mind.

Share the Word and Encourage Others

"Let the word of Christ dwell in you richly in all wisdom; teaching and admonishing one another in psalms and hymns and spiritual songs, singing with grace in your hearts to the Lord." Colossians 3:16

The word of Christ ought to dwell in us richly. This can be done through sharing God's word with others, as well as through song. In "teaching and admonishing one another" with the word of God, it gets more deeply fixed in our own memory. This was how the Israelite parents were to have God's law and commandments in their hearts. Notice the words of Moses to the Israelites:

"And these words, which I command you this day, shall be in your heart: And you shall teach them diligently to your children, and shall talk of them when you sit in your house, and when you walk by the way, and when you lie down, and when thou rise up." Deuteronomy 6:6-7 NKJV

There's something about sharing the word of God with others, whether in Bible study, in conversation or even in messaging someone with an encouraging text, which makes Bible passages easily remembered.

The first time I went out going door-to-door with a friend to give Bible studies, I had a short Bible lesson ready to be shared for the appointments we had made. That day, we had scheduled more than one appointment for Bible studies. I shared the same lesson with about three different contacts and by the time I had to share that same lesson at a later stage, I could easily remember the Bible passages and their references. I could also roughly recite what each passage said.

This is to illustrate the point that as one shares the words and passages from the Bible with others, the passages shared become more easily stored in the memory.

Scripture Songs

Psalms, hymns and spiritual songs are also a great tool to making scripture memorable. This was how the Jews remembered the psalms. Scripture songs are a great help for fixing passages of the Bible to one's mind:

> "As the children of Israel, journeying through the wilderness, cheered their way by the music of sacred song, so God bids His children today gladden their pilgrim life. There are few means more effective for fixing His words in the memory than repeating them in song. And such song has wonderful power. It has power to subdue rude and uncultivated natures; power to quicken thought and to awaken sympathy, to promote harmony of action, and to banish the gloom and foreboding that destroy courage and weaken effort." Education p.167

The human mind enjoys excitement; that is what makes the things we remember memorable. Scripture music appeals to this enjoyment and this makes it more effective as a tool for remembering God's word.

Prayer and God's Help

When it comes to memorising, it may be encouraging to consider that God Himself wants us to have His word in our hearts and minds. Storing up His word within us is how we gain understanding and all this is according to His will.

> "My son, if you accept My words and store up My commands within you, turning your ear to wisdom and applying your heart to understanding—indeed, if you call out for insight and cry aloud for understanding, and if you look for it as for silver and search for it as for hidden treasure, then you will understand the fear of the Lord and find the knowledge of God. For the Lord gives wisdom; from His mouth come knowledge and understanding." Proverbs 2:1-6 NIV

> "Now this is the confidence that we have in Him, that if we ask anything according to His will, He hears us. And if we know that He hears us, whatever we ask, we know that we have the petitions that we have asked of Him." 1 John 5:14-15 NKJV

Remember Christ's words, "without me, ye can do nothing." I would believe this to be the case with memorising also. When we prayerfully ask God to help us store up His word in our hearts, to hide His commandments within us, He will grant us this request. We may be confident in making this request because it is a prayer that is in line with His will.

Practical Suggestions

Below are some considerations on a few practical suggestions that have been of great help to some. It is highly likely that there are some practical methods, not mentioned here, which would work far more effectively for other minds. These, however, have also been found to be beneficial.

Memorising Passages

When memorising God's word, a good way to start is to memorise *passages* rather than scattered verses. This is mainly because verses are easier to remember when they are in the same passage and communicate an overall idea. This can be a psalm, a parable, or even a chapter. Of the Waldensian Christians, during the dark ages we read:

"Copies of the Bible were rare; therefore its precious words were committed to memory. Many were able to repeat large portions of both the Old and the New Testament. Thoughts of God were associated alike with the sublime scenery of nature and with the humble blessings of daily life. Little children learned to look with gratitude to God as the giver of every favor and every comfort." The Great Controversy p. 67

Bite-size Pieces

Many are intimidated at the idea of memorising, especially when they see others who are able to recite large passages. This is because they think that there is too much to remember. But no one needs to be intimidated. When memorising, one can break up verses or passages into manageable, "bite size," pieces and take them bit by bit to eventually memorise the whole.

A portion or phrase of a verse can be studied and reflected on in one day, until it becomes familiar in the mind. The rest can be done, in the same way, on the next day once the previous portion is memorised.

Here is an example if memorising Revelation 1:1; the verse can be broken up into parts and memorised over a few days. It reads:

"The Revelation of Jesus Christ, which God gave Him to show His servants--things which must shortly take place. And He sent and signified it by His angel to His servant John." Revelation 1:1 NKJV

The verse can be broken up into smaller segments to make it easy to remember. For example:

Sunday: *"The Revelation of Jesus Christ…"*
Monday: *"which God gave Him…"*
Tuesday: *"to show unto His servants…"*
Wednesday: *"things which must shortly take place …"*
Thursday: *"And He sent and signified …"*
Friday: *"by His angel …"*
Sabbath: *"to His servant John."*

For some, the smaller pieces may be remembered in a shorter time than for others. Whatever may be the case, it is helpful to memorise at a pace that is suited to how quickly one can remember and retain the words of the passage. Over time, this becomes easier to do.

One should remember that memorising is not merely to get the words fixed in the mind, but the actual *thoughts* and *ideas* placed by God in the Bible passages. This is why emphasis is placed on reflecting on a passage and giving it careful thought and consideration.

Scripture Memory Notes

Keeping a small note, with a Bible passage or text written on it, is a helpful device for memorising passages of scripture. This may be easily carried in the pocket and read whenever the opportunity is made. A new verse from a passage may be kept and memorised each day. Thus, bit by bit, the passage is becoming more fixed in the memory.

This method is also beneficial for reflecting on passages of scripture which one may have already memorised before. Keeping these notes helps one to keep a record of the verses & passages that they have memorised thus far.

Make it a Habit

Memorising, as a tool to abiding in Christ, is something that ought to be done often. As in most things, it requires perseverance and intentional dedication in order for it to eventually become a habit.

"That which at first seems difficult, by constant repetition grows easy, until right thoughts and actions become habitual." Ministry of Healing p.491

Once memorising becomes a part of one's routine, it will become easier to have more of Christ's words stored in the heart.

One Step at a Time

My advice to anyone who begins a memorising routine is always to start small, with a specific time set aside each day to memorise. This can be anything from 15 minutes before sleeping, to the first few minutes of the day after devotion, or even when riding on the taxi to work or school.

Whatever time of day one decides to start is not of too great importance, the point is really to begin. Once this is done regularly, it will become a more natural part of one's life.

"Repeated acts in a given course become habits. These may be modified by severe training, in afterlife, but are seldom changed. Once formed, habits become more and more firmly impressed upon the character." Mind, Character and Personality, book 2, p.599

Repetitive Reading

For a passage to become familiar, it may be helpful to read it numerous times. The mind becomes familiar with something that it does often. We may consider the idea of a travel route that one regularly takes. The more a person goes on a particular route over and over, not only does that way become more and more familiar, but new things may be seen with each trip that were not noticed before. Such is the case in reading as well.

Going over a passage or verse repeatedly, not necessarily in a parrot-like manner, but paying careful attention and thought to the passage each time it is read, makes it more and more familiar to the mind.

Emphasis may be placed on a different word or phrase with each reading, so as to grasp the thought in each of them. Example:

Reading 1: "**Abide** in Me, and I in you... "
Reading 2: "Abide **in** Me, and I in you... "
Reading 3: "Abide in **Me**, and I in you... "
Reading 4: "Abide in Me, and I **in** you... "
Reading 5: "Abide in Me, and I in **you**... "

With each attentive reading of the text, as emphasis is placed on a specific phrase or word, the overall thought behind the text comes through more forcefully. Having Bible passages stored in the mind allows one to thus meditate on them without having to open the pages. This is helpful to keep the mind occupied when walking, waiting or working.

Helpful Tools

Visual Aids

A helpful tool in fixing bible passages to memory, for children and for willing adults, is in the use of visual aids. These are things that enable one to visualise and imagine (and thus meditate) on what the passages of scripture speak of. An example of a good visual aid is in illustrations of the prophetic statue described in the second chapter of Daniel.

> *"The use of object lessons, blackboards, maps, and pictures, will be an aid in explaining [Bible] lessons, and fixing them in the memory." Education p.189*

Visual aids can include things such as drawings, sketches, or any other creative expression of the verses being memorised.

A friend of mine adopted a practice which has been a great help to me in memorising my favourite passages from books. My friend would make small animated sketches of each point in a passage she was memorising and then try to recite the passage from looking at the sketches she had made.

This method allowed her to use her imagination with the passages. More than one of the senses were involved in the process of memorising--seeing, hearing and drawing. The act of drawing and using the hand to illustrate the verses made the passages more memorable.

Quality More Than Quantity

The goal of memorising is not necessarily to have a large body of verses in the mind, without appreciating the meaning or the thought behind them. Usually, the reason we forget texts and passages after memorising them is because of trying to remember a large collection of verses, but neglecting to spend the time to recite and recall those previously memorised texts.

Making efforts to *retain* the verses already memorised is one of the most important parts of memorising.

> "*Young friends, the mountain-top cannot be reached by standing still, and wishing yourselves there. You can gain your object only by taking one step at a time, advancing slowly perhaps, but holding every step gained.*" Sons and Daughters of God p.333

We can achieve the goal of memorising by taking it one step at a time, advancing verse by verse. We must firmly *hold* and *maintain* each step of progress as it is made. This may seem like a slow advance at first, but as long as one persists they will find that more and more of God's word will be written in the heart and, most importantly, it will remain there.

The Blessing is in the Doing

A great portion of the blessing that comes from memorising lies in the very act of doing it. In the time spent going over God's word, and meditating on it, there is a wonderful communion with Him.

In this case, one can say that the journey is just as important as the destination.

What I have found is that the more one memorises, the more it is that other passages of scripture come together in the mind. This is part of how the Holy Spirit seeks to teach us.

"The Comforter, which is the Holy Ghost, whom the Father will send in my name, He shall teach you all things, and bring all things to your remembrance, whatsoever I ([Jesus]) have said unto you." John 14:26

Never Too Late to Start

Some may feel overwhelmed at the idea of memorising. Others who may have tried it before, without much success, may even be a bit intimidated by the idea; but, again, this does have to be the case.

"God is our refuge and strength, [and] a very present help in trouble." Psalms 46:1

Again, we take note of the fact that without Jesus we can do nothing. The opposite of this is also true. Like the apostle Paul, we can also testify to the fact that "I can do all things through Christ, who strengthens me." (Phil. 4:19). This includes memorising scripture.

With this in mind, there's no better time to start than the present. As mentioned previously, one can start bit by bit. Pick a favourite passage or text, a Bible promise you hold dear to your heart, or even a verse that has encouraged you in your reading of this book. This can be your starting point.

The greatest task in memorising is to get going. Once that is done, that which at first seemed difficult will soon become easy by constant repetition.

"For the Lord God will help me; therefore shall I not be confounded: therefore have I set my face like a flint, and I know that I shall not be ashamed." Isaiah 50:7

Diligence and Persistence

"Diligence and earnest fidelity are indispensable to success." Testi-

monies, vol. 4 p.453

Having gotten started in committing scripture to memory, it is as crucial for one maintain the habit. Very often, this requires diligence and commitment.

Fidelity (which is synonymous with commitment and faithfulness) involves not allowing things of lesser importance to divert an individual from their purpose. This is the case with the time set aside to memorise and recite scripture. Ensuring to make the most of the time made to memorise will help make the mind accustomed to the exercise.

Diligence involves being willing to keep going, even if one may stumble along the way. One should not be too hard on themselves if, after trying to memorise, they may have difficulty at first. The aim is to keep at it.

In the event where one may make missteps, they may gain success by getting right back on track and trying again. Diligence and heartfelt fidelity will prove to be fruitful for successfully retaining Bible texts and passages in the mind.

Questions on Chapter 5

Why is it important to memorise scripture? (p.84)

What are some of the methods that I can use to memorise scripture? (p.87-90)

How does sharing scripture with others help me to remember it? (p.89)

What practical things can I do to help me remember Bible passages better? (p.91-93)

Why is it that some things are more memorable than others, and how can I use this to memorise scripture? (p.94)

What is it better, quality or quantity? (p.95)

When is the best time to start memorising? (p.96)

6

Relentless Prayer

Importance of Prayer

Essentials of Prayer

What to Pray About

Some Practical Suggestions

God's promises to prayer

Importance of Prayer

There's an old and common English saying that goes something like: "familiarity breeds contempt." It basically presents the idea that when one has experienced something (or known someone) for a long time, the less they tend to appreciate it.

This experience is true with a number of things. This is, unfortunately, also the case with how some experience prayer. This has been true with me at times, when I thought I was clued up enough on the matter. Over time I have come to appreciate the thought that:

"If anyone thinks that he knows anything, he knows nothing yet as he ought to know." 1 Corinthians 8:2 NKJV

As we consider the subject of prayer, the hope is that it may lead to an appreciation of the real significance of prayer and radically impact ones individual experience of abiding in Christ.

Essential for Walking with God

"By faith Enoch was translated that he should not see death; and was not found, because God had translated him: for before his translation he had this testimony, that he pleased. But without faith it is impossible to please Him, for he that [comes] to God must believe that He is and that He is a rewarder of them that diligently seek Him." Hebrews 11:5-6

Enoch, who walked with God and held constant communion with Him, had the attitude of knowing that God is a rewarder of those who diligently seek Him. This was how Enoch pictured God; he had it fixed in His mind that God rewards those who actively pursue a closer relationship with Him. God says:

"Then you will call upon Me and go and pray to Me, and I will listen to you. And you will seek Me and find Me, when you search for Me with all your heart. I will be found by you, says the Lord..."
Jeremiah 29:12-14a

Those who walk with God have the attitude of diligently seeking Him. Such was the case with Enoch. If we are to have the same experience, we may do so by having the same attitude; we are to seek

God with all our hearts, believing that He will reward those who diligently seek Him.

Notice the experience of Daniel, the prophet.

"And I ([Daniel]) set my face unto the Lord God, to seek by prayer and supplications, with fasting, and sackcloth, and ashes:" Daniel 9:3

When Daniel felt that he had to draw closer to God, prayer and fasting became essential components. This was coupled with Bible study (Daniel 9:2).

From Daniel's experience, we learn that prayer is directly connected to seeking God. God also promises us that in seeking Him with all the heart, He will be found (Jeremiah 29:13).

Thus, prayer is an essential requirement for holding communion with God. Those who seek after God through diligent prayer will walk with Him as Enoch did.

"Prayer is the opening of the heart to God as to a friend. Not that it is necessary in order to make known to God what we are, but in order to enable us to receive Him. Prayer does not bring God down to us, but brings us up to Him." Steps to Christ p.93

"Why should the sons and daughters of God be reluctant to pray, when prayer is the key in the hand of faith to unlock heaven's storehouse, where are treasured the boundless resources of Omnipotence?" Ibid p.94

Connects Us to God

"Through sincere prayer we are brought into connection with the mind of the Infinite. We may have no remarkable evidence at the time that the face of our Redeemer is bending over us in compassion and love, but this is even so. We may not feel His visible touch, but His hand is upon us in love and pitying tenderness." Steps to Christ p.96

When we pray, we are drawing nearer to God. In so doing, we may be certain that we are encircled in His immediate presence. This is why the blessing of prayer is in the actual act of praying, more than only in the outcome. It is the communion with God that is to be sought after--the privilege of holding a one to one conversation with God. For this reason:

"We should be much in secret prayer. Christ is the vine, [you] are the branches. And if we would grow and flourish, we must continually draw sap and nourishment from the Living Vine; for separated from the Vine we have no strength." Early Writings p.73

Jesus' call to abide in Him is an invitation to have such an intimate connection with Him that we can be said to draw life directly from Him; as a branch from a vine. The same way communication with earthly friends strengthens the bond, even so the connection with our divine Friend is strengthened through prayer.

The words "abide in me, and I in you" are fulfilled through the heaven-ordained channel of prayer.

Power and Grace to Resist Temptation

"Be sober, be vigilant; because your adversary the devil walks about like a roaring lion, seeking whom he may devour." 1 Peter 5:8 NKJV

Peter's counsel for the church is for us to be vigilant and sober. This is because of the adversary of souls who is seeking whom he may devour. But how has Peter counselled us to carry out that watchfulness? He writes:

"The end of all things is at hand; therefore be serious and watchful in your prayers." 1 Peter 4:7 NKJV

"The darkness of the evil one encloses those who neglect to pray. The whispered temptations of the enemy entice them to sin; and it is all because they do not make use of the privileges that God has given them in the divine appointment of prayer... Without unceasing prayer and diligent watching we are in danger of growing careless and of deviating from the right path. The adversary seeks continually to obstruct the way to the mercy seat, that we may not by earnest supplication and faith obtain grace and power to resist temptation." Steps to Christ p.94

Satan has power over those who neglect the privilege of prayer. To "neglect" is not necessarily to completely disregard something, but rather to take it lightly--to treat it as unimportant. This means that one does not have to completely reject prayer in order to be overcome by the devil; rather, one just has to not regard it as something of real importance.

By prayer, we obtain the needed power to resist all of Satan's temptations. It is important to thus come to grips with the essential principles of prayer.

Essentials of Prayer

Faith[1]

> "Without faith it is impossible to please Him, for he who comes to God must believe that He is, and that He is a rewarder of those who diligently seek Him." Hebrews 11:6 NKJV

> "Therefore I tell you, whatever you ask in prayer, believe that you have received it, and it will be yours." Mark 11:24 ESV

God is pleased with the prayer of faith. When we pray, we are to actually believe that we do receive the things that God has promised, because He has promised them. This is the attitude of faith we may have when approaching God in prayer. Notice why we may have such confidence:

> "The assurance is broad and unlimited, and He is faithful who has promised. When we do not receive the very things we asked for, at the time we ask, we are still to believe that the Lord hears and that He will answer our prayers. We are so erring and short-sighted that we sometimes ask for things that would not be a blessing to us, and our heavenly Father in love answers our prayers by giving us that which will be for our highest good--that which we ourselves would desire if with vision divinely enlightened we could see all things as they really are.
>
> When our prayers seem not to be answered, we are to cling to the

Footnote:
1. More on faith, and how to exercise it, is discussed in chapter 8, Abiding Faith

promise; for the time of answering will surely come, and we shall receive the blessing we need most. But to claim that prayer will always be answered in the very way and for the particular thing that we desire, is presumption. God is too wise to err, and too good to withhold any good thing from them that walk uprightly. Then do not fear to trust Him, even though you do not see the immediate answer to your prayers. Rely upon His sure promise, 'Ask, and it shall be given you.'" Steps to Christ p.96

When we pray, we can trust God enough to believe that He will fulfil all that He has promised. This faith is to also be expressed in our actions. We are to talk and act as those who believe that God has answered, because His promises are certain.

"Our part is to pray and believe. Watch unto prayer. Watch, and co-operate with the prayer-hearing God. Bear in mind that "we are labourers together with God." 1 Corinthians 3:9. Speak and act in harmony with your prayers. It will make an infinite difference with you whether trial shall prove your faith to be genuine, or show that your prayers are only a form." Christ's Object Lessons p.146

Realising Your Need of God

"For I will pour water on him who is thirsty, and floods on the dry ground; I will pour My Spirit on your descendants, and My blessing on your offspring." Isaiah 44:3 NKJV

One of the ways in which God works is to bless those who genuinely realise their weakness and their need for His help. He pours floods of blessings on those who thirst for Him.

Oftentimes, when individuals come face to face with their unworthy condition, Satan may tempt us to think that we cannot approach God. He often tempts us with the feeling that we do not deserve to come to God. While this is true, we are more blessed when we realise that fact.

"When we are humble and contrite we stand where God can and will manifest Himself to us." Ministry of Healing p.513

Realising ones need for Christ comes with acknowledging how empty one is apart from God's help. This has been made a condition for receiving the blessings which God has to offer. He promises the blessing of His righteousness to those who thus "hunger and thirst" for Him.

"Blessed are they which do hunger and thirst after righteousness: for they shall be filled." Matthew 5:6

"Those who hunger and thirst after righteousness, who long after God, may be sure that they will be filled. The heart must be open to the Spirit's influence, or God's blessing cannot be received. Our great need is itself an argument and pleads most eloquently in our behalf. But the Lord is to be sought unto to do these things for us. He says, "Ask, and it shall be given you." And "He that spared not His own Son, but delivered Him up for us all, how shall He not with Him also freely give us all things?" Matthew 7:7; Romans 8:32." Steps to Christ p.95

Those who abide in Christ are those who, in their life and prayers, have a constant awareness of the fact that they can do nothing without Jesus. This acknowledgment is one of the conditions for answered prayer. When we are thus dependent on Him, He will pour out His blessings on those who thirst.

"Nothing is apparently more helpless, yet really more invincible, than the soul that feels its nothingness and relies wholly on the merits of the Saviour." The Ministry of Healing p.182

Confessing All Known Sins[2]

"If I regard iniquity in my heart, the Lord will not hear me." Psalms 66:18

"If we regard iniquity in our hearts, if we cling to any known sin, the Lord will not hear us; but the prayer of the penitent, contrite soul is always accepted. When all known wrongs are righted, we may believe that God will answer our petitions. Our own merit

Footnote:
2. The subject of confession is discussed further in chapter 9, What If I Fall.

will never commend us to the favor of God; it is the worthiness of Jesus that will save us, His blood that will cleanse us; yet we have a work to do in complying with the conditions of acceptance." Steps to Christ p.95

Jesus' death on the cross is a testimony to the fact that God is more than willing to pardon and cleanse us from all our unrighteousness. God has made the work of confession a necessary condition in order for us to experience the blessing of pardon.

"If we confess our sins, He is faithful and just to forgive us our sins, and to cleanse us from all unrighteousness." 1 John 1:9

While sin--cherished and un-confessed--cuts us off from receiving help from heaven; forgiveness is promised to those who do confess. Christ shed His blood to secure our pardon and from His death we can be sure that forgiveness is available for us. "The blood of Jesus Christ His Son cleanses us from all sin." *(1 John 1:7)*

Many professed believers, while believing in the existence of God and the truthfulness of His word, do not come to Him in confession of their sins because of not trusting that Christ would be willing to forgive them. For some it is because they think themselves too great a sinner for Jesus to forgive; for others it is the idea that they do not feel "bad enough" yet to trust that God will accept their confession as genuine.

There is also a class who, while they may perhaps confess, do not yet trust that God has fully forgiven them until they have done some great thing that makes them feel righteous. With these individuals, confession may often be made over and over again.

God offers us a different experience from all these. We have hope for forgiveness and this hope is not in ourselves. Our hope of forgiveness is secured in the worthiness and death of Jesus. This is why it is in our best interests to trustingly confess all our sins to God.

Such confession, in offloading all our sins at the foot of the cross and depending on the worthiness of Jesus, makes for fruitful and effectual prayer.

"While it is a disgrace to sin, it is no disgrace, but rather an honor,

to confess one's sins." Testimonies, vol. 5, p.509

Cherishing a Spirit of Forgiveness

"Whenever you stand praying, if you have anything against anyone, forgive him, that your Father in heaven may also forgive you your trespasses. But if you do not forgive, neither will your Father in heaven forgive your trespasses." Mark 11:25-26 NKJV

When we confess our sins, and desire God to forgive us entirely, we must be willing to give up any unforgiving attitude we may have against those who have done us wrong. This is essential for receiving God's forgiveness.

"If we expect our own prayers to be heard we must forgive others in the same manner and to the same extent as we hope to be forgiven." Steps to Christ p.97

Whether we get to experience God's forgiveness is influenced by our willingness to forgive those who have harmed us. It is for this reason that Jesus counsels us to pray for God to "forgive us our debts, as we forgive our debtors." (Matthew 6:12). Thus, one does more harm to their own soul when they hold a grudge and refuse to forgive those who have harmed them in the past.

Christ's sacrifice on the cross gives us an example of how God responds to those who have hurt Him and are unworthy of His forgiveness. God was willing to send His Son to die for us, even while we were His enemies (Romans 5:8-10). The fact that God did this, even before we wanted anything to do with Him, must be what drives us to be willing to forgive those who have wronged us. Hence Paul writes:

"Be kind to one another, tenderhearted, forgiving one another, even as God in Christ forgave you." Ephesians 4:32 NKJV

"For I ([God]) will forgive their iniquity, and I will remember their sin no more." Jeremiah 31:34 ESV

We are instructed to forgive others as God has forgiven us. When God forgives our iniquities, He does not bring up our sins ever again. This is to be the extent to which we forgive those who have harmed us; in not bringing up the past record of their sins.

Such an act of forgiveness should be done for the sake of Christ --in view at what He has done at Calvary in order to give us a chance at salvation. No one has ever been wronged like God was and yet His pain came from our own sins. His willingness to still forgive us should be our highest motive to forgive those who have harmed us.

Persistence

"Pray without ceasing," 1 Thessalonians 5:17

In order to hold constant communion with God, we are to keep an open line of communication with Him. This requires persistent, tireless prayer. With that being said, Jesus would not have us grow faint in prayer, especially when we do not see the things we are praying for come at the very time we pray for them. Speaking to His disciples:

"[Jesus] spake a parable unto them to this end, that men ought always to pray, and not to faint." Luke 18:1

When we note that the blessing of prayer is in the actual act, this will enable us to persist in prayer. Consider the following words carefully:

"We must show a firm, undeviating trust in God. Often He delays to answer us in order to try our faith or test the genuineness of our desire. Having asked according to His word, we should believe His promise and press our petitions with a determination that will not be denied.

God does not say, Ask once, and you shall receive. He bids us ask. Unwearyingly persist in prayer. The persistent asking brings the petitioner into a more earnest attitude, and gives him an increased desire to receive the things for which he asks. Christ said to Martha at the grave of Lazarus, "If thou wouldest believe, thou shouldest see the glory of God." John 11:40.

Our prayers are to be as earnest and persistent as was the petition of the needy friend who asked for the loaves at midnight (see Luke 11:5-13). The more earnestly and steadfastly we ask, the closer will be our spiritual union with Christ. We shall receive increased blessings because we have increased faith." Christ's Object Lessons p.145-6

From the above passage we find that God would not have us only praying every now and again, but God invites us to rather "unwearyingly persist in prayer". This draws us closer to Him and strengthens our faith. For this reason, God may sometimes delay in answering our prayers.

Praying without ceasing, however, does not mean to be unendingly in the practical act of prayer. Relentless and persistent prayer also includes maintaining a constant *attitude* of unbroken communicating with God. Notice how this is described below:

"When we permit our communion with God to be broken, our defence is departed from us. Not all your good purposes and good intentions will enable you to withstand evil. You must be men and women of prayer. Your petitions must not be faint, occasional, and fitful, but earnest, persevering, and constant. It is not always necessary to bow upon your knees in order to pray. Cultivate the habit of talking with the Saviour when you are alone, when you are walking, and when you are busy with your daily labor. Let the heart be continually uplifted in silent petition for help, for light, for strength, for knowledge. Let every breath be a prayer." The Ministry of Healing p.510

In the Name of Jesus

"Most assuredly, I say to you, whatever you ask the Father in My name He will give you. Until now you have asked nothing in My name. Ask, and you will receive, that your joy may be full." John 16:23-24 NKJV

Every promise of God is offered to us based on the sacrifice of Christ on our behalf. "For all of God's promises have been fulfilled in Christ with a resounding "Yes!" (2 Corinthians 1:20 NLT).

In claiming these promises, we are to claim them according to the merits and worthiness of Jesus; realising that we do not deserve them. This is the heart of what it means to pray in the name of Christ Jesus, accepting His sacrifice and all that it comes with.

> *"To pray in the name of Jesus is something more than a mere mention of that name at the beginning and the ending of a prayer. It is to pray in the mind and spirit of Jesus, while we believe His promises, rely upon His grace, and work His works."* Call Stand Apart p.27

> *"To pray in Christ's name means much. It means that we are to accept His character, manifest His spirit, and work His works. The Saviour's promise is given on condition. "If ye love Me," He says, "keep My commandments." He saves men, not in sin, but from sin; and those who love Him will show their love by obedience."* The Desire of Ages p.668

Praying in Christ's name calls us to take more thought when praying. It would do well for one to actually consider the value of praying in the name of Jesus. Consider why it is that, in claiming Jesus' name, we can be confident in approaching God in prayer.

By the Holy Spirit

> *"Likewise the Spirit helps us in our weakness. For we do not know what to pray for as we ought, but the Spirit Himself intercedes for us with groanings too deep for words. And he who searches hearts knows what is the mind of the Spirit, because the Spirit intercedes for the saints according to the will of God."* Romans 8:26-27 ESV

When we pray, the Holy Spirit intercedes on our behalf and presents our requests to God the Father in an eloquence far beyond our own. Our prayers are presented in accordance to the will of God, in request for what we would ask for, were our eyes divinely enlightened.

> *"We must not only pray in Christ's name, but by the inspiration of the Holy Spirit. This explains what is meant when it is said that the Spirit "maketh intercession for us, with groanings which cannot be uttered" (Romans 8:26). Such prayer God delights to answer. When with earnestness and intensity we breathe a prayer in the name of Christ, there is in that very intensity a pledge from*

God that He is about to answer our prayer "exceeding abundantly above all that we ask or think." Ephesians 3:20. Christ's Object Lessons p.147

When we cannot express ourselves, and we find ourselves at a loss for words in presenting our case before our Heavenly Father, the Holy Spirit is ready to take our heartfelt prayers to the throne of God. God delights in answering our earnest and genuine prayers

With Gratitude and Thankfulness of Heart

"Praise the Lord, my soul; all my inmost being, praise His holy name. Praise the Lord, my soul, and forget not all His bene-fits--who forgives all your sins and heals all your diseases, who redeems your life from the pit and crowns you with love and com-passion, who satisfies your desires with good things so that your youth is renewed like the eagle's" Psalm 103:1-5 NIV

God is constantly pouring out His blessings and benefits towards us as His children, more than we may possibly realise it in this life. He is worthy of praise for all that He has done and for all that continues to do for us.

In opening our hearts to God as to a friend, we have much to be thankful for. These expressions of our thankfulness are vital for a lively prayer life.

"Our devotional exercises should not consist wholly in asking and receiving. Let us not be always thinking of our wants and never of the benefits we receive. We do not pray any too much, but we are too sparing of giving thanks. We are the constant recipients of God's mercies, and yet how little gratitude we express, how little we praise Him for what He has done for us..." Call Stand Apart p.28

In our daily human interactions, we generally find it inappropriate for one who is constantly receiving favours and benefits to not ex-press their gratitude. We do not think too well of those who do not say "thank you" after we have done an act of kindness for them. In spite of this, how sparing are we when it comes to expressing grati-tude to God for His constant goodness towards us?

Our devotional exercises, our attitude in prayer and communion with God, should also include a spirit of sincere gratefulness for all He has done for us. This is an essential part of prayer.

What to Pray About

Having looked at the fundamentals of prayer, we can consider the "subject matter" that should make up our prayers; what are some of the things we should be praying for? We may consider a few:

Things in Your Actual Life

In opening our hearts to God as to a friend, we have the privilege of being as personal with Him as with a caring Father. Notice the psalmist's prayer:

"Hear the right, O Lord, attend unto my cry, give ear unto my prayer, that goes not out of feigned ([or pretending]) lips." Psalms 17:1

In our age of extreme superficiality, it has become rare to find authenticity in people. Much of how people relate to each other has been hampered by the effects of things such as social media, which have made people become less relational with one another. This condition has affected the way many individuals relate to God as well. The same way people relate to each other in a very detached and pretentious manner, God is also approached in this way too. As a God who knows our hearts, however, we can go to Him in honesty.

When we come to God in prayer, we never need to pretend. We can be "real" with God, as a friend mine would say. It is our privilege to come to God with the reverent confidence of knowing that we can pour out our hearts to Him. We can present to Him everything that concerns our actual, day-to-day life.

"Trust in Him at all times, O people; pour out your heart before Him; God is a refuge for us." Psalms 62:8 ESV

"Through nature and revelation, through His providence, and by the influence of His Spirit, God speaks to us. But these are not enough; we need also to pour out our hearts to Him. In order to

have spiritual life and energy, we must have actual intercourse with our heavenly Father. Our minds may be drawn out toward Him; we may meditate upon His works, His mercies, His blessings; but this is not, in the fullest sense, communing with Him. In order to commune with God, we must have something to say to Him concerning our actual life

[Jesus] taught His disciples how to pray. He directed them to present their daily needs before God, and to cast all their care upon Him. And the assurance He gave them that their petitions should be heard, is assurance also to us." Steps to Christ p.93

When we are happy or when sad, when in need of guidance or when facing a challenge at home, school & work; any affair of ones life may be presented and discussed with our caring God. There is nothing that may disturb our peace, or that may bring us gladness and joy, that is not a matter of concern to Him. God is never bothered or bored by our prayers.

We are invited to present our daily needs to God and to tell Him about the things that concern our actual life. Tell God about whatever it is you go through, both good and bad. Such prayers are essential for us to have communion with God in the fullest sense.

According to the Will of God

"Now this is the confidence that we have in Him, that if we ask anything according to His will, He hears us. And if we know that He hears us, whatever we ask, we know that we have the petitions that we have asked of Him." 1 John 5:14-15 NKJV

We are counselled to pray according to God's will. When we do so, we may be confident that He will grant us our requests.

Every promise that God makes is an expression of His will. God promises that "He will take care of you," (Psalm 55:22). Whenever we pray for His protection, we do so in harmony with His will because it is something that He has promised.

The instructions and promises found in the Bible reveal God's will to us. Since the will of God is revealed in His word, in praying according to His will we must be willing to also live according to the instructions of His word. In claiming a promise which God has made and in choosing to obey His word, we may be confident that we have the petitions that we have requested of Him.

Asking

"Ask, and it will be given to you; seek, and you will find; knock, and it will be opened to you." Matthew 7:7 NKJV

"The natural co-operates with the supernatural. It is a part of God's plan to grant us, in answer to the prayer of faith, that which He would not bestow did we not thus ask." The Great Controversy p.525

Consider this thought: there are things that God does not grant us, until we ask Him for them in faithful prayer. The same way good parents are willing to give good gifts to their children, our kind and compassionate Heavenly Father is waiting to bestow every needed blessing to His children. He has made it a condition that, in order to receive, we must first ask Him.

My father once said something to me that, though quite simple, really made an impression on me.

Growing out of my teenage years and having spent a few years in university, I started to develop the habit of not asking my parents for help with the things I needed; and I would try to solve matters by myself. This was until a certain point when I really needed something that was out of my hands. In this situation, I only let my father know about it at a much later stage. After helping me out, my father asked my why I had not told him about the matter earlier. After my poor excuse about independence and a host of other things, he said to me, "If you need something, tell me, and I will help you."

The reason this impressed me was because of how I saw it relate to God. How often do people try, by their own strength, to solve a problem that they are in before actually bringing it to God? My father would have been more accurate in saying: "I will help you... as far as I am able," but I want to believe that his sentiments are the same as God's. Hence Jesus says the words, "ask, and it shall be given to you" (Matthew 7:7)

"As a father has compassion on His children, so the Lord has compassion on those who fear Him." Psalms 103:13 NIV

It would not be inaccurate to imagine God saying to us today, "If you need anything, tell Me and I will help you." We can trust Him enough to ask Him for whatever we may need. God will grant us not just what we ask for, but will oftentimes supply our need in a manner that is far better than what we could have imagined with our limited vision. He is able "to do far more abundantly than all that we ask or think." (Ephesians 3:20)

Praise and Thanksgiving

"Oh, that men would give thanks to the Lord for His goodness, and for His wonderful works to the children of men! For He satisfies the longing soul, and fills the hungry soul with goodness." Psalm 107:8-9 NKJV

Generally speaking, we need to praise God more. Not only for what He has done for us, but also because of who He is as a kind and merciful God. We are to express our gratitude and adoration to Him for His consistent faithfulness towards us.

"Praise the Lord! Oh, give thanks to the Lord, for He is good! For His mercy endures forever." Psalm 106:1 ESV

When we meditate on the benefits that we receive, the everyday blessings which we often take for granted, these will make up the substance of our thanksgiving. For health, for the daily provisions, for prayers answered and for the forgiveness of sins, we may give thanks to God for all that He does for us.

Praying for the Holy Spirit

"In the great and measureless gift of the Holy Spirit are contained all of heaven's resources. It is not because of any restriction on the part of God that the riches of His grace do not flow earthward to men. If all were willing to receive, all would become filled with His Spirit." Christ's Object Lessons p.419

Through the Holy Spirit, every blessing of heaven is carried and made real to us. He is with us in His personal capacity as God and He brings with Him every needed blessing that heaven can offer. When we pray for the Holy Spirit, we can be sure that all that we need is found in Him. We are granted access to His blessings by the worthiness of Christ.

God is with us, personally, through the person of the Holy Spirit. "We fail many times because we do not realise that Christ is with us by His Spirit as truly as when, in the days of His humiliation, He moved visibly upon the earth." (*Lift Him Up*, p.175).

When we realise how much we need the presence and assistance of God the Holy Spirit, we will plead for Him the same way one who is thirsty pleads for water. Then shall we receive more of His presence in our lives. God promises:

"I ([God]) will pour water upon him that is thirsty, and floods upon the dry ground: I will pour my Spirit upon thy seed, and my blessing upon thine offspring." Isaiah 44:3

"Ask the Lord for rain in the time of the latter rain. The Lord will make flashing clouds; He will give them showers of rain, grass in the field for everyone." Zechariah 10:1 NKJV

"We cannot use the Holy Spirit. The Spirit is to use us. Through the Spirit God works in His people "to will and to do of His good pleasure." (Philippians 2:13). But many will not submit to this. They want to manage themselves. This is why they do not receive the heavenly gift. Only to those who wait humbly upon God, who watch for His guidance and grace, is the Spirit given. The power of God awaits their demand and reception. This promised blessing, claimed by faith, brings all other blessings in its train. It is given according to the riches of the grace of Christ, and He is ready to supply every soul according to the capacity to receive." The Desire of Ages p.672

The Holy Spirit awaits being asked for and received. In receiving God's Spirit, and permitting Him to work in our lives, we will receive all that is needed for our everyday lives and for living godly.

"Why [then] do we not hunger and thirst for the gift of the Spirit,

since this is the means by which we are to receive power? Why do we not talk of it, pray for it, preach concerning it? The Lord is more willing to give the Holy Spirit to us than parents are to give good gifts to their children. For the baptism of the Spirit every worker should be pleading with God." Testimonies, vol. 8, p.22

Praying for Others

"When you pray, say Our Father." Luke 11:2

"In calling God our Father, we recognize all His children as our brethren. We are all a part of the great web of humanity, all members of one family. In our petitions we are to include our neighbors as well as ourselves. No one prays aright who seeks a blessing for himself alone." Thoughts from the Mount of Blessings, p.105

One of the greatest and necessary subject matters for prayer is to intercede on behalf of others. The reason why Jesus could spend whole nights in prayer, and not run out of things to say, was because He was praying for others as well.

"When left alone, Jesus "went up into a mountain apart to pray." For hours He continued pleading with God. Not for Himself but for men were those prayers... In travail and conflict of soul He prayed for His disciples... For them the burden was heavy upon His heart, and He poured out His supplications with bitter agony and tears." The Desire of Ages, p.378

This can also be the character of our prayers. When our attention in prayer is not limited to our own needs and wants, but also praying for God to intervene on behalf of others, our prayer life will take on a much richer tone. Whenever those around us are in need of God's help, we can go to Him on their behalf.

This kind of prayer life will also be of benefit to the one who prays for others. Notice Job's case:

"The Lord turned the captivity of Job, when he prayed for his friends: also the Lord gave Job twice as much as he had before." Job 42:10

As mentioned earlier, the benefit of prayer extends beyond only receiving the outcomes of prayer, but also includes the privilege of talking with God. The conversation with God draws us closer to Him

When we pray for others, even when they may not have asked for it, it will result in blessings for them as well as for our own souls. Prayer of this nature draws us closer to God and deepens our love for our fellow man.

"Bless them that curse you, and pray for them which despitefully use you." Luke 6:28

Praying for others is not limited to our friends and loved ones alone, but even those who do us wrong are in need of our prayers. Praying for others is a practical act of service for them.

"There are many who long to help others, but they feel that they have no spiritual strength or light to impart. Let them present their petitions at the throne of grace. Plead for the Holy Spirit. God stands back of every promise He has made. With your Bible in your hands say, I have done as Thou hast said. I present Thy promise, "Ask, and it shall be given you; seek, and ye shall find; knock, and it shall be opened unto you." Christ's Object Lessons p.147

There are people all around us in need of prayers; family, friends, colleagues and fellow church members--many of whom face various challenges. We should make it a habit to include others in our prayers.

Keeping a list of people to pray for, something that can be reviewed weekly, is helpful in remembering individuals to pray for. A great blessing comes when you see God answering your prayers on behalf of others. Ultimately, the greatest thing to pray for, on behalf of others, is that they may be led closer to God and experience His salvation.

"Therefore I exhort first of all that supplications, prayers, intercessions, and giving of thanks be made for all men... For this is good and acceptable in the sight of God our Savior, who desires all men to be saved and to come to the knowledge of the truth." 1 Timothy 2:1-4 NKJV

Some Practical Suggestions

Below are some practical suggestions that may be of benefit to one's personal prayer life.

A Quiet Place

For private prayer, it is often best to be in a quiet place, where there is little or no distraction. Notice how Jesus started His day:

> *"In the morning, rising up a great while before day, He went out, and departed into a solitary place, and there prayed." Mark 1:35*

Christ's habit and daily routine involved waking up very early in the morning to go to a private place to pray. There was no distraction, no noise of the radio or TV in the background, no incoming cell phone messages to divert the attention from the open line of communication with His heavenly Father.

> *"Secret prayer is very important; in solitude the soul is laid bare to the inspecting eye of God, and every motive is scrutinized. Secret prayer! How precious! The soul communing with God! Secret prayer is to be heard only by the prayer-hearing God. No curious ear is to receive the burden of such petitions. In secret prayer the soul is free from surrounding influences, free from excitement. Calmly, yet fervently, will it reach out after God." Testimonies, vol.2 p.189-190*

In starting out the day, private prayer may be enjoyed in a quiet and undisturbed place. Early morning is often the best time for having personal time for communion with God. Before the activities of the day, we may gain strength for the day's tasks by dedicating our lives and our responsibilities to God.

> *"Consecrate yourself to God in the morning; make this your very first work. Let your prayer be, 'Take me, O Lord, as wholly Thine. I lay all my plans at Thy feet. Use me today in Thy service. Abide with me, and let all my work be wrought in Thee.' This is a daily matter. Each morning consecrate yourself to God for that day. Surrender all your plans to Him, to be carried out or given up as His providence shall indicate. Thus day by day you may be giving your*

life into the hands of God, and thus your life will be molded more and more after the life of Christ." Steps to Christ p.70

Sweet Hour of Prayer

It is very helpful to have a time set aside for daily, personal prayer and communion with God. King David did this too, he writes:

"Evening, and morning, and at noon, will I pray, and cry aloud: and He shall hear my voice." Psalm 55:17

"We, too, must have times set apart for meditation and prayer and for receiving spiritual refreshing. We do not value the power and efficacy of prayer as we should. Prayer and faith will do what no power on earth can accomplish. We are seldom, in all respects, placed in the same position twice. We continually have new scenes and new trials to pass through, where past experience cannot be a sufficient guide. We must have the continual light that comes from God." The Ministry of Healing p.509

Whether it is in the morning, at noon or in the evening, having a set time for personal prayer and devotion does one good. Each day demands a renewal of strength that can come only from thus communing with God. Nothing of lesser importance should be allowed to interfere with this time.

Calm, Sincere and Simple Prayer

"Prayer is the most holy exercise of the soul. It should be sincere, humble, earnest--the desires of a renewed heart breathed in the presence of a holy God. When the supplicant feels that he is in the divine presence, self will be forgotten. He will have no desire to display human talent; he will not seek to please the ear of men, but to obtain the blessing which the soul craves." Testimonies vol.5 p.201

We do not ever need to impress God in our prayers, whether with loud cries or eloquent speeches. We may offer up our petitions to Him in our own simple, natural language; with a calm and sincere reverence. God welcomes us to freely express ourselves to Him as to a caring and compassionate Father.

The Example of Elijah

"[Elijah] was a man subject to like passions as we are, and he prayed earnestly that it might not rain: and it rained not on the earth by the space of three years and six months." James 5:17

Elijah was a man who possessed no special powers or qualities that would give him any advantages which we do not have. He was subject to the same struggles as us. In his prayers, Elijah prayed earnestly and God heard--and answered--his request.

We can learn what earnest prayer looks like from Elijah's example on mount Carmel. The book of 1 Kings 18:17-39 narrates a conflict which took place between Elijah and the prophets of Baal regarding the worship of the true God. The contest was to prove who the true God was between Baal and Jehovah. Each of the prophets were meant to pray to his god to spark a fire on an altar that had been set up. The difference between Elijah's prayer and the prayers of Baal's prophets is a striking contrast which shows the kind of prayers that the true God accepts.

"Baal's priests have screamed and foamed and leaped, from early morning until late in the afternoon; but as Elijah prays, no senseless shrieks ([or screams]) resound over Carmel's height. He prays as if he knows Jehovah is there, a witness to the scene, a listener to his appeal. The prophets of Baal have prayed wildly, incoherently. Elijah prays simply and fervently, asking God to show His superiority over Baal, that Israel may be led to turn to Him." Prophets and Kings p.152

"And it came to pass at the time of the offering of the evening sacrifice, that Elijah the prophet came near, and said, 'Lord God of Abraham, Isaac, and of Israel, let it be known this day that you are God in Israel, and that I am thy servant, and that I have done all these things at thy word. Hear me, O Lord, hear me, that this people may know that you are the Lord God, and that thou hast turned their heart back again.'

Then the fire of the Lord fell, and consumed the burnt sacrifice, and the wood, and the stones, and the dust, and licked up the water that was in the trench." 1 Kings 18:36-38

Elijah's prayer was simple and sincere, claiming the promises of God. He prayed with a childlike trust, for the glory and honour of God; not simply for his own selfish interests. God answered his simple prayer with power. This may be our experience also, in praying with a calm, yet eager, trust to the God of heaven.

"By calm, simple faith the soul holds communion with God and gathers to itself divine rays of light to strengthen and sustain it to endure the conflicts of Satan. God is our tower of strength." Testimonies, vol.2 p.189

God's Promises to Prayer

Prayer offers us an intimate connection with Christ; so intimate a connection that it can be likened to His illustration of the branch to a vine. This experience is essential to abiding in Christ, without whom we can do nothing. In inviting us to come to Him through prayer, God promises to answer:

"Call to Me, and I will answer you, and show you great and mighty things, which you do not know." Jeremiah 33:3 NKJV

Jesus, while walking this earth in His humanity, sustained His connection with God the Father by prayer. We may have the same experience too.

"Because the life of Jesus was a life of constant trust, sustained by continual communion, His service for heaven was without failure or faltering. Daily beset by temptation, constantly opposed by the leaders of the people, Christ knew that He must strengthen His humanity by prayer. In order to be a blessing to men, He must commune with God, from Him obtaining energy, perseverance, steadfastness." Gospel Workers p.255

Jesus' prayer life gave force to the success of His ministry. When we purposefully and intentionally take advantage of the privilege that is ours in prayer, our experience will not be much different from His:

"Now to Him who is able to do far more abundantly than all that we ask or think, according to the power at work within us, to Him be glory in the church and in Christ Jesus throughout all genera-

tions, forever and ever. Amen." Ephesians 3:20-21

Questions on Chapter 6

Why is prayer essential? (p.100)

What is prayer? (p.101)

What are the essential conditions for answered prayer? (p.103-111)

What attitude should I have in prayer? (p.105)

Why should I confess all my sins when I pray? (p.107)

Will God forgive me if I refuse to forgive others? (p.108)

Why does it seem like God sometimes delays to answering our prayers? (p.109)

What does it mean to pray in Jesus' name? (p.112)

What can I pray about? (p.112)

What do I do if I feel like I cannot pray? (p.100, 103, 104, 112)

Can I tell God everything that I am going through, and everything that I feel? (p.112, 120)

What does it mean to pray according to God's will? (p.113)

How important is it to praise God in prayer? (p.111, 115)

What practical things can I do to improve my prayer life? (p.119)

What example of prayer do we find in Elijah's experience? (p.121)

What has God promised to those who pray? (p.122)

7

Abiding Faith

❦

The Importance of Faith

What is Faith?

The Power Contained in God's Word

Experienced by Exercising Faith

Exercising Faith

Trusting in God

Great Faith is Persistent

Faith and Expectation

The Case of Abraham

How Faith Grows and Develops

Full Assurances of Faith

What is Presumption?

A Warning Against Unbelief

Overcoming Unbelief

A Case of Little Faith

In Summary

The Importance of Faith

Looking forward to the time of His coming, Jesus asks the question, "when the Son of man comes, shall He find faith on the earth?" (Luke 18:8). In the book of Revelation, those who are found ready for Christ's coming at the end of the world are characterised as keeping the commandments and having the faith of Jesus (Revelation 14:12). One of the most important elements in the Christian journey, and in the experience of abiding in Christ, is the element of genuine faith.

All who will be found abiding in Christ at His return would have learnt the lesson of how to exercise faith.

> "By faith Enoch was translated that he should not see death; and was not found, because God had translated him: for before his translation he had this testimony, that he pleased God. But without faith it is impossible to please Him: for he that cometh to God must believe that He is, and that He is a rewarder of them that diligently seek Him." Hebrews 11:5-6

> "And Enoch walked with God: and he was not; for God took him." Genesis 4:24

As one who walked with God, Enoch is described as having pleased God. The only way to really please God is by faith and it is impossible to do so without it. This is why Enoch is listed in the faith hall of fame.

For us to have the same experience that Enoch had, the experience of walking with God, we must have the same quality of faith too. This is why the subject of faith is vital for having a healthy Christian experience and maintaining communion with Christ.

> "The knowledge of what the Scripture means when urging upon us the necessity of cultivating faith, is more essential than any other knowledge that can be acquired. We suffer much trouble and grief because of our unbelief, and our ignorance of how to exercise faith. We must break through the clouds of unbelief. We cannot have a healthy Christian experience, we cannot obey the gospel unto salvation, until the science of faith is better understood, and until

more faith is exercised. There can be no perfection of Christian character without that faith that works by love, and purifies the soul." The Review and Herald, October 18, 1898 par. 7

Outside of faith, one cannot have the experience of abiding in Christ--of holding unbroken communion with Him. Faith is an essential ingredient and it is important to understand what it really means in order to exercise it. This is why Paul prays for the church "that Christ may dwell ([may abide]) in your hearts by faith…" (Ephesians 3:17)

What is Faith?

"Now faith is the substance of things hoped for, the evidence of things not seen." Hebrews 11:1

Although many may know what the *definition* of faith is, the lack of faith in their experience shows that few really understand what that definition actually *means*.

For us to get a better, practical understanding of what the meaning of faith is, we will consider an experience of one who is described as having "great faith".

The Roman Centurion

"Now when Jesus had entered Capernaum, a centurion came to Him, pleading with Him, saying, 'Lord, my servant is lying at home paralyzed, dreadfully tormented.' And Jesus said to him, 'I will come and heal him.'" Matthew 8:5-7 NKJV

When the Roman centurion came to Jesus on behalf of his servant, Jesus' first and natural response was that He would go and heal him. Jesus, in His humanity, could not be in all places at once. Thus, the promise to heal the servant already meant a lot. But notice the centurion's response:

"The centurion answered and said, 'Lord, I am not worthy that You should come under my roof. But only speak a word, and my servant will be healed.'" Matthew 8:8 NKJV

According to the centurion, if Jesus would only speak, his servant would be healed. The man had confidence in Christ's word. He con-

127

sidered the word as having the power and ability to heal the servant even if Jesus was not there in person. The Roman centurion trusted that the word, by itself, was able to accomplish this work. Then notice Jesus' response:

> "When Jesus heard it, He marveled, and said to those who followed, 'Assuredly, I say to you, I have not found such great faith, not even in Israel!'... Then Jesus said to the centurion, 'Go your way; and as you have believed, so let it be done for you.' And his servant was healed that same hour." Matthew 8:10, 13 NKJV

Jesus refers to the centurion's attitude and confidence in Him as "great faith". The centurion's response thus gives us a practical demonstration of what faith is.

To exercise faith means to believe and trust that God's word is able and powerful enough, by itself, to do what it speaks. Great faith, like that of the centurion, *expects* God's word to do that.

Through the centurions encounter we also learn the crucial point that God's word, and the promises that it contains, is the foundation of all true faith. Hence it could be said:

> "Faith comes by hearing, and hearing by the word of God." Romans 10:17 NKJV

The Power of God's Word

Few people understand the power that is in the word of God. Understanding the power contained in God's word is important primarily because our faith is in proportion to our trust in that power. "Faith comes by hearing, and hearing by the word of God," this means that the scriptures are the source if our faith. To get a glimpse of the power of God's word, and the faith that comes with knowing that power, it is necessary for the Bible itself to teach us.

Creative Power

The Bible illustrates how God created the entire universe by nothing other than His spoken word. The power to create was contained in the word and the extent of that power was such that He could create the entire universe with the word and nothing else.

"By the word of the Lord were the heavens made; and all the host of them by the breath of His mouth...For He spake, and it was done; He commanded, and it stood fast." Psalms 33:6, 9

In the first chapter of Genesis we see the power of God's word. When He said "let there be light", the light came to existence as a real and tangible thing by His command. This is because God's word creates what it speaks! The light existed as an actual thing from the moment God spoke it and the word, by itself, brought the light into being.

"God... quickens the dead, and calls those things which be not as though they were." Romans 4:17 NKJV

When God speaks of something, even if that thing has never existed before, the thing comes into being by the power of His word. He speaks of "the things which be not," the things which do not exist, "as though they were;" and when He speaks of them, they actually come into being. This is because:

"God is not a man, that He should lie, nor a son of man, that He should repent. Has He said, and will He not do? Or has He spoken, and will He not make it good?" Numbers 23:19 NKJV

Unlike humanity, God is able to carry out His word. When a human speaks of something and that thing does not exist or come to fulfilment, what they have spoken is a lie. But God's word is powerful and He is far greater than humans. When God speaks of something, He is more than able to bring it into being, furthermore, making it good.

Does Not Rely on Circumstance

"For God, who commanded the light to shine out of darkness, hath shined in our hearts, to give the light of the knowledge of the glory of God in the face of Jesus Christ." 2 Corinthians 4:6

When God said "let there be light", it was at a time when the Earth was formless and "darkness was upon the face of the deep" (Genesis 1:2-3). The universe was in perfect darkness and, until that point, light had never existed. Yet, even through these circumstances, when God spoke light into reality, "there was light." The word of God could not be limited by any opposing circumstance. This is the word in which we are called to put our trust.

The Unstoppable Word

"For as the rain comes down, and the snow from heaven, and do not return there, but water the earth, and make it bring forth and bud, that it may give seed to the sower and bread to the eater, so shall My word be that goes forth from My mouth; it shall not return to Me void, but it shall accomplish what I please, and it shall prosper in the thing for which I sent it." Isaiah 55:10-11 NKJV

The Bible describes God's word as being alive and powerful (Hebrews 4:12). When it leaves His mouth, the word goes on a mission to accomplish what God has spoken. By itself, God's word accomplishes the thing spoken of and it does not go back to Him until it has done what it set out to do. Thus, when God makes a promise, the word itself is the power that will fulfil that promise. Whenever God speaks, His word is unstoppable!

Upholds All Creation

The same power that was in God's word to create the heavens and the earth is the same power by which Christ still *maintains* the whole universe today. We are told that,

"The heavens and the earth which are now preserved by the same word, are reserved for fire until the Day of Judgment and perdition of ungodly men." 2 Peter 3:7 NKJV

The reason why the world still spins on its axis, and the sun still shines, is because of the power that holds them up. That power is God's word. Even today, He is consistently "upholding all things by the word of His power" (Hebrews 1:3). This is why:

"It is easier for heaven and earth to pass, than one tittle of the law ([God's word]) to fail." Luke 16:17

This can be our confidence--that as long as the world is still standing, God's promises will never fail! You can put your trust in God's

promises as firmly as a builder lays his foundation on the solid
ground.

Experienced by Exercising Faith

Although God's creative word is powerful and unstoppable, whether
or not we get to experience that power is determined by how we receive that word--whether or not we receive that word in faith.

> *"For this reason we also thank God without ceasing, because when
> you received the word of God which you heard from us, you wel-
> comed it not as the word of men, but as it is in truth, the word of
> God, which also effectively works in you who believe." 1 Thessalo-
> nians 2:13 NKJV*

The word of God works, effectively so, in those who believe--in those
who have faith. This very point is the reason why the early Hebrew
Christians were reminded about ancient Israel in the wilderness:

> *"Let us therefore fear, lest, a promise being left us of entering into
> ([God's]) rest, any of you should seem to come short of it. For unto
> us was the gospel preached, as well as unto them ([the Israelites in
> the wilderness]): but the word preached did not profit them, not
> being mixed with faith in them that heard it." Hebrews 4:1-2*

It is possible that, although God makes a promise, we may still fall
short of experiencing it. This was the case with the ancient Israelites
who left Egypt. When the word of God is not mingled with the faith
of the hearer, it does not profit the one who hears it.

The gospel is "the power of God unto salvation", but this is re-
stricted only "to everyone that believes" (Romans 1:16). That is to
say that the unbelieving individual, while still in unbelief, does not
experience the power of the gospel as contained in the word of God.

Exercising Faith

With all that we have discussed thus far, we can consider some principles of how to exercise faith. This is so that we may experience the
power of God's word through faith.

> *"Looking unto Jesus the author and finisher of our faith..." He-*

brews 12:2

Due to the fact that without Him we can do nothing, Jesus is also the author and the finisher of our faith. Everything needed for our salvation, even the faith that grabs hold of Christ's righteousness, comes from God Himself.

"God has dealt to every man the measure of faith." Romans 12:3

"Faith that enables us to receive God's gifts is itself a gift, of which some measure is imparted to every human being. It grows as exercised in appropriating ([taking hold of]) the word of God." Education p.253

Since Jesus has granted the gift of faith to everyone, each individual may exercise faith. It is not a unique ability that only a special group of people have. Our duty is to understand how we may exercise that faith. What we will find is that faith is not a complex thing; faith is plain and simple, yet still very powerful.

"How to exercise faith should be made very plain." Ibid

"Faith is simple in its operation and powerful in its results." Mind Character and Personality, book 2 p.532

Faith is a Response to the Promises of God's Word

From the example of the Roman Centurion, we learnt that to have faith is to depend on God's word (alone) to carry out the thing which it speaks. Faith thus expects the word to carry out the thing spoken, by its own power. From that we gather some vital principles regarding faith as a positive response to the word of God:

"To every promise of God there are conditions. If we are willing to do His will, all His strength is ours. Whatever gift He promises, is in the promise itself. "The seed is the word of God." Luke 8:11. As surely as the oak [tree] is in the acorn [seed], so surely is the gift of God in His promise. If we receive the promise, we have the gift." Education p.253

In receiving the promises of God, we receive the very thing that the word of God contains in that promise--even though we cannot yet see and touch it. This is how it is that faith, itself, is the substance--the actual material--of the things hoped for.

Faith responds to God's word by accepting, and embracing, the thing which God has promised. Thus, we are encouraged to:

> *"Place no dependence upon changeable feelings, but plant your feet upon the sure platform of the promises of God: 'Thou hast said it; I believe the promise.' This is an intelligent faith." Our High Calling p.124*

When God makes a promise, faith accepts that promise as true, and that the promise brings with it the very thing spoken of. So when God promises us His forgiveness, we may trust that we do receive and possess that very thing because we have the promise that contains it. We may even thank God for what we now have.

Faith Accepts and Follows God's Will

> *"The just shall live by faith." Romans 1:17*

> *"[Jesus] answered and said, "It is written, 'Man shall not live by bread alone, but by every word that proceeds from the mouth of God.'" Matthew 4:4 NKJV*

In order to live by faith, we must live by *every* word that proceeds from the mouth of God. Thus, the same attitude we have--in taking God's promises to be true--must be the same attitude towards His commandments and instructions also. This is genuine faith in God's word.

Every Promise is Given on Condition of Obedience

The promises of God must be received together with His commandments. His instructions must be received as with the promises. Obedience to God's will, as it is shown to us in His commandments, is the highest condition for receiving the blessings of His promises; and faith accepts all of God's word. Thus,

> *"Whatsoever we ask, we receive of Him, because we keep His commandments, and do those things that are pleasing in His sight." 1 John 3:22*

Real faith accepts God's promises. The willingness to do His will, those things that are pleasing in His sight, is the condition to receiving every one of the sure promises; and the promises are trustworthy.

Faith is Separate from Feeling

Due to the fact that faith is dependent on God's word, and the word only, faith thus has nothing to do with feelings and emotions. These two are separate and distinct things.

"For we walk by faith, not by sight." 2 Corinthians 5:7

Exercising faith means taking God's word to be true, regardless of the circumstances around us and the feelings within us.

"True faith lays hold of and claims the promised blessing before it is realised and felt...Here is faith, naked faith, to believe that we receive the blessing, even before we realise it...The very time to exercise faith is when we feel destitute of the Spirit. When thick clouds of darkness seem to hover over the mind, then is the time to let living faith pierce the darkness and scatter the clouds. True faith rests on the promises contained in the Word of God, and those only who obey that Word can claim its glorious promises." Early Writings p.72

Thus, when our feelings are against us and when sadness & depression cloud the mind, even at that same time we can claim the promises of God's word. The word of God is unchanging.

"You are not to wait for wonderful emotions before you believe that God has heard you, feeling is not to be your criterion, for emotions are as changeable as the clouds. You must have something solid for the foundation of your faith. The word of the Lord is a word of infinite power, upon which you may rely, and He has said, 'ask, and ye shall receive.'" Selected Messages, book 1, p.328

Faith Acts

True faith is always expressed, either in words or in actions. This was the case with the Roman centurion.

"When Jesus has entered Capernaum, a certain centurion came to Him, pleading with Him, saying, 'Lord, my servant is lying at home paralyzed, dreadfully tormented.'" Matthew 8:6 NKJV

Because the centurion was confident in the power contained in God's word, he himself went to Christ. His faith in Christ's word was expressed by his efforts to go to Christ, as well as in him saying: "Lord, speak the word only, and my servant shall be healed." Had he said, "God's word is powerful", and yet not gone to Christ to claim that word, it would have been evidence of unbelief.

This is the Spirit of Faith

"I will walk before the Lord in the land of the living. I believed, therefore have I spoken: I was greatly afflicted." Psalms 116:9-10

Although David was greatly afflicted, he still spoke words of courage that he would "walk before the Lord in the land of the living". The reason he spoke this way, even in his affliction, was because he believed in God. "I believed," he says, and "therefore have I spoken."

This attitude is what Paul later refers to as "the spirit of faith."

"We, having the same spirit of faith (according as it is written: 'I believed, and therefore have I spoken") we also believe, and therefore speak.'" 2 Corinthians 4:13

The spirit of faith is to talk and act as if God's promises are true, regardless of any affliction that we may be going through.

The spirit of unbelief is the exact opposite; it is to talk and act as if God's promises were *not* true. The reason why many fall short of experiencing God's promises is because of their expressions of doubt and unbelief.

"Those who talk faith and cultivate faith will have faith; but those who cherish and express doubts will have doubts." Mind, Character and Personality, book 2 p.534

"Take the word of Christ as your assurance. Has He not invited you to come unto Him? Never allow yourself to talk in a hopeless, discouraged way. If you do you will lose much. By looking at ap-

pearances and complaining when difficulties and pressure come, you give evidence of a sickly, enfeebled faith. Talk and act as if your faith was invincible. The Lord is rich in resources; He owns the world. Look heavenward in faith. Look to Him who has light and power and efficiency." Christ Object Lessons p.146

Faith is a Choice, an Action of the Will

From the previous point, we also draw the important principle that faith is the outcome of a decision made to trust God, based on His promises. We must *choose* to trust His promises despite the circumstance or our emotions. This means putting one's will on God's side.

"At times the masterly power of temptation seems to tax our will power to the uttermost, and to exercise faith seems utterly contrary to all the evidences of sense or emotion; but our will must be kept on God's side. We must believe that in Jesus Christ is everlasting strength and efficiency." Our High Calling p.124

When circumstances appear to oppose God's promises we can, and must, choose to trust Him still. This is not at all to say that any feelings of assurance should be thrown aside.

"A feeling of assurance is not to be despised; we should praise God for it; but when your feelings are depressed, do not think that God has changed. Praise Him just as much, because you trust in His word, and not in feelings. You have covenanted to walk by faith, not to be controlled by feelings. Feelings vary with circumstances" ibid.

Trusting in God

"You believe that there is one God. You do well. Even the demons believe--and tremble!" James 2:19 NKJV

True faith has more to it than to only believe that God exists, and to acknowledge the truthfulness of His word. True faith also involves submission to God and trusting ourselves fully to His care.

"There is a kind of belief that is wholly distinct from faith. The existence and power of God, the truth of His word, are facts that

even Satan and his hosts cannot at heart deny... Where there is not only a belief in God's word, but a submission of the will to Him; where the heart is yielded to Him, the affections fixed upon Him, there is faith--faith that works by love and purifies the soul." Steps to Christ p.63

Thus, true faith has to do with putting ones trust in God, to place our entire dependence on Him. This trust is expressed in following His will, and we can place our full weight on the promises of God's word.

"Faith is trusting God--believing that He loves us and knows best what is for our good. Thus, instead of our own, it leads us to choose His way." Education p.253

True faith is expressed in an abiding trust. This kind of faith is willing to obey God's will, even when it seems to not make sense; realising that God loves us too much to do us any harm.

A Simple, Childlike Trust

"Faith is simple in its operation and powerful in its results. Many professed Christians, who have a knowledge of the sacred Word, and believe its truth, fail in the childlike trust that is essential to the religion of Jesus. They do not reach out with that peculiar touch that brings the virtue of healing to the soul" S.D.A Bible Commentary, vol. 6 p.1074

The simple trust and confidence that a little child has in his parents, taking their word as truth, is the same simple trust and confidence that we are to exercise in the promises of God's unchanging word.

"Jesus called them unto Him, and said, 'Suffer little children to come unto Me, and forbid them not: for of such is the kingdom of God. Verily I say unto you, Whosoever shall not receive the kingdom of God as a little child shall in no wise enter therein.'" Luke 18:16-17

The child of a good parent simply trusts his parent, and would never question or doubt whether his caring father or mother could be trusted. In the same way, we are to have a simple, childlike trust towards our Father in Heaven.

"Like as a father pities his children, so the Lord pities them that fear Him. For He knows our frame; He remembers that we are dust." Psalms 103:13-14

Great Faith is Persistent

In Matthew 15:21-28 we are shown an example of a woman to whom Christ says, "O woman, great is your faith." (Matthew 15:28). The great faith of the woman was seen in her persistence.

"Behold, a woman of Canaan came out of the same coasts, and cried unto [Jesus], saying, 'Have mercy on me, O Lord, thou son of David; my daughter is grievously vexed with a devil.'" Matthew 15:22

We can consider some points from this woman's experience as another example of what great faith looks like.

The woman was a Canaanite and the Jews had no favour for non-Jews (John 4:9). The woman recognised her unworthiness. The fact that she even came to Christ, who was a Jewish man, was a gamble on her part.

The Canaanite woman depended on the mercy of God. She realised that she did not deserve Christ's help, but she had a hope in the fact that He is merciful (See Psalms 147:11).

Even though the Canaanite woman thus came to Jesus, the responses she received from Him made it seem as though He refused to help her, or to even give her any attention. He apparently ignored her and "answered her not a word..." (Verse 23). Yet, she still continued to plead.

She cried to the disciples and even they asked Jesus to "send her away, for she cries out after us." They were annoyed by her appeals because they also saw her as unworthy.

Jesus then continues to express words that suggested that He would not help anyone who was not an Israelite.

"Then she came and worshiped Him, saying, 'Lord, help me.' But He answered and said, 'It is not good to take the children's bread, and throw it to the little dogs." Matthew 15:25-26 NKJV

Following her constant appeals, Jesus responded in a manner that expressed the prejudiced attitude that the Jews of that time had against the Canaanites. Yet, the woman still continued to plead.

"This answer ([from Jesus]) would have utterly discouraged a less earnest seeker. But the woman saw that her opportunity had come. Beneath the apparent refusal of Jesus, she saw a compassion that He could not hide. "Truth, Lord," she answered, "yet the dogs eat of the crumbs which fall from their masters' table." The Desire of Ages p.401

Despite all the painful suggestions that implied that Jesus refused to help, the woman persisted in prayer. She claimed the blessings not because she deserved them, but because of the mercy of God. Because of her persistent dependence, regardless of the apparent refusal from Christ, He said to her: "O woman, great is your faith!" (Matthew 15:28.). This is the faith that is needed today.

"I asked... why there was no more faith and power in Israel. He said, "[You] let go of the arm of the Lord too soon. Press your petitions to the throne, and hold on by strong faith. The promises are sure. Believe [you] receive the things [you] ask for, and [you] shall have them." I was then pointed to Elijah. He was subject to like passions as we are, and he prayed earnestly. His faith endured the trial. Seven times he prayed before the Lord, and at last the cloud was seen. I saw that we had doubted the sure promises, and wounded the Saviour by our lack of faith." Early Writings p.73

Great faith is persistent, regardless of any apparent refusal from God. Hold on to the promises of God in steady, enduring faith.

Faith and Expectation

True faith always has an expectation that the promises of God will come to fulfilment, and that this will happen by the power of the word itself.

"Therefore I tell you, whatever you ask in prayer, believe that you have received it, and it will be yours." Mark 11:24 ESV

One who truly trusts in the word of God has an expectation that it will be fulfilled. When we receive the word of God, we are assured that we receive the thing promised. Faith then becomes sight when the promises are realised.

> *"[Abraham and his household] all died in faith, not having received the promises, but having seen them afar off, and were persuaded of them, and embraced them, and confessed that they were strangers and pilgrims on the earth." Hebrews 11:13*

Genuine faith means to have such a confidence in the promises of God that, when claiming them, we may look forward to them with hopeful expectation; even to embrace, confess and speak about them.

When God speaks of His forgiveness for our sins, we may be persuaded of the fact and also go on to speak as those who have been made righteous by that word.

The Case of Abraham

Abraham's experience can be considered as another case study of great faith. In the book of Romans, Paul uses Abraham's case as an example of one who was made righteous through faith. We can draw a few practical principles of faith from this example.

Abraham Had a Trustful Perspective of God

The idea that Abraham had of God, what he thought about Him, had a great impact on his faith. He believed in God as:

> *"God, who gives life to the dead and calls those things which do not exist as though they did." Romans 4:17 NKJV*

Abraham's idea of God was that He is able to raise the dead and that God can speak of something that does not exist and, by His word, bring that thing into existence. This was the picture of God that Abraham had in his mind. Thus Abraham could trust God:

> *"...being fully persuaded that, what [God] had promised, He was able also to perform." Romans 4:21*

Abraham Trusted God, Despite the Circumstances

When Abraham was 99 years old, God promised him that he would be the father of many nations (Genesis 17:1, 4-5). This was a seemingly hopeless situation, but not to Abraham:

"who, contrary to hope, in hope believed, so that he became the father of many nations, according to what was spoken, "So shall your descendants be." Romans 4:18 NKJV

Even though the situation seemed hopeless for Abraham to have a son, Abraham still believed. Faith, saving faith in God, does not look to the circumstances. It depends entirely on God's word.

Abraham's Faith Was Based Only on God's Word

Abraham's faith was not based on how hopeful things seemed to be, but was based entirely on the promise of God. He "believed in hope…according to that which was spoken [by God]" (verse 18).

Like the Centurion, Abraham depended on the promise of God *only*. This is the faith of Abraham, and this must be the quality of our faith also. The word of God must be our assurance. This is *genuine* faith.

Abraham Was Not Weak in Faith

"And being not weak in faith, [Abraham] considered not his own body now dead, when he was about an hundred years old, neither yet the deadness of Sarah's womb." Romans 4:19

When God promised Abraham a child, Abraham did not spend time thinking about the fact that he and Sarah were beyond the age of child bearing. He did not pay attention to these "realities;" He did not regard them, but he trusted in the promises of God.

Had Abraham not done this, he would have been "weak in faith." Weak faith, as opposed to strong faith, focusses more on the circumstance that are seemingly against the promises of God.

Abraham Was Strong in Faith

"[Abraham] staggered not at the promise of God through unbelief;

but was strong in faith, giving glory to God." Romans 4:20

Unbelief causes one to fall short of the promises of God; but this was not the case with Abraham. He was strong in faith, thus giving glory to God. Strong faith gives God glory:

"Whoever offers praise glorifies Me; and to him who orders his conduct aright I will show the salvation of God." Psalms 50:23 NKJV

When God made promises to Abraham, Abraham went about his life as though he had already seen the promised blessing fulfilled. As a result of this, He could praise God for it.

This is the mark of strong faith; to give glory to God in praise whenever He makes a promise. This is because when we have the promise, we just as surely have the blessing (whether or not we see or feel it).

Fully Persuaded of the Ability of God

Abraham was "fully persuaded that, what [God] had promised, He was able also to perform." Romans 4:21

When it came to how the promises were going to be fulfilled, Abraham was convinced that God has the ability to make His promises happen. Abraham was not concerned with the "how" part, but he had a confidence in the ability of the almighty God.

How Faith Grows and Develops

"We are bound to thank God always for you, brethren, as it is fitting, because your faith grows exceedingly, and the love of every one of you all abounds toward each other, so that we ourselves boast of you among the churches of God for your patience and faith in all your persecutions and tribulations that you endure." 2 Thessalonians 1:3-4 NKJV

From the experience of the Thessalonians we learn that faith can grow, and that it can do so "exceedingly". How does faith grow?

"Faith comes by hearing, and hearing by the word of God." Ro-

mans 10:17 NKJV

*"[Faith] grows as exercised in appropriating ([in taking hold of])
the word of God. In order to strengthen faith, we must often bring
it in contact with the word." Education 253*

Faith, dependence on the word of God only, grows as it is exercised.
To strengthen our faith, God often brings us into situations that require us to believe on His word--to claim and receive His promises
with all that they contain. In order to claim those promises, we must
be familiar with them by daily studying God's word.

The Bible is filled with scenarios that reveal the power of God's
word--from when God said, "'let there be light,' and there was
light..."(Genesis 1:3) to the very last verses.

The Importance of Developing Faith

*"If you do not cultivate faith, its importance will gradually lose
its place in your mind and heart. You will have an experience like
that of the foolish virgins, who did not supply oil for their lamps,
and their light went out. Faith should be cultivated. If it has become weak, it is like a sickly plant that should be placed in the
sunshine and carefully watered and tended." Mind, Character and
Personality, book 2 p.534*

When faith has become weak, it can be cultivated and developed
only by exercising the little faith that is already there.

How is this to be exercised? Paul has said, "I have believed, [and]
therefore have I spoken" (2 Cor. 4:13). This is the spirit of faith--to
express confidence in the sure promises of God's word, whether or
not we necessarily feel anything. Thus by exercising faith, more faith
is developed.

*"Those who talk faith and cultivate faith will have faith; but those
who cherish and express doubts will have doubts." Ibid*

*"If we would give more expression to our faith, rejoice more in
the blessings that we know we have,--the great mercy and love of
God,--we should have more faith and greater joy." The Ministry of
Healing p.252*

There is no holiness in constantly talking of our difficulties and looking to others for pity and sympathy. This is the spirit of unbelief--to talk and act is though God's words were not true.

"Let us take heed to our words. Let us talk faith, and we shall have faith. Never give place to a thought of discouragement in the work of God. Never utter a word of doubt. It is as seed sown in the heart of both speaker and hearers, to produce a harvest of discouragement and unbelief." Evangelism p.633

It is important here to re-emphasise the point that we must *choose* to trust God. When feelings seem to oppose God's promises, when tough circumstances surround us, we may still *decide* to trust God; having realised that His word is reliable. Faith is an action of the will, "I *will* trust God, even in the midst of trial."

Exhorting One Another by the Word

"Take heed, brethren, lest there be in any of you an evil heart of unbelief, in departing from the living God." Hebrews 3:12

The Hebrew Christians were warned about the danger of unbelief. Unbelief causes us to depart from God; not exercising faith pushes us further and further away from Him. To prevent this from happening, a word of counsel is given:

"But exhort one another daily, while it is called 'Today'; lest any of you be hardened through the deceitfulness of sin." Verse 13

Cultivating faith must be a daily exercise. A way to do this is when believers encourage each other with the word of God daily. Admonishing others with the promises of scripture prevents them from becoming hardened through unbelief, and it also impacts the one who does the admonishing. Thus, in daily encouraging others with the word, our own faith develops and strengthens.

Full Assurances of Faith

God is very well acquainted with our human condition, even our tendencies to doubt. In view of this, He has provided us with enough for us to have what the apostle Paul refers to as "the full assurance of faith." Through the many assurances which God has given, that His word can be trusted, we may have a firm confidence and faith in Him. We will consider a few:

The Sacrifice of Christ

"He that spared not His own Son, but delivered Him up for us all, how shall He not with Him also freely give us all things?" Romans 8:32

The sacrifice and death of Jesus on the cross is the ultimate guarantee of God's willingness to provide for every one of our needed blessings. If God the Father gave all of heaven in the gift of His own Son, how can we question whether He is willing to fulfil His promises and provide for all our needs?

"God demonstrates His own love toward us, in that while we were still sinners, Christ died for us." Romans 5:8 NKJV

While we were still His enemies, wanting nothing to do with Him, God was willing to give His Son for us. The death of Jesus shows us God's willingness to save, and the resurrection of Jesus shows God's power, His ability, to fulfil every one of His promises to those who put their trust in Him.

"Because we are the gift of His Father, and the reward of His work, Jesus loves us. He loves us as His children. Reader, He loves you. Heaven itself can bestow nothing greater, nothing better. Therefore trust." The Desire of Ages p.483

God Swore by Himself

"For when God made a promise to Abraham, because He could swear by no one greater, He swore by Himself, saying, "Surely blessing I will bless you, and multiplying I will multiply you." Hebrews 6:13-14 NKJV

Even though God cannot lie, when He made a promise to Abraham, God went the extra mile to even swear to Abraham; and He swore by the greatest thing that He could find--Himself. That is to say, God put Himself on the line as the pledge for His promises.

"And so, after [Abraham] had patiently endured, he obtained the promise." Hebrews 6:15

The reason God went so far as to put Himself on the line as an oath of surety to His promises was because of how confident God is that He is able to fulfil them. He wants us to have the same great confidence in His word. Notice this idea:

"When people take an oath, they call on someone greater than themselves to hold them to it. And without any question that oath is binding. God also bound Himself with an oath, so that those who received the promise could be perfectly sure that He would never change His mind. So God has given both His promise and His oath. These two things are unchangeable because it is impossible for God to lie. Therefore, we who have fled to Him for refuge can have great confidence as we hold to the hope that lies before us." Hebrews 6:16-18 NLT

"The honour of His throne is staked for the fulfilment of His word unto us." Christ's Object Lessons p.148

Because God has sworn by Himself, the honour of His everlasting throne is at stake. If He does not fulfil any of His promises, this throne must lawfully be given up. Thus, we have the assurance that the promises of God are as certain and as sure as His eternal throne.

The Evidences of Past Promises

Since the beginning of creation, God's promises have never been found to fail. At the end of building the temple at Jerusalem, which God promised would take place, king Solomon exclaimed:

"Blessed be the Lord, who has given rest to His people Israel, according to all that He promised. There has not failed one word of all His good promise, which He promised through His servant Moses." 1 Kings 8:56 NKJV

There has never been a time when the promises of God have failed. His track record knows no failure. For this reason, we can put our trust in Him, more than we put our trust in our earthly friends.

When we spend time in reflecting on this fact, and how God has been faithful in the past, our hope will be strengthened.

"[God] is well pleased when we urge past mercies and blessings as a reason why He should bestow on us greater blessings. He will more than fulfil the expectations of those who trust fully in Him. The Lord Jesus knows just what His children need, how much divine power we will appropriate for the blessing of humanity; and He bestows upon us all that we will employ in blessing others and ennobling our own souls." The Ministry of Healing p.513

Prophecy

Prophecy is a powerful witness to the truthfulness of God's word. When we study prophecy, and see its fulfilment, confidence in the power and consistency of God's word is established.

"And now I have told you before it come to pass, that, when it is come to pass, ye might believe." John 14:29

Jesus does not want us to believe Him blindly. Through prophecy, He has given us enough to be able to intelligently put our trust in Him. We see the certainty of God's prophetic word through the epistle of Peter. While writing about his personal experience with Jesus, Peter also gave evidence to the power of God's words.

Peter testified to the fact that he had a *real* experience with Jesus. We learn of the lives of great men through the eyewitness accounts of those who lived during their times. In the same way, we have evidence of the truthfulness of Christ's life, death and resurrection through the testimony of the apostles. Says Peter:

"For we have not followed cunningly devised fables, when we made known unto you the power and coming of our Lord Jesus Christ, but were eyewitnesses of His majesty." 2 Peter 1:16

Peter was not writing about a story he had heard from someone, but told of his own experience as an eyewitness. Like John, he wrote about "that which was from the beginning, which we have heard, which we have seen with our eyes, which we have looked upon, and our hands have handled, of the Word of life" (1 John 1:1). Because of this fact, we can take the reality of Christ's life as factual. Peter then continues with the following thought:

"We have also a more sure word of prophecy; whereunto [you] do well that [you] take heed, as unto a light that shineth in a dark place, until the day dawn, and the day star arise in your hearts."
2 Peter 1:19

Beyond the fact that we have the definite eyewitness accounts of the apostles, Peter argues the fact that the word of prophecy is more trustworthy than their own eyewitness accounts. Even though Peter had a physical experience with Jesus, God's prophetic word is "more sure".

The additional idea presented is that when our experiences and circumstances seem to argue against the promises of God's word, we may rest assured that the word of prophecy is "more sure". It would do well for us to receive it as our source of light, shining in a dark and skeptical world.

What is Presumption?

We have understood that faith means to depend on the word of God *only* to bring about the thing which it has promised and that faith expects the word of God to do so. Thus, faith is fully reliant on the word of God and nothing else. With this in mind, we want to understand, and guard against, presumption.

"Faith is in no sense allied to presumption. Only he who has true faith is secure against presumption. For presumption is Satan's counterfeit of faith." The Desire of Ages p.126

The same way any counterfeit always has a similarity to an original, even so presumption--the false version of faith--very closely resembles faith. Yet the two are distinct and separate things. Consider the following passage:

"Faith claims God's promises, and brings forth fruit in obedience. Presumption also claims the promises, but uses them as Satan did, to excuse transgression. Faith would have led our first parents to trust the love of God, and to obey His commands. Presumption led them to transgress His law, believing that His great love would

save them from the consequence of their sin. It is not faith that claims the favor of Heaven without complying with the conditions on which mercy is to be granted. Genuine faith has its foundation in the promises and provisions of the Scriptures." Ibid

Genuine faith is based on the promises and the provisions of what God has said in His word. With this in mind, we learn that presumption can take one of two main forms:

To Claim God's Promises Without Obedience

God's promises are all given on the condition that we follow His will. To expect to receive the promises of God, while still choosing to disobey that will, is presumption. This is seen in the example of the children of Israel soon after leaving Egypt.

God had promised the Israelites that if they would trust in Him He would give them the land of Canaan.

"Behold, the Lord thy God hath set the land before thee: go up and possess it, as the Lord God of thy fathers hath said unto thee;, 'fear not, neither be discouraged.'" Deuteronomy 1:21

Before the Israelites entered Canaan, the Land of Promise, 12 men were sent to spy out the land. When they returned, 10 of them gave a discouraging report about the size of the men in the Promised Land. They looked at the circumstances and spoke words of unbelief as to the possibility of possessing the land which God had promised. This doubtful report caused the children of Israel to murmur against God and against Moses. (See Numbers 14:1-11, Deuteronomy 1:26-28)

In their unbelief and murmuring, the Israelites distrusted God. They saw it better to have died in Egypt and thus, by their unbelief, they disqualified themselves from receiving the promises. For this reason God denied them entrance into Canaan. He set them to wander in the wilderness of Sinai for 40 years. (Numbers 14:22-35, Deuteronomy 1:34-36)

Hearing this, the Israelites thought to rather take the land over by their own power. Moses, reminding them of this experience, says to them:

"Then you answered and said to me, 'We have sinned against the Lord; we will go up and fight, just as the Lord our God commanded us.' And when everyone of you had girded his weapons of war, you were ready to go up into the mountain." Deuteronomy 1:41 NKJV

Even though God now told them that they would no longer enter Canaan, they still attempted to go up, "according to all that the Lord… commanded." They claimed the (previous) promises of God, that they would enter Canaan, but this promise was of no effect due to their unbelief. Thus:

"The Lord said to [Moses], 'Say to them, Do not go up or fight, for I am not in your midst, lest you be defeated before your enemies.' So I spoke to you, and you would not listen; but you rebelled against the command of the Lord and presumptuously went unto the hill country. Then the Amorites who lived in that hill country came out against you and chased you as bees do and beat you down in Seir as far as Hormah." Deuteronomy 1:42-44

Thus we see an illustration of presumption in the case of the Israelites--that presumption means to try and claim the promises of God's word, while still being in disobedience to His instruction. Presumption means to expect the provisions of God's word on our own terms, and not according to His will.

To Claim, From God, What He Has not Promised

The second expression of presumption is to depend on God and expect from Him that which He has not promised. It is very similar to faith, but because it is not founded on the word of God, it is not faith at all.

"When our prayers seem not to be answered, we are to cling to the promise; for the time of answering will surely come, and we shall receive the blessing we need most. But to claim that prayer will always be answered in the very way and for the particular thing that we desire, is presumption." Steps to Christ p.96

The reason this would be presumption is primarily because God has not promised this--He has not promised to answer our prayers exactly as and when we desire them to be answered. Faith is founded and based on the promises of God. Without this word, faith would have no foundation.

With these two principles in mind, we are able to discern between genuine faith and presumption.

Other Instances of Presumption

Other instances of presumption, under the previous two descriptions we have mentioned, also include the following cases:

To Follow Christ Without Fully Obeying Him

To be a Christian, the experience of walking with God, is not merely to adopt the title of "Christian". It includes living a life in complete harmony with God's revealed will.

> "A mere profession of discipleship is of no value. The faith in Christ which saves the soul is not what it is represented to be by many. 'Believe, believe,' they say, 'and you need not keep the law.' But a belief that does not lead to obedience is presumption. The apostle John says, 'He that saith, I know Him, and keepeth not His commandments, is a liar, and the truth is not in him.' (1 John 2:4). Let none cherish the idea that special providences or miraculous manifestations are to be the proof of the genuineness of their work or of the ideas they advocate. When persons will speak lightly of the word of God, and set their impressions, feelings, and exercises above the divine standard, we may know that they have no light in them." Thoughts from the Mount of Blessings p.146

It is presumptuous to claim to be a Christian, while still living in disobedience to the will of God. Obedience, driven by faith, is the true mark of whether one is a disciple of Christ or not.

To Assign to God What He has not Said

> "But the prophet, which shall presume to speak a word in my name, which I have not commanded him to speak, or that shall speak in the name of other gods, even that prophet shall die." Deuteronomy 18:20

Many expect things from God based on a faulty understanding of His word and His character. Individuals associate God with ideas which have nothing to do with Him. In so doing they thus presume to speak in His name.

This kind of presumption also led to Eve's fall in the Garden of Eden when she said to Satan: "God said, 'You shall not of the fruit... neither shall you touch it, let you die." Genesis 3:3. God had not said that they should not touch the fruit, and Satan used Eve's addition to God's word to her destruction.

God has given us His word by, which we may test all things. In laying our confidence in His sure word, we have a secure foundation for our faith.

To Rely on False Evidences for Faith

One of the major ways in which presumption reveals itself is through depending on signs, impressions and emotions as assurances to God's promises. Notice how this existed even in Jesus' day:

> *"The Pharisees and Sadducees came to Jesus and tested Him by asking Him to show them a sign from heaven." Matthew 16:1 NIV*

When the Pharisees and Sadducees did not want to believe in Jesus as the Messiah, they asked Him for a sign. They already had evidences from the Old Testament scriptures, however, and that should have been enough to convince them.

At times individuals demand a sign, a miracle or "proof," when they are reluctant to believe the evidence that has already been presented to them. But notice Jesus' response to this attitude in the Pharisees:

> *"'An evil and adulterous generation seeks for a sign, but no sign will be given to it except the sign of Jonah.' So He left them and departed." Matthew 16:4 ESV*

It is presumptuous to depend on signs, feelings (good or bad) or any other thing--besides God's word--as a foundation for our faith.

> *"Faith is not feeling. 'Faith is the substance of things hoped for, the evidence of things not seen.'[Hebrews 11:1.] True faith is in*

no sense allied to presumption. Only he who has true faith is se-cure against presumption, for presumption is Satan's counterfeit of faith." Gospel Workers p.260

A Warning Against Unbelief

The spirit of faith is to talk and act as though God's promises are true, because they are. The spirit of unbelief is the exact opposite of this.

Unbelief may receive the word of God, but it does not believe that God's word is powerful enough to carry out what it speaks. The spirit of unbelief is to talk and act as if God's promises were *not* true. This is shown in speaking about the opposing circumstances as having more power than God's word.

"Take heed, brethren, lest there be in any of you an evil heart of unbelief, in departing from the living God." Hebrews 3:12

Unbelief is a dangerous place to be in. It draws us away from the living God, and thus we want to guard against it. We may consider some of the dangers of not choosing to take God at His word:

Unbelief Cuts Us Off From the Power of God's Word

Faith puts us in direct contact with the power of God, the same power that He used to create the universe (Romans 1:16-17, 20). Unbelief, on the other hand, cuts us off from that power.

In one account, when Jesus' friend Lazarus was sick, word was sent to Him.

"When Jesus heard that, He said, 'This sickness is not unto death, but for the glory of God, that the Son of God might be glorified thereby.'" John 11:3-4

In this incident, Jesus did not immediately go to where His sick friend was, and Lazarus eventually died. Jesus said to His disciples: "I go, that I may awake him out of sleep."

To Jesus, Lazarus' death was only temporary.

"Jesus, again groaning in Himself, came to the tomb. It was a cave, and a stone lay against it. Jesus said, 'Take away the stone.' Mar-

tha, the sister of him who was dead, said to Him, 'Lord, by this time there is a stench, for he has been dead four days.' Jesus said to her, 'Did I not say to you that if you would believe, you would see the glory of God?'" John 11:38-40 NKJV

In response to Christ's instructions, Martha spoke of the opposing circumstances--the fact that after four days Lazarus' body would have started decomposing. But Jesus made it clear that a condition to seeing the glory of God, His power, was to have faith in Him. This is the basic reason why many do not get to experience God's power today.

> *"But many have not a living faith. This is why they do not see more of the power of God. Their weakness is the result of their unbelief. They have more faith in their own working than in the working of God for them. They take themselves into their own keeping. They plan and devise, but pray little, and have little real trust in God. They think they have faith, but it is only the impulse of the moment. Failing to realise their own need, or God's willingness to give, they do not persevere in keeping their requests before the Lord." Christ's Object Lessons p.145*

Unbelief, in trusting anything other than the power of God's word alone, cuts us off from experiencing His power.

> *"[Jesus] did not [do] many mighty works there because of their unbelief." Matthew 13:58*

> *"In order to fight successfully in the battle against sin, you must keep close to Jesus. Do not talk unbelief; you have no excuse for doing this... Unbelief always separates the soul from Christ." In Heavenly Places p.122*

Dishonours God

God has given Himself as a pledge to fulfil His word and He "is not a man that He should lie; neither the son of man, that He should repent" (Numbers 23:19). Unbelief dishonours God, because in not trusting Him, or taking Him at His word, it causes us to respond to Him as though He were a liar.

154

"Many of us walk by sight and not by faith. We believe the things that are seen but do not appreciate the precious promises given us in God's Word; and yet we cannot dishonor God more decidedly than by showing that we distrust what He says and question whether the Lord is in earnest ([sincere]) with us or is deceiving us." Faith and Works p.35

Leads to Sin

Sin is the transgression of the law of God (1 John 3:4). It is nothing more than going against what God has said. To decide to take God at His word is faith and this is always expressed in obedience to that word.

Unbelief, on the other hand, is a distrust of God's word and this lays the foundation for not obeying that word. Unbelief will always result in actions that go contrary to God's word.

It is for this reason that Paul says: "for whatsoever is not of faith is sin." (Romans 14:23)

Overcoming Unbelief

"Lord, I believe; help thou mine unbelief." Mark 9:24

Together with the assurances of faith already mentioned, Jesus has given us strong helps for overcoming unbelief. It must here be restated that "faith is simple in its operation and powerful in its results." We do not need to look for anything complicated in order to exercise faith.

By the Word of God

"In order to strengthen faith, we must often bring it in contact with the Word." Education, p.254

"So then faith comes by hearing, and hearing by the word of God." Romans 10:17

The Bible is the foundation of faith. Faith comes through a daily, continual contact with the word of God and choosing to trust the promises that it contains. When we see the evidences of God's power and love in the lives of its various characters, we learn to trust and accept that love for ourselves.

Letting the Mind Dwell on the Promises

"This I recall to my mind, therefore have I hope. It is of the Lord's mercies that we are not consumed, because His compassions fail not." Lamentations 3:21-22

It is not merely in knowing about the word of God that develops faith, but it is in contemplating on it--taking time to think about its promises and the evidences of God's power. For us to have faith, we must recall to mind the evidences of what God has done for us and what He has promised us in His word. Then we will have hope also.

Exercise Faith Until You Have Faith

"Faith grows by conflicts with doubts; virtue gathers strength by resistance to temptation." Mind, Character and Personality, book 2 p.673

"If you want faith, talk faith; talk hopefully, cheerfully." Testimonies, vol. I, p. 699

The more we express our faith, despite our feelings, is the more it grows. Unbelief, similarly, grows as it is expressed. Therefore, even though we may have had unbelief before, faith is still within our power to exercise today.

The best way to develop and increase faith is to have faith, to talk and act as though God's words are the truth. "I believed, therefore have I spoken" (2 Corinthians 4:13). This is because our thoughts are affected by what we say, thus the more we talk and express faith, the more the feelings of doubt lose their strength.

"It is a law of nature that our thoughts and feelings are encouraged and strengthened as we give them utterance. While words express thoughts, it is also true that thoughts follow words. If we would give more expression to our faith, rejoice more in the blessings that we know we have,--the great mercy and love of God,--we should have more faith and greater joy." The Ministry of Healing, p.251

Prayer

Trust between earthly friends grows the more they learn to confide in each other. Even so, the more one opens up the heart to God as to a friend, the more one grows in trust towards Him and His word.

> *"In order for a man's faith to be strong, he must be much with God in secret prayer." Testimonies, vol. 4, p.236*

The reason many are still in unbelief is due to not being personal with God through spending time with Him in secret prayer. It is not easy to trust a God with whom you are not intimate. Jesus made Himself fully vulnerable to humanity on the cross, and we have the freedom to pour out our hearts to Him just the same.

In bringing our most personal burdens to God, even concerning any unbelief we may be going through, our faith will be strengthened.

A Case of Little Faith

In an occasion when Jesus' disciples got to witness Him walking on water, we get to see a case of "little faith;" which is very closely related to unbelief. Seeing Jesus on the water, we read the following about Peter:

> *"Peter answered [Jesus] and said, 'Lord, if it is You, command me to come to You on the water.' So He said, 'Come.' And when Peter had come down out of the boat, he walked on the water to go to Jesus. But when he saw that the wind was boisterous, he was afraid; and beginning to sink he cried out, saying, "Lord, save me!" Matthew 14:28-30 NKJV*

Peter had enough faith in Christ to ask Him to call him onto the water. But when Peter saw the circumstances changing, he started to lose confidence in the power of the word that had called him.

> *"And immediately Jesus stretched forth His hand, and caught him, and said unto him, O thou of little faith, wherefore didst thou doubt?" Matthew 14:31*

Little faith is confident enough in God's word to ask Him for things, as Peter did. But little faith is easily shaken by circumstances, even when God's word has already spoken. Such a faith does not stand firm when difficulties arise.

> *"Wherefore didst thou doubt?" said Christ to the sinking Peter. The same question may be addressed to us. Why do we dishonor God with our shameful unbelief? The Lord has pledged Himself to give us strength to enable us to stand."* The Review and Herald, June 9, 1896

Even though Jesus had said "come", Peter looked at the challenging circumstances more than at the power of God's word. In doing the same when we experience difficulty, we dishonour God. Looking at the assurances of His promises, we never have reason to distrust God.

> *"As we search the Scriptures, we find ground for confidence, provision for sufficiency. It is our privilege to say boldly, yet humbly, 'The Lord is my helper, therefore I shall not be moved from my steadfastness...' Let us pledge ourselves before God and the angels of heaven that we will not dishonor God by speaking words of discouragement or unbelief. If we talk faith, we shall have faith; we shall be confirmed in faith."* Ibid

In Summary

Faith is essential for an experience of abiding in Christ. It is needed at every step because we need to walk with Christ moment by moment. It is necessary for every part of one's life, whether small or great.

> *"Faith is needed in the smaller no less than in the greater affairs of life. In all our daily interests and occupations the sustaining strength of God becomes real to us through an abiding trust."* Education p.255

Having looked at all that we have covered concerning faith, we can thus summarise the overall principles of faith in these terms:

To Trust God, and Believe His word

Faith is a positive response to the words of a loving God. In confidence, we choose to take God at His word--whether it is a commandment or a promise. Thus may we live by *every* word that proceeds from the mouth of God; this is living by faith.

To Act & Speak as Though God's Word is Trustworthy

Faith, a confidence in the power of God's word, is expressed in words and actions. We may go along cheerfully knowing that when we have the promises, we have the blessings that they contains. In so doing, we have the actual substance of the thing hoped for.

> *"To abide in faith is to put aside feeling and selfish desires, to walk humbly with the Lord, to appropriate His promises, and apply them to all occasions, believing that God will work out His own plans and purposes in your heart and life." Faith I Live By p.122*

Trusting God Despite Circumstances & Emotions

Faith involves taking God's word, and the word only, as the assurance; not the apparent circumstances, not how we feel, not how things seem to be looking, but the word *only*. This is genuine faith.

> *"Although the fig tree shall not blossom, neither shall fruit be in the vines; the labour of the olive shall fail, and the fields shall yield no meat; the flock shall be cut off from the fold, and there shall be no herd in the stalls: Yet I will rejoice in the Lord, I will joy in the God of my salvation. The Lord God is my strength, and He will make my feet like hinds' feet, and He will make me to walk upon mine high places." Habakkuk 3:17-19*

Questions on Chapter 7

What is faith? (p.127, 158)

What does great faith look like? (p.138, 140)

How can I have faith? (p.127)

How do I exercise faith? (p.131, 132-136)

What is the relationship between faith and the Bible? (p.127, 128-131)

Can I trust the Bible as God's word? (p.128, 145-147)

How do I experience the power of God's word? (p.132)

What do I do if I do not have faith? (p.131, 142)

What if I feel like I do not have faith? (p.134, 155)

How do I strengthen and grow my faith? (p.142)

What assurances has God given for me to trust Him in faith? (p.144)

What is presumption? (p.148)

What does presumption look like? (p.151)

What is unbelief (p.153)

How can I overcome unbelief? (p.155)

What does little faith look like? (p.157)

What are the overall principles of Biblical faith? (p,158)

8

Triumph over Temptation

The Reality of Temptation

Understanding Temptation

The Factors at Play

Meeting Temptation

The Weapons of Our Warfare

Practical Counsel for Resisting Temptation

The Temptation of Trials

God's Promises to the Tempted

The Reality of Temptation

In the experience of ancient Israel's exodus from Egypt, God brought His people out of their bondage with signs and wonders that testified of His power to save. The apostle Paul recounts their experience to the church at Corinth. The Israelites experienced God's power when He parted the Red sea--they ate a daily supply of manna and even drank water as it was supplied from a rock. These experiences were to point them to Jesus, their true deliverer (1 Corinthians 10:1-4).

While this was the case, it is unfortunate that a majority of those who experienced the deliverance from Egypt did not make it to the Promised Land of Canaan. Because of their rebellion, most of those who were saved from Egyptian slavery died in the desert.

"With most of them God was not well pleased, for their bodies were scattered in the wilderness." 1 Corinthians 10:5

Paul relates the wilderness experience to teach us an important point; that abiding in Christ does not do away with the responsibility to remain faithful and neither does it remove the possibility of falling. Israel's wilderness experience was a warning "to the intent that we should not lust after evil things as they also lusted." (1 Corinthians 10:5).

"Therefore let him who thinks he stands take heed lest he fall." 1 Corinthians 10:12 NKJV

To those who think themselves to be standing firm, spiritually, the encounter of the Israelites in the desert is presented as a message of caution.

Throughout the Bible, appeals are made for the Christian to "endure unto the end" as an essential requirement for being finally saved at the close of earth's history (Matthew 24:13). Our experience of abiding in Christ is meant to reach its highpoint when we "hold the beginning of our confidence steadfast to the end" (Hebrews 3:14). Paul thus adds the caution for the reader to "take heed lest he falls" in order to stress the principle of continuous faithfulness.

The Israelites were delivered from Egyptian bondage before traveling the wilderness of Sinai. Even though God had saved them then, however, they were eventually led astray. Paul outlines the causes of them falling away in order for us to avoid the same. In recounting this experience to the church at Corinth, a crucial point is made to the person who may regard themselves to be "standing":

> *"No temptation has overtaken you except such as is common to man; but God is faithful, who will not allow you to be tempted beyond what you are able, but with the temptation will also make the way of escape, that you may be able to bear it." 1 Corinthians 10:13 NKJV*

Temptation, being "common to man," is a reality faced by every individual. None are beyond its reach. This counsel to the Corinthian church brings about the importance of understanding temptation, especially for those seeking to abide in Christ.

In understanding temptation, perhaps the most important consideration is the fact that God has made a "way of escape" to enable us to triumph over it. It is very necessary to remember Jesus' words to His disciples, that "without me, you can do nothing." The way of escape comes from God Himself and "God is faithful." Understanding temptation, and how we may experience God's way of escape, is the subject of our consideration; thus, "let him that thinks he stands take heed lest he falls"

Understanding Temptation

From James' letter to the early Christian church, we learn some important points that help us understand temptation and how it can be overcome. He writes:

> *"Each one is tempted when he is drawn away by his own desires and enticed. Then, when desire has conceived, it gives birth to sin; and sin, when it is full-grown, brings forth death." James 1:14-15 NKJV*

Here is outlined what it means to be tempted. When one is drawn away and enticed by their desires, that person is experiencing temptation. Temptation happens when our natural desires, (also called "lusts" in some Bible versions) give out an invitation for us to do something. The idea of being "drawn away" may be imagined as though these desires are pulling one in a certain direction. In the original language of the letter, the word for being "drawn away" is also used to represent a fisher, or hunter, attracting his prey with bait. In the same way, humanity is pulled by the internal desires to follow a direction that eventually leads to death.

As will be seen, these desires may take on various forms, but the point to be noted is that temptation happens when the desires from within give out an invitation and draw one away to follow a particular course of action.

Forces Within, Forces Without

While we are generally faced with the reality of being "drawn away and enticed" by our natural inward desires, we also face a force outside of us that works to tempt us to follow forbidden paths. This was seen in the life of Jesus in His humanity as our example here on earth.

When He began His public ministry, Jesus prepared Himself for His mission by entering into a 40-day season of fasting and prayer. After His baptism He went into a wilderness, spending the time in isolation and devotion with His heavenly Father.

> *"Then Jesus was led up by the Spirit into the wilderness to be tempted by the devil. And when He had fasted forty days and forty nights, afterward He was hungry. Now when the tempter came to Him, he said, 'If you are the Son of God, command that these stones become bread.'" Matthew 4:1-3 NKJV*

While Jesus had been fasting, Satan came to Him to tempt Him. Jesus had not eaten for close to six weeks and at the point of His greatest hunger, Satan enticed Jesus by appealing to His appetite.

What must be noted in the encounter between Jesus and the devil is the fact that Satan brought the temptation to Jesus. That is to say, the devil was the one who initiated the temptation. This is why Matthew rightly refers to the devil as "the tempter." This is one of the roles Satan plays in the conflict between good and evil.

Jesus was "in all points tempted like as we are, yet without sin" (Hebrews 4:15). In His humanity, Jesus experienced temptation in the exact same way that we do. Thus, as with Jesus' experience, Satan also works to draw us away into a path that leads to sin and death.

Much can be learned from Jesus' temptation, and how he gained the victory. For now we note the point that the temptation, the invitation to sin, came from Satan and not from God.

"Temptation is enticement to sin, and this does not proceed from God, but from Satan and from the evil of our own hearts. 'God cannot be tempted with evil, and He Himself tempteth no man.' James 1:13, R.V." Thoughts from the Mount of Blessings p.116

We learn, therefore, that we are tempted from two main sources. The inward desires are the forces within us that draw us away, while Satan is also an external force, inviting us to sin. As the tempter, Satan works tirelessly to lead humanity to go against God's will.

These two forces (Satan and our evil desires) work hand-in-hand in the sense that Satan tempts us by appealing to our inward, human desires. From outside of us, Satan takes advantage of the fact that we are drawn away by our desires. It is through these desires that Satan makes attempts to lead humanity to sin.

The Factors at Play

It is helpful to understand what factors are at play when it comes to understanding why we get tempted. The question may be asked; "why do our desires naturally draw us away from the will of God? Why is it that, if God created us, we have these seemingly uncontrollable desires?" The answer to these is found in understanding the condition of humanity before and after Adam and Eve disobeyed God in the Garden of Eden.

When God created the earth, He made humanity just right; "God saw everything that He had made," including humanity, "and behold it was very good." (Genesis 1:31). Adam and Eve were made without any defects.

"God created man in His own image; in the image of God He created him; male and female He created them." Genesis 1:27 NKJV

God created human beings with all the qualities necessary to reveal His image. Humanity was created with physical, mental and spiritual powers, which were designed to work together in revealing God's character. In their perfect humanity, Adam and Eve's thoughts and feelings were in harmony with God's will and, before the fall, all these powers worked well together.

> *"Man was originally endowed with noble powers and a well-balanced mind. He was perfect in his being, and in harmony with God. His thoughts were pure, his aims holy." Steps to Christ p.17*

The harmony between the mind of God and of mankind was seen in the assignment God had given to Adam in naming all of the animals. "Whatever Adam called each living creature that was its name" (Genesis 2:19). Adam's mind was in total agreement with the mind of God.

Adam was created with a perfect and well-functioning body, also referred to as his flesh (Genesis 2:21). Adam and Eve's bodies, although different, were complementary to each other and designed by God with all their senses functioning perfectly. Thier physical nature was among the things that God declared to be "very good."

To Adam was also given the ability to appreciate "every tree… that is pleasant to the sight and good for food." (Genesis 2:9) Thisability included the sense of sight, God-given taste-buds and a healthy appetite. Adam's perfect humanity included his emotions and the ability to show his passion and affection toward his wife, Eve. This affection was expressed when he said of Eve, "This is now bone of my bones, and flesh of my flesh." (Genesis 2:23)

Moreover, God blessed Adam with a powerful mind. "Adam gave names to *all* cattle, to the birds of the air, and to *every* beast of the field." (Genesis 2:20 Emphasis added). His mind also had the ability to think through complex scenarios and arrive at a right conclusion. This is what we would call judgement, or the ability to reason.

All these elements were a part of human nature since creation: the ability to reason, the appetites & passions, as well as the flesh. They all had their specific purpose and functions in the nature of humanity.

"Our natural inclinations and appetites... were divinely appointed, and when given to man, were pure and holy. It was God's design that reason should rule the appetites, and that they should minister to our happiness. And when they are regulated and controlled by a sanctified reason, they are holiness unto the Lord." Child Guidance p.378

God's plan for how these different aspects of our nature would work included the fact that the reasoning powers of the mind were meant to have control over the appetites, the passions and the flesh. This is crucial to note. As a part of God's plan, the mind was meant to be the "higher power" in humanity, over the "lower powers" of the desires, appetites and emotions etc.

The Power of Choice

The greatest of the "powers" that God gave to Adam and Eve, the one that distinguished them from all the animals, was their power of choice. The ability to choose one's own actions may otherwise be referred to as the *will*, and this was built into humanity.

"[The will] is the governing power in the nature of man, the power of decision, or of choice. Everything depends on the right action of the will. The power of choice God has given to men; it is theirs to exercise." Steps to Christ p.47

God gave humanity the opportunity to exercise the will, the power of choice, by giving the first pair an instruction relating to the tree of the knowledge of good and evil.

"The Lord God planted a garden eastward in Eden, and there He put the man whom He had formed. And out of the ground the Lord God made every tree grow that is pleasant to the sight and good for food. The tree of life was also in the midst of the garden, and the tree of the knowledge of good and evil... Then the Lord God took the man and put him in the Garden of Eden to tend and keep it. And the Lord God commanded the man, saying, "Of every tree of the garden you may freely eat; but of the tree of the knowledge of good and evil you shall not eat, for in the day that you eat of it you shall surely die." Genesis 2:8-9, 15-17 NKJV

Placing the tree of the knowledge of good and evil in the Garden of Eden was not a random act on God's part. The pair was given the choice to either obey or disobey God. The trees of the garden, the tree of life and the tree of the knowledge of good and evil, were the signs of humanity's choice.

When Adam and Eve sinned, their transgression was not merely in consuming the fruit. Their sin was in the choice they made to go against the revealed will of God.

> *"In Eden, God said to Adam concerning the tree of knowledge, "In the day that thou eatest thereof thou shalt surely die." (Genesis 2:17) "And the serpent said unto the woman, ye shall not surely die..." Adam listened to the voice of Satan speaking through his wife; he believed another voice than that which spoke the law in Eden." Be Like Jesus p.133*

In the two options placed before Adam and Eve, the results of disobedience had been clearly presented. In choosing to disobey, they thus chose the consequences that came with the decision.

How Humanity Broke at the Fall

Having considered the various factors that make up our human nature, what we will notice is the fact that Adam and Eve's choice to go contrary to the will of God had drastic consequences on their human nature. This human nature is what we, as their descendents, have inherited.

> *"Through disobedience, [Adam's] powers were perverted, and selfishness took the place of love. His nature became so weakened through transgression that it was impossible for him, in his own strength, to resist the power of evil." Steps to Christ p.17*

After Adam disobeyed, the powers that God had given him lost their goodness and perfection. Humanity "broke", so to say, and the powers that God had given--the reason, the appetites and, the flesh--no longer functioned as God had initially intended.

This change in human nature is immediately seen in Adam's relation to God and Eve after his fall. Before sin, Adam could freely have a face-to-face conversation with God (Genesis 2:15-17). This changed when he disobeyed. After the fall, we are told that:

> When "they heard the sound of the Lord God walking in the garden in the cool of the day... Adam and his wife hid themselves from the presence of the Lord God among the trees of the garden." Genesis 3:8 NKJV

As a result of choosing to disobey God and His instruction, Adam's nature became wicked. "The wicked flee when no one pursues" (Proverbs 28:1). In fleeing from God and attempting to hide from His presence, Adam gave evidence of the wickedness that now found its place in him. By their disobedience, Adam and Eve became what is also referred to as being "carnal, sold under sin" (Romans 7:14). This condition is described thus:

> "The carnal mind is enmity against God: for it is not subject to the law of God, neither indeed can be." Romans 8:7

> "When man transgressed the divine law, his nature became evil, and he was in harmony, and not at variance, with Satan." The Great Controversy p.505

When humanity broke, the condition that resulted affected how their powers worked. Adam and Eve now had a nature that was in opposition to God and His law. With that being the case, their God given appetites and lusts (or desires) became corrupted to follow after things which were opposed to God's will. These desires became selfish and corrupt.

The apostle Peter thus describes the desires of humanity as "fleshly lusts, which war against the soul" (1 Peter 2:11). The desires which God had given to be a blessing to humankind now became a curse. The apostle James, also, refers to these as "the evil desires at war within you" (James 4:1).

Note here the idea of an internal warfare that goes on. In Peter's description, the selfish desires of the flesh are represented as the enemy. This is because the "lusts of the flesh" want to do what the mind knows to be unlawful. Thus, these powers (the mind and the lusts of the flesh) may often be in conflict.

This conflict is not only limited to being between the desires of the flesh and one's own mind, but the conflict also extends to include choosing between the selfish desires and the will of God. Hence it can be said that:

"The sinful nature wants to do evil, which is just the opposite of what the Spirit wants. And the Spirit gives us desires that are the opposite of what the sinful nature desires. These two forces are constantly fighting each other, so you are not free to carry out your good intentions." Galatians 5:17 NLT

The Mind Now Subject to the Desires

The unfortunate effects of the fall include the fact that in the war that goes on within humanity, the mind lost its power to rule over the desires of the flesh. Human nature became damaged, resulting in the mind (the reason and the will) being weaker than the lower powers of appetite and passion (the desires of the flesh).

In his letter to the Romans, Paul describes this condition in the life of what he terms a "wretched man" who needs to be "delivered from this body of death" (Romans 7:23). Placing himself in such a person's shoes, Paul writes:

"For I know that in me (that is, in my flesh) nothing good dwells; for to will is present with me, but how to perform what is good I do not find. For the good that I will to do, I do not do; but the evil I will not to do, that I practice." Romans 7:18-19 NKJV

Notice, again, the factors at play in this scenario: the flesh (with its appetites and desires) as well as the mind. While an individual wants, or "wills", to do what is good, he finds himself still doing what he knows to be wrong. The will and the flesh are in a battle where the enemy is the flesh in which "nothing good dwells". Paul continues:

"I delight in the law of God according to the inward man. But I see another law in my members, warring against the law of my mind, and bringing me into captivity to the law of sin which is in my members." Verse 22

The man Paul describes illustrates the condition of fallen humanity.

The internal war is seen in the "law" that is within the body being in conflict with the "law" of the mind. In this battle, the mind is held captive to the "law" that is within the body. The person described is convicted of his need to do right; he "delights in the law of God according to the inward man." Though this is the case, his mind is "brought into captivity" to do what his desires tell him to do, despite his good intentions.

The reality of this experience is seen in an example of one trying to kick the smoking habit. She is well aware of the dangers that the habit causes. Year after year she makes a resolution to stop smoking, she "wills to do good"; but as the story goes, she finds herself overpowered by the craving which strengthens every time it is indulged. Despite the mind saying no, the power of the corrupted appetite brings her into captivity. This is the internal conflict in all human beings .

What does all of this have to do with temptation? Consider this thought:

> "Sin has degraded the faculties of the soul. Temptations from without find an answering chord within the heart, and the feet turn imperceptibly toward evil." The Ministry of Healing p.451

Having understood temptation as an invitation that centres on the desires, we note that the reason these desires do draw us away so strongly is because of our broken condition. A key feature of this brokenness is the fact that the mind is now subject to the lusts of the flesh, so that "you are not free to carry out your good intentions."

Sin Results in Submitting to the Desires

After defining what temptation is, James continues to explain the results of giving in to the invitations given by the desires:

> "Each one is tempted when he is drawn away by his own desires and enticed. Then, when desire has conceived, it gives birth to sin; and sin, when it is full-grown, brings forth death." James 1:13 NKJV

When one consents to the invitation of their selfish desires, it results in disobeying God. "When the desire has conceived" it gives birth to sin, "the transgression of the law" (1 John 3:4). This is also referred to as "fulfiling the lusts of the flesh" (Galatians 5:16)

Thus, while temptation is the invitation to sin, being "drawn" and "enticed" by the inward desires is not, in and of itself, a sin. The "lusts of the flesh" give out an invitation to follow a forbidden path. When a person consents to follow that path, then they transgress the law and commit sin. Hence it can be said that:

> *"Temptation is not sin; the sin lies in yielding. To the soul who trusts in Jesus, temptation means victory and greater strength."* Christ Triumphant p.218

The choice made to follow the lusts of the flesh may not always get the opportunity to manifest itself outwardly. This is why it is possible for one to commit sin in their heart. The choice made to comply and agree to the selfish desire begins within the mind. This is why Jesus spoke of sins proceeding from within:

> *"From within, out of the heart[s] of men, proceed evil thoughts, adulteries, fornications, murders."* Mark 7:21 NKJV

Jesus also illustrates this principle with the example of a man who, in his heart, entertains and submits to impure thoughts:

> *"You have heard that it was said, 'You shall not commit adultery.' But I say to you that everyone who looks at a woman with lustful intent has already committed adultery with her in his heart."* Matthew 5:27-28 ESV

The words "lustful intent" here express the idea of the choice made to entertain the sinful imaginings. Here Jesus shows the depth of His law as relating to the heart and not simply the external expressions of disobedience. In every instance, sin is conceived in the choice made to accept the invitation to go contrary to God's will.

Our Choice to Make
In the daily contest between the flesh and the Spirit, our God-given power of choice still remains intact. While temptations give out

an invitation to sin, all are left with the choice of whether or not they will yield and consent to that invitation. Thus, every temptation comes with a choice that must be made. We are left to choose to either fulfil the lusts of the flesh or to choose the will of God.

"No man can be forced to transgress. His own consent must be first gained; the soul must purpose the sinful act, before passion can dominate over reason, or iniquity triumph over conscience. Temptation, however strong, is never an excuse for sin." Messages to Young People *p.67*

Since all are faced with a choice when they are tempted, none can truly say that they were *made* to sin. While, at times, external pressure may be put on an individual to compel them to transgress, the choice to do so always lies with the individual. This is why being tempted is not an excuse for disobedience. The choice always remains as to whether one will choose the right or not.

Many, however, while still choosing to do right, still find themselves doing wrong. Like the man described by Paul, who is held captive to his desires, they cannot carry out their good intentions. Note the statement below:

"The tempted one needs to understand the true force of the will. This is the governing power in the nature of man - the power of decision, of choice. Everything depends on the right action of the will." The Ministry of Healing *p. 176*

Everything depends on the *right* action of the will! That is to say, there is a wrong way to exercise the will. Thus, overcoming temptation is not merely the result of "will power." Simply having good intentions, or making a choice to do what is right, is not what gives the victory; but it is in making the choice *rightly*!

For some time in my experience, I did not understand what the right action of the will was, and this came with its experience of defeats. Many learn the hard way that their "promises and resolutions are like ropes of sand," and that to obtain victory over temptation takes more than only making a resolution to live right.

How to rightly exercise the will in the battle with temptation will be seen as we proceed towards the subject of *Meeting Temptation*. In chapter 1 (*Consecration*) we discussed the role of exercising the will in order to allow Christ in the heart. The principle there described will be found to be the same for meeting temptation as well.

How Satan Takes Advantage

It may be necessary to note here just how Satan takes advantage of our desires, "the lusts of the flesh", in order to trap us in his deceptions. As noted before, some of the desires we have were placed there by God himself. To get humanity to fall, however, Satan takes advantage by suggesting that we can best fulfil these desires by disobeying God. He did this when he tempted Eve in the Garden of Eden.

God had placed in Eve a natural desire for wisdom and personal advancement. During her conversation with Satan, Eve was led to believe that the forbidden fruit was "good for food and… desirable to make one wise." After this change in her attitude towards the tree, she "took of its fruit and ate." (Genesis 3:6) Satan deceived Eve to believe that she had to cross the path of disobedience in order to fulfil her desire. This is Satan's policy today.

The difference between our experience and Eve's is that our desires have since been corrupted to lust after evil things; for example:

> *"The desire to accumulate wealth is an original affection of our nature, implanted there by our heavenly Father for noble ends."*
> Counsels on Stewardship p.148

While God had place in us a desire to accumulate wealth, His intention was for it to be for noble ends. This desire has since been perverted for selfish ends. Such is the case with most of the desires which God had initially given to humanity at the creation.

The desire for love has been perverted with sexual immorality, the desire for beauty has been corrupted with vanity & proud adornment, the desire for pleasure has been perverted with gluttony & greed, and so on.

Since humanity broke at the fall, Satan takes advantage of the God-given (yet damaged) desires to lead us into temptation.

"Satan finds in human hearts some point where he can gain a foot-hold; some sinful desire is cherished, by means of which his temptations assert their power." The Great Controversy p.623

The Way of Escape is Provided

Jesus' words "without me you can do nothing" cover every single aspect of the Christian life. This includes resisting temptation. Thus, our hope of overcoming temptation rests on our intimate bond with Him. This point should never be forgotten.

"Unless we become vitally connected with God, we can never resist the unhallowed effects of self-love, self-indulgence, and temptation to sin… Without a personal acquaintance with Christ, and a continual communion, we are at the mercy of the enemy, and shall do his bidding in the end." The Desire of Ages p.324

In view of this, Paul gives the assurance that God has provided and laid out a way of escape for all who are tempted. God has made it possible for us to be freed from the "captivity" of the lusts and appetites. As stated earlier,

"No temptation has overtaken you except such as is common to man; but God is faithful, who will not allow you to be tempted beyond what you are able, but with the temptation will also make the way of escape, that you may be able to bear it." 1 Corinthians 10:13 NKJV

In His way of escape, God allows no one to be tempted beyond what they may endure through His strength. This means that no matter how strong your personal weaknesses may be, there is a sure way of escape from these weaknesses. If we are to be kept from falling into temptation, it is crucial to understand and to follow God's way.

Through His power

As previously seen, after Adam and Eve sinned, humanity has been completely unable to do right in our own strength. Nevertheless, God "knows our frame; He remembers that we are dust" (Psalm103:14). This is why, in His was of escape, God has provided His power to meet the helplessness and weakness of every individual. And this power is in no short supply!

"Abundant grace has been provided that the believing soul may be kept free from sin; for all heaven, with its limitless resources, has been placed at our command. We are to draw from the well of salvation." God's Amazing Grace p.181

As we consider the practical steps for dealing with temptation, it is important to be mindful of the power that God will gladly make available to the tempted. In keeping in mind Christ's limitless power we may face temptation with our confidence placed on Him. This attitude has an effect on one's experience.

"To go forward without stumbling, we must have the assurance that a hand all-powerful will hold us up, and an infinite pity be exercised toward us if we fall." Sons and Daughters of God p.145

Meeting Temptation

Ever since my earliest years of school, I was often among the smallest of my friends. In primary school I was an easy target for being teased and harassed, which made me very insecure. Before going to high school, I was anxious about how I would survive there. Obviously everyone would be older and larger than me and, additionally, the high school I would be attending was rumoured to be full of gangs and bullies (which I later found to be an exaggeration).

The year I was to begin high school, I had a neighbour whose children had already been attending the school a few years before me. My parents, together with the neighbours, thought it a good idea to have us all travel together as their children. This was an answer to my prayers. My neighbour's son was a senior in the high school. When we arrived at school, I would walk with him and all my fears of being bullied were removed. I considered him to be my "protection", and this gave me a sense of boldness when walking the school grounds.

The confidence I had when walking with my neighbour, trusting somewhat in his ability to take care of me, is a small illustration of the confidence we may have when we are conscious of the fact that we are walking with God. In the battles with temptation, we are never left alone. God promises:

"Fear not, for I am with you; be not dismayed, for I am your God. I will strengthen you, yes, I will help you, I will uphold you with My righteous right hand." Isaiah 41:10 NKJV

Christianity is a daily experience of walking with God. Communion with Christ means that, while we may still get tempted, God Himself is with us. The battle may be faced and overcome in His strength.

"We fail many times because we do not realise that Christ is with us by His Spirit as truly as when, in the days of His humiliation, He moved visibly upon the earth." Lift Him Up p.157

"The closer we are to God, the safer we are, for Satan hates and fears the presence of God." Our High Calling p.96

God's Role: He Will Alert

Those who have given themselves to abide in Christ have the privilege of Christ's Spirit being there to alert them whenever they are tempted. When one is tempted, and a battle goes on between the flesh and the Spirit, God first steps in to warn us of our danger. He alerts us to the fact that we are tempted so that we may choose His way.

"When you are tempted, He will show you a way out so that you can endure." 1 Corinthians 10:13 NLT

"Your ears shall hear a word behind you, saying, "This is the way, walk in it," whenever you turn to the right hand or whenever you turn to the left." Isaiah 30:21 NKJV

But how does God alert us? Whenever an individual is being "enticed" by their desires, the Holy Spirit speaks to us through the voice of conscience. The conscience is the "still small voice" that brings us to the sense of what is right and wrong. This is how the Holy Spirit makes appeals to every tempted child of God.

"Conscience is the voice of God, heard amid the conflict of human

passions; when it is resisted, the Spirit of God is grieved." Faith I Live By p.58

Usually, whenever one is tempted, the struggle they face is to choose between the strong invitations of the passions, as opposed to doing what is right. In this conflict, the "conscience" is stirred up and warns the tempted one of the danger. This warning comes from God. This is why it is risky to go against ones conscience, because doing so grieves the Holy Spirit. Let nothing cause you to violate your conscience:

"Allow no taunts, no threats, no sneering remarks, to induce you to violate your conscience in the least particular, and thus open a door whereby Satan can come in and control the mind." Sons and Daughters of God p.211

"Do not grieve the Holy Spirit of God, by whom you were sealed for the day of redemption." Ephesians 4:30 NKJV

While God speaks to us through the voice of conscience, He never compels anyone to obey. God respects our power of choice. Whenever He alerts us to our danger in temptation it is also to reveal our duty to us and get us to choose it--to follow His way of escape. We are to respond to God's voice when it speaks to us.

"The Holy Spirit will not compel men to take a certain course of action. We are free moral agents; and when sufficient evidence has been given us as to our duty, it is left with us to decide our course." Fundamentals of Christian Education p.124

"We want to become so sensitive to holy influences that the lightest whisper of Jesus will move our souls." That I May Know Him p.361

When Tempted, Submit

In his epistle, James gives helpful guidance on what *our* part is when facing temptation. The apostle expands on what we noted earlier as "the right action off the will". His counsel to the church is as follows:

"Do you think that the scripture said in vain, 'the spirit that dwells in us lusts to envy?' But He gives more grace." James 4:5-6a AKJV

James makes mention to what he calls "the spirit that dwells in us." This is "the spirit of man which is in him," (1 Corinthians 2:11) and not the Spirit of God. The point James makes about the spirit of man is that it "lusts to envy." Naturally, we are inwardly "drawn away of our own lusts, and enticed" to envy and to various other unholy desires.

The crucial point to be noted, however, is that while "the spirit that dwells in us lusts," God gives more grace! This means that the grace that is needed to overcome the inward lusts and desires is greater than those lusts themselves. The remedy is greater that the problem!

God's grace is His enabling power. Paul learnt that God gives "more grace" when, in his season of trial, God spoke to Paul, saying: "My grace is sufficient for you, for *My strength* is made perfect in weakness." (2 Corinthians 12:9, emphasis added)

"But how do I access this grace?" one may ask. James continues:

"'God resists the proud, but gives grace to the humble.' Submit yourselves therefore to God. Resist the devil, and he will flee from you." James 4:6-7 NKJV

While God's grace is available to everyone; not all get to experience its power. Those who do experience God's enabling power are referred to as "the humble". This outlines the condition for receiving power from God to face temptation and overcome the "spirit that lusts to envy."

The grace which enables us to deny "worldly lusts" (Titus 2:11) comes to those who, when faced with temptation, humble themselves to God. The humble are those who submit to God, surrendering themselves entirely over to His will. Jesus, while praying in the garden of Gethsemane, submitted to His Father when He prayed "not My will but Yours be done." (Luke 23:42). This is how He "humbled Himself and became obedient to the point of death" (Philippians 2:8).

Thus, James urges us to "submit yourselves therefore to God" when we are tempted. This is how to gain the victory.

"Jesus gained the victory through submission and faith in God, and by the apostle He says to us, 'Submit yourselves therefore to God. Resist the devil, and he will flee from you. Draw nigh to God, and He will draw nigh to you.' We cannot save ourselves from the tempter's power; he has conquered humanity, and when we try to stand in our own strength, we shall become a prey to his devices; but 'the name of the Lord is a strong tower: the righteous runneth into it, and is safe.' Satan trembles and flees before the weakest soul who finds refuge in that mighty name." The Desire of Ages p.131

Whenever temptation comes and the decision must be made between the lusts of the flesh or the will of God, at that point we must submit to God. This is how we receive the grace and power from God to keep us from falling.

"As soon as we incline our will to harmonize with God's will, the grace of Christ stands ready to co-operate with the human agent." In Heavenly Places p.27

We are to co-operate with God when facing the battle with temptation. When we are tempted, God will alert us to our danger by His Spirit and offer us power to resist the tempter. When He does so, we are to choose His way of escape--we are to submit to following His will. Thus, all the power of God comes to our assistance when we sincerely pray the prayer, "not my will but Yours be done." Another author expresses it thus:

"When we are tempted the Holy Spirit will try to alert us, and if we quickly submit to God, He will then have the right to control our spirit and give us the victory." Davis, M. What shall I do to Inherit Eternal Life, [sp]

The Right Action of the Will
To further illustrate the point os submitting to the will of God, consider the case of two people with a smoking addiction. One of these is a growing Christian and the other is not. Over time, these two individuals learn of the hazardous effects of smoking on the lungs and on their health in general. Upon learning this, they both make

the resolution to quit smoking. The non-Christian decides to quit because he wants to preserve his health; he wants to cut down on the expense of smoking and, above all, wants to live longer. The Christian on the other hand, while she also wants to live longer, is moved by a different motive:

"Your body is the temple of the Holy Spirit who is in you, whom you have from God, and you are not your own? For you were bought at a price; therefore glorify God in your body and in your spirit, which are God's." 1 Corinthians 6:19-20 NKJV

The Christian's desire to quit smoking, in contrast to that of her friend's, is driven by a motive much higher than merely preserving her own life. While they both make a good decision to cut out the habit, the Christian is moved by an ambition to follow and co-operate with the will of God. This is what makes the difference.

Because the Christian's decision is based on the intention to do God's will and to please Him, she receives power from God. Her friend, on the other hand, is left with having to carry out the resolution in his own strength.

"As the will of man co-operates with the will of God, it becomes omnipotent. Whatever is to be done at His command may be accomplished in His strength. All His biddings are enabling's." Christ's Object Lessons p.333

Thus we learn that it is not only in making a decision to do good that gives the power to obey, but power comes to those who make the choice to do good because it is *God's will*. This is the right action of the will! I emphasise this point because of how easy it is to miss. God invests His power on behalf of those who choose to do His will, because it is His will!

Whenever one is tempted, the decision must be made to choose God's way of escape and to submit completely to Him. In the conflict with temptation and sinful desires, when the choice is made to "co-operate with the will of God" because it is His will, omnipotent power is supplied to us to enable us to escape.

Resist the Devil

After counselling the church to submit to God, so as to receive power from Him, James highlights the importance of resisting the temptation. When we are tempted, the power that God gives is for the purpose of resisting the devil and his invitations to sin.

During a discussion on this very subject, a lady once asked a very practical question on facing temptation. "Let's say I'm tempted," she stated, "and I submit to God and pray the prayer, 'Not my will by Yours be done',... then what?" The answer is simple; "Resist the devil."

This point is well illustrated in the experience of Joseph in Egypt. Joseph, a servant of God, was a slave in the house of Potiphar (a leader of Egypt's security forces). When Joseph advanced in his work and became Potiphar's personal assistant, Mrs Potiphar "cast longing eyes on Joseph, and she said [to him], 'Lie with me.'" (Genesis 39:7)

Joseph, who lived to honour God, turned down Potiphar's wife's invitation for him to sleep with her. In his response to her invitation, he insists; "How can I do this great wickedness, and sin against God?" (Genesis 39:9). The primary reason behind Joseph's decision was his unwillingness to disobey God. He was committed to doing what he knew to be God's will: "You shall not commit adultery." (Exodus 20:14)

Mrs Potiphar, however, did not back down easily: "She kept putting pressure on Joseph day after day". While this was the case "He refused to sleep with her, and he kept out of her way as much as possible." (Genesis 39:10 NLT).

Notice Joseph's very intentional efforts in responding to the temptation. He did not only refuse to give in to the temptation. After choosing to do the will of God, he went a step further to keep away from her as far as possible. Joseph "resisted the devil" and the temptation that came with being around Potiphar's wife.

Joseph's steps to purposefully avoid the temptation were also seen when Potiphar's wife came to Joseph in a more forceful manner. When no-one was in the house and the two of them were left alone,

"She caught him by his garment, saying, "Lie with me." But he left his garment in her hand, and fled and ran outside." Genesis 39:12 NKJV

When this happened, Joseph went further than merely saying no. He did not just stand there, in the face of temptation, but Joseph ran away! This is our duty as well.

The reason why many are overcome in times of temptation, even after supposedly submitting to the will of God, is primarily because they still remain in the presence of the temptation. After submitting to the will of God when tempted, it is usally also necessary to "run away" from the temptation as did Joseph.

"Run from anything that stimulates youthful lusts." 2 Timothy 2:22 NLT

To the question regarding what to do after submitting to God, this is the point: the moment God alerts us to a temptation, and one makes the conscious decision to co-operate with His will, that very moment is the best time to remove oneself from the temptation as soon as possible. We are never to negotiate with temptation or with the tempter.

Depending in the temptation, avoiding sin may not mean running away in the literal sense. "Resisting the devil" may, however, involve blocking the links to websites that are harmful to spiritual life, not going to places where one is easily influenced to do wrong, and so on. All this is to be done in the strength we receive when we make the choice to co-operate with the will of God.

Escape Quickly

A close friend of mine narrates a humorous, but very real, experience of how he gained the victory over an intemperate eating habit he once had with cake. Now, there is nothing inherently wrong with cake, but for my friend it was a weakness which he would overindulge. After being personally convicted of his unhealthy habit, he prayed to God to help him overcome.

One evening, while going to the fridge to get something to drink, it was to his surprise that his mother had brought home his favourite--cake. Although he was not hungry, and it may have been far from meal time, when he saw the cake, as he states, his "taste buds started doing things." He even forgot that he came to get the drink.

At this point, my friend was tempted. His appetite was "drawing him" to eat the cake, even though he was very convicted not to. With the fridge still open in front of him, my friend prayed for strength to overcome the invitation and the temptation. "Not my will but Yours" he prayed, knowing that he could not resist the temptation in his own strength.

To make a long story short, after he prayed this prayer, with the cake still in front of him, he eventually gave in and ate it. Even though he prayed the prayer for strength he was overcome by the temptation and went against his conscience.

But why was that the case? It makes sense as we continue.

After claiming forgiveness, and picking himself up, my friend later experienced a second encounter with the same temptation. On this occasion, my friend went to the fridge to look for something to drink and, again, there it was on the shelf--the cake that easily beset him. This time, unlike at first, he quickly shut the fridge door.

While his weakness was aroused again, my friend narrates how he rushed to his bedroom and began to pray. He knelt by his bedside in prayer for roughly an hour! He pleaded with God for the grace and strength needed to overcome his craving. There was a very real battle going on between the conscience and the fleshly desires. Through prayer and faith, my friend claimed the promise of strength to bear the temptation, and he received this.

"When temptations and trials rush in upon us, let us go to God and agonize with Him in prayer. He will not turn us away empty, but will give us grace and strength to overcome, and to break the power of the enemy." Early Writings p.46

After praying, he later called his niece and sent her to fetch him the drink that he had earlier tried to get for himself. He avoided being where his weakness would be at its most severe and this is how he gained the victory. I believe he has since gained the victory over the intemperate cake struggle.

As seemingly small as it may be, this experience illustrates the need of escaping quickly when faced with temptation. There is no safety in negotiating with the tempter. Thus, when enticed by the lusts of the flesh within, or by the tempter himself, there is no better time than the present to flee to the throne of grace "to obtain mercy, and find grace to help in time of need." Hebrews 4:15

> "It is not safe for us to linger to contemplate the advantages to be reaped through yielding to Satan's suggestions. Sin means dishonor and disaster to every soul that indulges in it; but it is blinding and deceiving in its nature, and it will entice us with flattering presentations. If we venture on Satan's ground we have no assurance of protection from his power. So far as in us lies, we should close every avenue by which the tempter may find access to us." Thoughts from the Mount of Blessing p.118

The reason my friend was able to overcome his temptation the second time was because the moment God alerted him, he submitted to God's will and resisted the devil. When he saw the cake, immediately he shut the fridge door, he immediately fled the scene of temptation and went to his room, and he immediately wrestled with God in prayer!

While temptations may vary for each person, and Satan adapts his attempts to each ones peculiar weaknesses, this principle is applicable for all temptations. We are at our safest when, should we meet with temptation, we flee and not negotiate with the enticement to sin.

> "Bear in mind that it is none but God that can hold an argument with Satan." S.D.A. Bible Commentary Vol. 5 p.1083

Surrender and Trust
When we choose God's way, and surrender fully to His will, it is always necessary to *trust* that He will fulfil what He has promised in availing His limitless power. Consecration, surrendering to the will of God, always goes together with trust. We can be confident that God's power to resist temptation is available to us at the exact

moment we make the decision to co-operate with His will.

"In the whole Satanic force there is not power to overcome one soul who in simple trust casts himself on Christ." Christ's Object Lessons p.157

Having confidence in God's power, and in His willingness to save us in the battle with temptation, has a significant effect on whether or not one experiences that power. While we may be weak in our own strength, God has assured us that "He gives power to the weak and strength to the powerless" (Isaiah 41:29 NLT). You can put your trust in Him, no matter how strong the temptation.

"Temptations to the indulgence of appetite possess a power which can be overcome only by the help that God can impart. But with every temptation we have the promise of God that there shall be a way of escape. Why, then, are so many overcome? It is because they do not put their trust in God. They do not avail themselves of the means provided for their safety. The excuses offered for the gratification of perverted appetite, are therefore of no weight with God." Counsels on Diet and Foods p.154

Confusing the Still Small Voice

Submitting to God immediately when tempted is crucial because this is also when we hear His voice most distinctly. Consider this:

"If the voice of Jesus is not heeded at once, it becomes confused in the mind with a multitude of other voices." S.D.A. Bible Commentary Vol.7 p.967

When God alerts us to our danger in the time of temptation, not submitting to Him immediately gives way for the tempter to confuse us. This is a part of how Satan persuaded Eve to disobey in Eden.

Before Satan came to Eve, it was settled in her mind that "of the fruit of the tree which is in the midst of the garden, God has said, 'You shall not eat it, nor shall you touch it, lest you die.'" (Genesis 3:2). After a very short discussion with the serpent, however, her attitude towards the tree of the knowledge of good and evil changed:

"The woman [now] saw that the tree was good for food, [and] that

it was pleasant to the eyes, and a tree desirable to make one wise, she took of its fruit and ate." Genesis 3:6 NKJV

Eve expressed her conviction when she said, "God has said 'You shall not eat of it;" but by lingering by the tree and allowing the serpent to have her attention, her ideas of what to do became confused. This is the result of not heeding the voice of Jesus at once. The conscience, which is clear when it first brings conviction, becomes difficult to discern when not followed immediately.

A personal experience I once had may be helpful in further illustrating this point.

One of the biggest struggles in my Christian journey, one in which God has since given the victory, was with overeating. After learning about God's aspirations for us to glorify Him, "whether we eat or drink", adopting a shift to a health conscious lifestyle and diet was not a great struggle for me. The greatest challenge, however, arose later on the point of intemperance and overeating. My appetite was a major obstacle here.

"Even health reformers can err in the quantity of food. They can eat immoderately of a healthy quality of food." Testimonies, vol.2 p.365

When, after a good meal, I knew that I had eaten enough, I would still have a craving to go for second servings (or even third). After I became convicted on this point, whenever I would want to overeat beyond what I knew I needed, my conscience would begin to alert me to the fact that I was being tempted. In not heeding the voice at once, however, it was easy to give way to a multitude of other voices; "But it's healthy food after all," "just once more," "it's not that big a deal," and so on.

Giving in to the appetite would not seem that problematic after silencing the voice of conscience. After indulging my appetite, however, the Holy Spirit would again bring conviction through the voice the conscience.

"The office of the Holy Spirit is distinctly specified in the words of Christ: "When He is come, He will reprove the world of sin, and

of righteousness, and of judgment." John 16:8. It is the Holy Spirit that convicts of sin." Acts of the Apostles p.52

It was not until I made a wholehearted surrender of this struggle to God that I gained the victory. When, in the face of temptation, I *immediately* submitted to God and resisted the devil, I received all the strength that was necessary to escape the temptation.

This is why we are to submit quickly and not silence the voice of God when it alerts us to our danger. We should be ready to submit to the will of God whenever He makes known His will to us--and this is how we may gain the victory. As stated earlier:

> *"We want to become so sensitive to holy influences that the lightest whisper of Jesus will move our souls." That I May Know Him p.361*

A Caution About Conscience and Impressions

It is crucial to note here that while God may warn us through the conscience, the conscience is not the ultimate revealer of His will. That is to say, our consciences are very limited and it is unsafe to place our entire dependence on them as our main guide as to what is right and wrong.

When the Bible speaks about the conscience, it speaks of both a "good conscience" (Acts 23:1) and an "evil conscience" (Hebrews 10:22). Our conscience, the sense of what is right and wrong, is heavily influenced by what we have been taught to be right or wrong. This influence includes upbringing, culture, social norms and religious morals. Our consciences, however, are not the ultimate guides as to our duty. Whether or not ones conscience is led by God is always to be confirmed by God's word above all.

> *"Take your conscience to the Word of God, and see if your life and character are in accordance with the standard of righteousness which God has there revealed. You can then determine whether or not you have an intelligent faith, and what manner of conscience is yours." Our High Calling p.143*

One of Satan's tricks is to lead some to disobey God because they have not yet felt "convicted." At times the statement is made, "I see what the Bible says concerning this and that point, but if God really wants me to do it, He will first convict me." This is a dangerous position to take.

On the other hand, Satan leads others to "teach man-made ideas as commands from God" (Matthew 15:9). Some enforce man-made rules on others as a standard to be obeyed because they are strongly convicted about them in their own consciences, but cannot adequately base them on the scriptures.

While both may be sincere in following their consciences, they deceive themselves in placing their conscience above God's word. These become easy prey to temptation.

> "It is not enough for a man to think himself safe in following the dictates of his conscience... The question to be settled is, 'Is the conscience in harmony with the Word of God?' If not, it cannot safely be followed, for it will deceive. The conscience must be enlightened by God. Time must be given to a study of the Scriptures and to prayer. Thus the mind will be stablished, strengthened, and settled." Our High Calling p.143

> "Satan takes advantage of an unenlightened conscience, and thereby leads men into all manner of delusions, because they have not made the Word of God their counselor. Many have invented a gospel of their own in the same manner as they have substituted a law of their own for God's law." Mind Character and Personality, book.1 p.323

When we speak about the Holy Spirit speaking to us through the conscience, we may discern His voice most clearly when our conscience is informed and tested by the scriptures. The Bible, as mentioned earlier, is the ultimate expression of God's will. Whether or not one is led by the Spirit of God must always be examined by the word of truth, these always work together.

> "When He, the Spirit of truth, has come, He will guide you into all truth; for He will not speak on His own authority, but whatever He hears He will speak; and He will tell you things to come." John 16:13 NKJV

The Weapons of our Warfare

In any war, the weaponry of an army can determine whether or not they gain victory. In our contest with "fleshly lusts which war against the soul," we are assured of weapons at our disposal which are powerful enough for us to come out victorious.

> *"(For the weapons of our warfare are not carnal, but mighty through God to the pulling down of strong holds;) Casting down imaginations, and every high thing that exalts itself against the knowledge of God, and bringing into captivity every thought to the obedience of Christ." 2 Corinthians 10:4-5 NKJV*

For every tempted soul, God has made a way of escape from "every high thing that exalts itself against the knowledge of God;" whether that is from one's own desires or from the tempter. In our warfare, the weapons on our side are mighty. God has provided weapons that will not easily be overcome. These are offered for us to meet every stronghold that may attempt to bind an individual.

We will take a brief look at the weapons which God has made ready at hand to bring every thought to the obedience of Christ.

The Word of God

When Jesus was tempted, His backup against Satan's enticements was always "it is written;" the word of God was His greatest defence. He had the experience described by the psalmist:

> *"Your word I have hidden in my heart, that I might not sin against You." Psalm 119:11 NKJV*

God's word is "living and powerful" (Hebrews 4:12), and the same word that kept Jesus from giving in to temptation is available to us as well.

> *"When assailed by temptation, look not to circumstances or to the weakness of self, but to the power of the word. All its strength is yours." The Desire of Ages p.123*

But how do we access the power of God's word? Well, we have noted that God avails His power to the tempted one who submits to His will. As the will of an individual thus co-operates with the will of God, they obtain the needed power. The Bible plays a crucial role here because God's will is most clearly revealed in it.

> *"Indeed you are called a Jew, and rest on the law, and make your boast in God, and know His will... being instructed out of the law." Romans 2:17-18 NKJV*

The Jews had the privilege of knowing what God's will was because they were instructed "out of the law;" which includes the writings of Moses and the Old Testament scriptures. This also includes the 10 commandments; as the Psalmist writes, "I delight to do Your will, oh my God, and Your law is within my heart." (Psalm 40:8). This means that for us to have an understanding of God's will, in order to meet temptation, we need His word to be in our hearts also.

Here is how God's word, and its power, works in us when we are tempted. When tempted, we are to claim God's promises and choose His will as expressed and revealed in His word. In so doing, we run to the source of God's power. As with Jesus, when we say, "not my will but Yours be done," at that moment of temptation, power is provided for us to escape and to resist the devil.

> *"By the word of Your lips, I have kept away from the paths of the destroyer. Uphold my steps in your paths, that my footsteps may not slip" Psalm 17:4-5 NKJV*

Prayer

> *"Watch and pray that you may not enter into temptation. The spirit indeed is willing, but the flesh is weak." Matthew 26:41 ESV*

In Jesus' words to His disciples, He shows the power of prayer as a defence against temptation. The counsel Jesus gives is for His followers to be on guard and maintain a deep prayerful life; this is what will keep them from entering in to temptation.

> *"When it becomes the habit of the soul to converse with God, the power of the evil one is broken; for Satan cannot abide near the soul that draws nigh unto God." Our High Calling p.96*

"The reason why so many are left to themselves in places of temptation is that they do not set the Lord always before them. When we permit our communion with God to be broken, our defence is departed from us. Not all your good purposes and good intentions will enable you to withstand evil. You must be men and women of prayer. Your petitions must not be faint, occasional, and fitful, but earnest, persevering, and constant." The Ministry of Healing p.510

Prayer is a powerful weapon not only for keeping us from temptation, but also as way of escape in the moments of temptation. In the garden of Gethsemane, while Jesus was tempted to turn back from going to the cross, He prayed for strength three times. He is our example of what victories may be gained when, in the times of temptation and trial, we go to God in prayer

*"By faith and prayer all may meet the requirements of the gospel…
'The eyes of the Lord are over the righteous, and His ears are open unto their prayers.' (1 Peter 3:12) Cry unto the Lord, tempted soul. Cast yourself, helpless, unworthy, upon Jesus, and claim His very promise. The Lord will hear. He knows how strong are the inclinations of the natural heart, and He will help in every time of temptation."* Testimonies, vol. 5p.177

Practical Counsel on Resisting Temptation

Avoiding Forbidden Paths
Part of the Lord's Prayer, the model prayer which Jesus outlines to His disciples, includes the words "lead us not into temptation, but deliver us from evil." (Matthew 6:13) The prayer is for God's guidance to keep us from straying into directions that may lead to temptation.

In praying this prayer, we also have the responsibility to co-operate with God by also avoiding forbidden paths.

"While we are not to be dismayed by trial, bitter though it be, we should pray that God will not permit us to be brought where we shall be drawn away by the desires of our own evil hearts. In offer-

ing the prayer that Christ has given, we surrender ourselves to the guidance of God, asking Him to lead us in safe paths. We cannot offer this prayer in sincerity, and yet decide to walk in any way of our own choosing. We shall wait for His hand to lead us; we shall listen to His voice, saying, "This is the way, walk ye in it." Isaiah 30:21." Thoughts from the Mount of Blessing p.117

In the work of self-examination, it is important to be honest with oneself about the influences that take advantage of our weaknesses. Once these are identified, it is necessary to avoid them, and not give them access to us.

"So far as in us lies, we should close every avenue by which the tempter may find access to us." Ibid p.118

Remember, we are tempted when we are drawn away by our internal desires, but also by the things outside of us that we may allow to get our attention. This is why it is important to be aware of what one allows into their minds, either in the choice of entertainment, friendships, places of recreation and so on. This is how we wisely keep from falling into temptation.

"I will behave wisely in a perfect way... I will set nothing wicked before my eyes." Psalm 101:2-3 NKJV

"Those who would not fall a prey to Satan's devices, must guard well the avenues of the soul; they must avoid reading, seeing, or hearing that which will suggest impure thoughts. The mind must not be left to dwell at random upon every subject that the enemy of souls may suggest. The heart must be faithfully sentineled, or evils without will awaken evils within, and the soul will wander in darkness." Acts of the Apostles p.518

Cut it Out

In the Sermon on the Mount, Jesus uses a blunt illustration to explain the importance of doing away with things that cause a person to fall into sin. He instructs:

"If your right eye causes you to sin, pluck it out and cast it from you; for it is more profitable for you that one of your members per-

ish, than for your whole body to be cast into hell. And if your right hand causes you to sin, cut it off and cast it from you; for it is more profitable for you that one of your members perish, than for your whole body to be cast into hell." Mathew 5:29-30 NKJV

Jesus' words make the point that there are things in a person's life that may be a direct cause of their struggle with a particular sin. In order to ensure that one does not lose their shot at eternity, Jesus counsels us to cut these off and remove them.

The metaphor of the "eye" and the "arm" notes the fact that the things which are an obstacle to a person's spiritual life may not always be evil in themselves (because God created the eye and the arm). Television, for example, has no inherent evil in it; neither does the Internet, social media and so on. Many people, however, do find themselves bound to immoral addictions which they access directly through these mediums and, for that reason, would need to "cut them off". The point is not limited to these examples, however.

Wherever a thing easily takes advantage of a person's weakness, and causes them to sin, is it better for that thing to be cut off and removed.

"Let us lay aside every weight, and the sin which so easily ensnares us, and let us run with endurance the race that is set before us." Hebrews 12:2 NKJV

At times, doing away with things that lead one to sin may seem painful--even as painful as losing a limb. That is a testament to how attached we can become to our selfish desires. The peace gained from trusting Christ, however, is far greater than the pain of separating from things which lead us to sin.

Sometimes, the things that need to be cut off include evil associations whose influence strongly leads to sin. God has intended that His children be the salt of the earth and witness to others through friendship. There are, however, instances where a non-believer has a stronger influence over the believer. This is partly why God instructed the Israelites to not marry idol worshipers. Relationships with individuals whose influence leads one to dishonour God are among the things that also must be cut off:

"Turn from the one who has ventured to present wrong practices to you. Resolutely turn from the tempter, saying, I must separate from your influence; for I know you are not walking in the footsteps of our Saviour." Sons and Daughters of God p.164

In Jesus' words, He notes that it is "more profitable" to do away with the obstacles in the way of our walk with Him. We gain more than we lose by cutting out the weights that slow us down spiritually, especially for being better equipped to "run with endurance the race set before us" (Hebrews 12:1-2).

Avoiding Idleness

One of the most notable experiences that marked the reputation of King David, during his reign over Israel, was his sin of adultery with Bathsheba, the wife of a man named Uriah. David's moral fall as the leader of the nation involved him attempting to cover up his sin and eventually plotting Uriah's death. His one sin resulted in adversity for God's people, as well as a household with intense conflict and broken relationships.

The events that led up to the fall of David offer us an important lesson.

"It happened in the spring of the year, at the time when kings go out to battle, that David sent Joab and his servants with him, and all Israel; and they destroyed the people of Ammon and besieged Rabbah. But David remained at Jerusalem." 2 Samuel 11:1 NKJV

At the time when kings go to war, David was meant to be in the battlefield as leader of Israel. Under David's leadership, Israel had a good track record thus far, "they destroyed the people of Ammon and besieged Rabbah." David thus felt confident that he could send the armies without him. He began to be to be self-reliant and this opened the door for temptation.

"David was surrounded by the fruits of victory and the honours of his wise and able rule. It was now, while he was at ease and unguarded, that the tempter seized the opportunity to occupy his mind." Patriarchs and Prophets p.718

While the rest of his army was away, David stayed behind in his royal home. In his time of ease and idleness, Satan found a window to tempt the king,

"Then it happened one evening that David arose from his bed and walked on the roof of the king's house. And from the roof he saw a woman bathing, and the woman was very beautiful to behold. So David sent and inquired about the woman. And someone said, "Is this not Bathsheba, the daughter of Eliam, the wife of Uriah the Hittite?" Then David sent messengers, and took her; and she came to him, and he lay with her, for she was cleansed from her impurity; and she returned to her house. And the woman conceived; so she sent and told David, and said, "I am with child." 2 Samuel 11:2-5 NKJV

David is said to have risen from his bed in the evening. This is to say that during the day he had been sleeping, if not lying in bed. In his time away from war, he spent the day in idleness and it was then, when David had nothing to do, that the first steps were taken leading up to his moral fall.

A common statement is made that "an idle mind is the devil's workshop." The idea behind this statement is simply that when a mind is not occupied with meaningful activity, Satan will offer it something to do.

"When in ease and self-security he let go his hold upon God, David yielded to Satan and brought upon his soul the stain of guilt. He, the Heaven-appointed leader of the nation, chosen by God to execute His law, himself trampled upon its precepts. He who should have been a terror to evildoers, by his own act strengthened their hands." Patriarchs and Prophets p.718

The lesson to be gained from David's fall is the importance of avoiding idleness in order to not fall into temptation. The first steps in the downward course of David's fall began in the times when he was idle and unguarded, and thus Satan easily "seized the opportunity to occupy his mind."

Do not Give Satan a Chance

"Give no opportunity to the devil." Ephesians 4:17 ESV

In any war, no military ever gives their enemy an opportunity to gain the upper hand. In the warfare against the lusts of the flesh and the devil, we are also not to give him any room to easily tempt us. For this reason, we are to shun the very earliest suggestions of temptation, even when they begin in one's own mind.

"The first time the temptation comes, meet it in such a decided manner that it will never be repeated." Sons and Daughters of God p.164

"If we would not commit sin, we must shun its very beginnings. Every emotion and desire must be held in subjection to reason and conscience. Every unholy thought must be instantly repelled." Testimonies, vol.5 p.177

Decide Beforehand

The first chapter, the book of Daniel recounts the event of Israel's captivity and defeat by the Babylonian king, Nebuchadnezzar. As a teenager and a part of Israel's royal family, Daniel was taken captive by the Babylonian king, to be brought up and educated in the Babylonian way of life. Part of this new system included a diet which went against the prescribed diet which God gave to His people in Leviticus 11. When the Babylonian diet was offered to Daniel and his fellow captive youth, they made a bold resolution:

"Daniel purposed in his heart that he would not defile himself with the portion of the king's delicacies, nor with the wine which he drank; therefore he requested of the chief of the eunuchs that he might not defile himself." Daniel 1:8 NKJV

Daniel had made a personal decision to follow God's will, even as it related to what was on his plate. In choosing to follow God's will in this regard, Daniel humbly--yet tactfully--made the request to be served with alternative food. This request was at the risk of disrespecting the king, but he chose to honour God above man.

Daniel received courage and power from God to face the temptation set before him because before the temptation came, he had already purposed it in his mind that he would not give in. He submitted to the will of God beforehand and when the temptation did come, he was able to meet it.

We, too, are to consciously make the choice that if "such and such" a temptation arises, we intend to follow God's will. Thus we will not be left confused in the hour of temptation.

The Temptation of Trials

Throughout the scriptures, the word that is translated "temptations" is not only limited to the experience of being enticed to sin. The experiences of difficulty and trials are also referred to as temptation. The Bible teaches that those who abide in Christ will also experience these kinds of temptations. Speaking to the church, the apostle James says the following:

> "My brethren, count it all joy when ye fall into diverse temptations; Knowing this, that the trying of your faith worketh patience. James 1:2-3
> "But let patience have its perfect work, that you may be perfect and complete, lacking nothing" James 1:4 NKJV

The temptations which James refers to here are those that try our faith (other versions note this as "the testing of your faith"). Sometimes, in order to purify and develop our characters, God may permit us to go through these difficult experiences.

> "What is temptation? It is the means by which those who claim to be the children of God are tested and tried. We read that God tempted Abraham, that He tempted the children of Israel. This means that He permitted circumstances to occur to test their faith and lead them to look to Him for help. God permits temptation to come to His people today that they may realise that He is their helper. If they draw nigh to Him when they are tempted, He strengthens them to meet the temptation." In Heavenly Places p.251

In speaking of such temptations, James encourages us to "count it all joy" when we find ourselves in these kinds of situations. That is because the trials of our faith are used as a part of God's work to refine and purify His true followers, even as a fire purifies a precious metal in the refining process. When we remember that "God will not allow you to be tempted above what you are able" we may be confident that He would never place us in a situation which He knew we could not be able to bear in His strength.

"God permits us to be placed under circumstances that will test us, to increase our love and to perfect our trust in Him. Through self-denial and suffering with Christ, we grow in grace and in the knowledge of the truth. Trials will come, but they are an evidence that we are children of God. Paul passed through great trials, but he did not despair as though his Father in heaven were dead. He rejoiced in tribulation; for he desired, through participations in the sufferings of Christ, to be conformed to his image. Let this hero of faith speak for himself. He says, "I take pleasure in infirmities, in reproaches, in necessities, in persecutions, in distresses for Christ's sake." [2 Corinthians 12:10.]" Gospel Workers (1892) p.441

Trials are God's Instruments

Paul describes the experience of those who have faith in Jesus and how that influences their outlook on trials and tribulations. He writes:

"Having been justified by faith, we have peace with God through our Lord Jesus Christ... And not only that, but we also glory in tribulations, knowing that tribulation produces perseverance; and perseverance, character; and character, hope." Romans 5:1, 3-5 NKJV

Those who have been justified by believing in Jesus may rejoice when faced with tribulation. This is because the tribulations we face are the Lord's instruments to produce the attributes of His character in us.

This means that God does not send trials in our lives as a sign of His displeasure towards us. On the contrary--the difficulties of life are His means of developing faith, trust and endurance, in His people.

"Trials and obstacles are the Lord's chosen methods of discipline and His appointed conditions of success... Often He permits the fires of affliction to assail [His people] that they may be purified."
The Ministry of Healing p.471

To those who follow Christ, trials always achieve a greater good for them.

Job was a faithful servant of whom God could boast about to Satan. "Have you considered My servant Job," God said, "that there is none like him on the earth, a blameless and upright man, one who fears God and shuns evil?" (Job 1:8). While this was the case, God still permitted Job to go through the severe trial of losing his accumulated wealth, his loved ones and his health.

Throughout his period of temptation, however, while also weighed down with confusion and pain, Job still expressed words of trust in God. "Though He slay me," he says, "yet will I trust Him." (Job 13:15).

While Job's friends tried to throw blame on him, and accuse him of suffering as a punishment for his sins, he insisted: "For I know that my Redeemer lives, and He shall stand at last on the earth."(Job 19:25)

When we realise that the trials we face are permitted by God to work out His will in us, we also--like Job--may remain hopeful in God. Every trial that He permits His faithful children to undergo will always, ultimately, work together for their good.

"And we know that all things work together for good to those who love God, to those who are the called according to His purpose."
Romans 8:28 NKJV

The words "all things" literally mean *all things*. Both the positive and seemingly negative experiences work in favour of those who have surrendered themselves to God. Seeing trials from this perspective kept Jesus going and we may also cherish the same hope.

"The Father's presence encircled Christ, and nothing befell Him but that which infinite love permitted for the blessing of the world. Here was His source of comfort, and it is for us. He who is imbued with

the Spirit of Christ abides in Christ. Whatever comes to him comes from the Saviour, who surrounds him with His presence. Nothing can touch him except by the Lord's permission. All our sufferings and sorrows, all our temptations and trials, all our sadness and griefs, all our persecutions and privations, in short, all things work together for our good. All experiences and circumstances are God's workmen whereby good is brought to us." The Ministry of Healing p.488

God's Promises to the Tried and Tempted

"Trust ye in the Lord for ever: for in the Lord Jehovah is everlasting strength." Isaiah 26:4

"The prayer, 'Bring us not into temptation,' is itself a promise. If we commit ourselves to God we have the assurance, He "will not suffer you to be tempted above that ye are able; but will with the temptation also make a way to escape, that ye may be able to bear it." Thoughts from the Mount of Blessing p.118

"Christ's example shows us that our only hope of victory is in continual resistance of Satan's attacks. He who triumphed over the adversary of souls in the conflict with temptation understands Satan's power over the race, and has conquered in our behalf. As an overcomer, He has given us the advantage of His victory, that in our efforts to resist the temptations of Satan we may unite our weakness to His strength, our worthlessness to His merits. And sustained by His enduring might, under strong temptation, we may resist in His all-powerful name and overcome as He overcame." In Heavenly Places p.251

Walk in the Spirit

Since we still have the fallen condition of our human nature, there will constantly be an internal conflict between the flesh and the Spirit. To those who are in the Spirit, however, this battle does not have to be one that ends in defeat.

"Walk in the Spirit, and you shall not fulfil the lust of the flesh." Galatians 5:14 NKJV

While "the flesh lusts against the Spirit and the Spirit against the flesh", we are promised that our fellowship with God's Spirit will enable us to not submit to the lusts of the flesh.

God the Holy Spirit, as the third person of the Godhead, comes to the aid of all those who are tempted--to help them to resist. He is our greatest source of strength.

> *"In describing to His disciples the office work of the Holy Spirit, Jesus sought to inspire them with the joy and hope that inspired His own heart. He rejoiced because of the abundant help He had provided for His church...Sin could be resisted and overcome only through the mighty agency of the Third Person of the Godhead, who would come with no modified energy, but in the fullness of divine power." The Desire of Ages p.671*

When we walk in the Spirit, when we abide in Christ, the promise is that we shall not fulfil the lusts of the flesh. But what does it mean to walk in the Spirit? Notice how Paul describes this:

> *"There is therefore now no condemnation to those who are in Christ Jesus, who do not walk according to the flesh, but according to the Spirit... For those who live according to the flesh set their minds on the things of the flesh, but those who live according to the Spirit, the things of the Spirit." Romans 8:1, 5 NKJV*

To walk in the flesh means to "set your mind on the things of the flesh." This is true with walking in the Spirit also. Thus, to walk in the Spirit means that the choices we make are motivated by what is in harmony with the Spirit of God and not what our flesh desires. When this is our daily mindset, we "walk in the Spirit" and thus will not fulfil the lusts of the flesh. Moment by moment, we may consciously surrender our lives to following God's will.

The Power That Works in You

When we come to Christ and give our lives over to His will, He puts His Spirit into our hearts. Note this promise:

> *"I will give you a new heart and put a new spirit within you; I will take the heart of stone out of your flesh and give you a heart of*

flesh. I will put My Spirit within you and cause you to walk in My statutes, and you will keep My judgments and do them." Ezekiel 36:26-27 NKJV

When we choose to follow Christ, He puts a new spirit in us--a new attitude that now desires to do right. Whenever one finds themselves loving righteousness, and hating iniquity, it is evidence that God is working in their heart. He works to gives us new desires.

God follows this up with the promise to put His Spirit within us so that He may enable us, from within, to do His will. Like Paul, we can say "yet not I, but Christ lives in me" (Galatians 2:20). Notice Paul's prayer:

"I bow my knees to the Father of our Lord Jesus Christ... that He would grant you, according to the riches of His glory, to be strengthened with might through His Spirit in the inner man, that Christ may dwell in your hearts through faith;... that you may be filled with all the fullness of God." Ephesians 3:14-19 NKJV

We can experience the fullness of God working in our own hearts! This experience is also referred to as being "partakers of the divine nature." Peter describes how the Holy Spirit's work in our hearts enables us to escape the corrupting influence of our lusts and sinful desires. He notes:

God has "given to us exceedingly great and precious promises, that through these you may be partakers of the divine nature, having escaped the corruption that is in the world through lust." 2 Peter 1:4-5 NKJV

As we walk in the Spirit, and do not fulfil the lusts of the flesh, we become partakers of the divine nature. Day by day, as we mind the things of the Spirit and choose God's will, He weakens the force of the temptations that would easily beset us. More and more, we escape the corruption that comes from indulging the lusts of the flesh. This is experienced all through the power of God the Holy Spirit working within us.

"It is by the Spirit that the heart is made pure. Through the Spirit the believer becomes a partaker of the divine nature. Christ has

given His Spirit as a divine power to overcome all hereditary and cultivated tendencies to evil, and to impress His own character upon His church." *The Desire of Ages p.671*

Questions on Chapter 8

Will I still get tempted if I walk with God? (p.162)

What is temptation? (p.163)

What are the two main sources of temptation? (p.164)

Why do I get tempted and naturally desire to do wrong? (p.165, 168-170)

What was the original relationship between our reason, the will and our passions & appetites? (p.165-167)

What's wrong with our human nature? (p.168, 170)

What is the difference between sin and temptation? (p.163-164, 171)

Is it a sin to be tempted? (p.171)

What does God do when I am tempted? (p.175, 176-177, 202)

What should I do when I am tempted? (p.172, 178-185)

What tools has God given to help me to resist temptation? (p.190-191)

How can I keep from falling when I am tempted? (p.192-197, 202)

Why does God sometimes allow trials to come in my life? (p.198)

Is it possible to not fall when I am tempted? (p.172, 175, 201)

What promises has God given for us whenever we are tempted? (p.201)

9

What if I Fall?

❧

The Possibility of Falling

How Christ Regards Those Who Fall

Rising From a Fall

Promises to the Fallen

The Possibility of Falling

Paul's words, "let him that thinks he stands take heed lest he falls" (1 Corinthians 10:13), highlight the reality that falling into sin is a real possibility--even for those who think that they are standing. While we seek to never fall throughout our walk with God, it is important to know what God's word counsels for those who may fall.

> *"For a righteous man may fall seven times and rise again, but the wicked shall fall by calamity." Proverbs 24:16 NKJV*

The difference between a righteous and an unrighteous person is not that the righteous are unable to fall. Those who abide in Christ are also at risk of being overcome by temptation and sin. What sets these apart from the unrighteous, however, is that should the righteous fall by taking their eyes off of Jesus they may still rise up again!

> *"The pen of inspiration, true to its task, tells us of the sins that overcame Noah, Lot, Moses, Abraham, David, and Solomon, and that even Elijah's strong spirit sank under temptation during his fearful trial. Jonah's disobedience and Israel's idolatry are faithfully recorded. Peter's denial of Christ, the sharp contention of Paul and Barnabas, the failings and infirmities of the prophets and apostles, are all laid bare by the Holy Ghost, who lifts the veil from the human heart. There before us lie the lives of the believers, with all their faults and follies, which are intended as a lesson to all the generations following them." Testimonies vol. 4 p.12*

The Bible never covers up the moral falls of even the most celebrated of God's servants. The shortfalls of these pioneers are recorded throughout Biblical history as lesson books for us. Their experiences reveal to us the things that lead the righteous to fall and, moreover, how God works in lifting up the fallen. Their experiences are important for us to note.

We may draw encouragement from the fact that those who may fall into sin do not need to remain in that condition. "Without Me, you can do nothing," Christ says; *He* lifts up the fallen. We will thus consider how to experience His restoration, in the unfortunate event of falling into sin.

Things That Cause a Fall

"Whoever commits sin also commits lawlessness, and sin is law-lessness. And you know that [Jesus] was manifested to take away our sins, and in Him there is no sin. Whoever abides in Him does not sin. Whoever sins has neither seen Him nor known Him." 1 John 3:4-6 NKJV

In the previous chapter, we learnt that abiding in Christ is our greatest safeguard against falling into temptation. John draws from the same idea, that those who abide in Christ--while they maintain an intimate communion with Him--do not transgress His law. Hence, in the event that one does fall and commit sin, it is because they have chosen to come out of Christ.

Thus, the idea is not that those who sin do not, or have never, walked with Christ; rather, in the choice to go against the will of God, the choice comes with detaching oneself from Him.

Since maintaining a vital connection with Christ is essential for not falling, the opposite is also true; the cause of many a fall stems from not maintaining the vital connection with Christ. Notice how this idea is discussed in the epistle to the Hebrews:

"Let us lay aside every weight, and the sin which so easily ensnares us, and let us run with endurance the race that is set before us, looking unto Jesus, the author and finisher of our faith... looking carefully lest anyone fall short of the grace of God." Hebrews 12:1-2, 15 NKJV

In order to lay aside the sins that ensnare us, we are encouraged to "look unto Jesus;" to consider Him. But Paul emphasises how this is not just considering Jesus in a casual manner. We are told that when looking unto Jesus, it should be by "looking carefully" (other versions even say "looking diligently"). This is so that we do not fall short of God's grace.

Knowing this, we get to understand the primary cause of individuals falling into sin--especially those who may have been abiding in Christ. The choice to give in to temptation, and transgress God's law, comes as the result of taking one's focus off Christ and not "looking diligently" to Him. To get humanity to fall, then, Satan constantly works through various ways to divert our minds from "looking unto Jesus" consistently. Notice his diverse tactics:

> "When the mind dwells upon self, it is turned away from Christ, the source of strength and life. Hence it is Satan's constant effort to keep the attention diverted from the Saviour and thus prevent the union and communion of the soul with Christ. The pleasures of the world, life's cares and perplexities and sorrows, the faults of others, or your own faults and imperfections--to any or all of these he will seek to divert the mind. Do not be misled by his devices." Steps to Christ p.71

Through the various ways in which Satan leads believers to fall, his main tactic is to cause individuals to lose focus of Christ and thus not abide in Him.

Various experiences throughout Biblical history illustrate the point above. Through a season of doubt and fear, the prophet Elijah distrusted God and, through deception, Satan led Eve to eat of the forbidden fruit. David's idleness and self-trust resulted in an adulterous affair with Uriah's wife and Peter, in a moment of panic, denied his Lord on the eve of the crucifixion.

Even today, our adversary attempts to divert our focus away from Jesus--the source of our spiritual strength. Whether it is through a momentary slip, or gradual spiritual decline which comes by neglecting personal prayer and Bible study, Satan seeks to lead us to eventually fall.

In a piece on the secret to abiding in Christ, the songwriter Leoni Gardner puts it these words:

> "So now I know Your meaning, when You spoke about the vine;
> Connection must be constant, Your precious life with mine;
> I see it all so clearly now, since I have through it through;
> I only ever fall in sin, when I take my eye off You!"
> Leoni Gardner, The Abiding Secret

How Christ Regards Those who Fall

God's attitude towards the failures of His children is very different to how humans treat those who hurt them. When God's people were in a rebellious condition, and the temple was in ruins as a result, He still sent them prophets to call them back to Himself. During a time of reform, the prophet Micah expressed these words of confidence in God's deliverance:

"Do not rejoice over me, my enemy; when I fall, I will arise; when I sit in darkness, the Lord will be a light to me. I will bear the indignation of the Lord, because I have sinned against Him, until He pleads my case and executes justice for me. He will bring me forth to the light; I will see His righteousness." Micah 7:8-9 NKJV

Micah here refers to sinning against God as falling. When one of God's people find themselves in this fallen state, Christ Himself pleads their case; He wants to bring them out of that condition. While sin has the terrible result of separating an individual from God, Jesus works to reconcile fallen humanity with God. Note John's words to the church:

"My little children, these things I write to you, so that you may not sin. And if anyone sins, we have an Advocate with the Father, Jesus Christ the righteous. And He Himself is the propitiation for our sins, and not for ours only but also for the whole world." 1 John 2:1-2 NKJV

An advocate is someone who is on your side and wants to see you come out as innocent. Immediately when humanity sinned, Jesus stepped in to avail salvation for mankind. As our advocate, He wants to deliver us.

When a child fails or becomes disobedient earthly parents often scold and shout at the child; but that is not how Jesus treats us. Rather, in His compassion, Jesus seeks to save that which is lost. We may be assured of God's infinite pity towards the fallen. Christ died for the fallen and it is sinners that need His salvation most; hence:

"God showed His great love for us by sending Christ to die for us while we were still sinners." Romans 5:8 NLT

"We shall often have to bow down and weep at the feet of Jesus because of our shortcomings and mistakes; but we are not to be discouraged. Even if we are overcome by the enemy, we are not cast off, not forsaken and rejected of God. No; Christ is at the right hand of God, who also maketh intercession for us." Steps to Christ p.64

Jesus does not give up on us, or sharply cut us off, in the event that one falls into sin. *"If through manifold temptations we are surprised or deceived into sin, He does not turn from us and leave us to perish. No, no, that is not our Saviour."* (S.D.A. Bible Commentary, vol. 7 p.948). As an advocate, He longs to lift up those who have fallen. Regardless of how far fallen and defiled a person may be, God's "grace is sufficient for you" (2 Corinthians 12:9).

"Jesus is amply able to save the very hardest and the most wicked and defiled sinner." Testimonies on Sexual Behavior, Adultery, and Divorce p.143

Jesus Himself spoke the message that "God so loved the world that He gave His only begotten Son, that whoever believes in Him should not perish but have everlasting life" (John 3:16). Take a moment to think about those words. Although the "world" is a reference to the general population of the Earth, it also refers to humanity's condition as a result of sin. The apostle John highlights that "the whole *world* lies in wickedness." (1 John 5:19). God, in His love, gave His Son for those that are in this condition; and He does not want any to perish.

If--in the event of taking one's focus off Jesus--one happens to fall in to sin, Christ's mission is to lift them up. When such a person realises their transgression, they are in a better position to receive and experience Christ's restoration.

"Remember this. If you have made mistakes, you certainly gain a victory if you see these mistakes and regard them as beacons of warning. Thus you turn defeat into victory, disappointing the enemy and honouring your Redeemer." Christ's Object Lessons p.332

Come to Jesus

"The next day John saw Jesus coming toward him, and said, 'Behold! The Lamb of God who takes away the sin of the world!'" John 1:29 NKJV

John the Baptist, in introducing Jesus to the world as the Messiah, identifies Him as the Lamb of God whose primary mission involves removing sin from the lives of those who lie in wickedness. To take away the sins of humanity was a part of His identity. Even His very name is His mission statement; His parents were to "call His name Jesus, for He will save His people from their sins" (Matthew 1:21).

This goes to re-emphasise the idea stressed throughout this entire book:

"As the branch cannot bear fruit of itself, unless it abides in the vine, neither can you, unless you abide in Me ([Jesus])... for without Me you can do nothing."

Our inability to accomplish anything noteworthy in the Christian walk is most true when it comes to taking away our own sins. Jesus came to set captives free from their bondage to sin. Thus, to all who have fallen, the greatest need is to come to Jesus--the Lamb of God who can take all your sins away.

At times, when individuals fall, they feel that they cannot come to Jesus until they have made themselves right first; but in so doing, they start at the wrong place. "Behold" Jesus--He is the Lamb of God and the remover of our sins. God Himself invites all that have fallen to "look to Me, and be saved, all you ends of the earth! For I am God, and there is no other" (Isaiah 45:22).

To all who have fallen, John encourages us to consciously regard Jesus as the given sacrifice to take away our transgressions. We are to think about what Christ has done for sinners. If, after falling, you realise your great need and your powerlessness to correct your faults, Jesus invites you to come to Him.

"He is also able to save to the uttermost those who come to God through Him, since He always lives to make intercession for them." Hebrews 7:25 NKJV

"Let us therefore come boldly to the throne of grace, that we may obtain mercy and find grace to help in time of need." Hebrews 4:16 NKJV

Make No Delay to Come

Throughout the history of ancient Israel, God's chosen people, they often became rebellious and disobedient. At a time, when they were described as a "sinful nation, [and] a people laden with iniquity" (Isaiah 1:4), God Himself makes the effort to restore them. In calling them to Himself as their only hope of deliverance, He pleads:

"'Come now, let us settle the matter,' says the Lord. 'Though your sins are like scarlet, they shall be as white as snow; though they are red as crimson, they shall be like wool.'" Isaiah 1:18 NKJV

Regardless of how gruesome their sins may have been, God urges His people to come to Him immediately. He offers to purify them. The same invitation is given today; God wants to "settle the matter."

Jesus is constantly working, through His Holy Spirit, to draw the sinful and the fallen to Himself. The fact that an individual *wants* to forsake their sins is evidence of that work. We are not to resist the drawing of God's Spirit by looking to ourselves and mourning over our condition. "Come *now*" is God's invitation to those whose sins are red like crimson.

"Some seem to feel that they must be on probation, and must prove to the Lord that they are reformed, before they can claim His blessing. But they may claim the blessing of God even now. They must have His grace, the Spirit of Christ, to help their infirmities, or they cannot resist evil." Steps to Christ p.52

At times, after falling into sin, individuals feel that they cannot even approach God. Some wait until they can prove how sorry they are before coming to Him; but this is a mistake. We are never to wait until we feel "right enough" to come to Jesus. He does not accept us because of our goodness. While we are to realise how unworthy we are of His favour, it is when we are fallen that we need Him most. For this reason;

"Jesus loves to have us come to Him just as we are, sinful, helpless, dependent. We may come with all our weakness, our folly, our sinfulness, and fall at His feet in penitence. It is His glory to encircle us in the arms of His love and to bind up our wounds, to cleanse us from all impurity." Ibid

In spite of how far fallen one may be, Christ is urging us to come to Him *immediately*. Our only hope of deliverance from the sins that so easily beset us is in responding to Jesus' invitation to come to Him. If you fall, make no delay to come back to Jesus. He came to deliver us from evil.

God Offers Pardon

"Seek the Lord while He may be found, call upon Him while He is near. Let the wicked forsake his way, and the unrighteous man his thoughts; let him return to the Lord, and He will have mercy on him; and to our God, for He will abundantly pardon." Isaiah 55:6-7 NKJV

To all those who are wicked and unrighteous, God's prophet gives the invitation to return to God. He encourages us with the promise of God's nearness and the fact that those who seek God will find Him. The use of the word "return" points to the idea that these wicked ones had once been acquainted with God before they chose an unrighteous direction.

We are assured that God has an abundance of pardon that He is willing to give to those who do forsake their sins and come back to Him. He is willing to forgive, freely. For those who may regard this as too good to be true, that an offended God would be willing to love and pardon sinful human beings, God further goes on to assure us that:

"'My thoughts are not your thoughts, nor are your ways My ways,' says the Lord. 'For as the heavens are higher than the earth, so are My ways higher than your ways, and My thoughts than your thoughts.'" Isaiah 55:8-9 NKJV

If anyone has fallen in to sin, Jesus offers a free and full forgiveness.

To receive this, He invites us to come to Him.

I've come to learn that it is a common tendency for individuals to regard God in human terms--to think of God as though He is like us human beings. When a person is offended or hurt by someone, even by a loved one, people often seek to make the offender feel the pain that they have caused. But God is not like that. He is not vengeful; on the contrary, God is doing all that He can to restore fallen and sinful humanity. Hence the prophet writes:

> *"Who is a God like You, pardoning iniquity and passing over the transgression of the remnant of His heritage? He does not retain His anger forever, because He delights in mercy. He will again have compassion on us, and will subdue our iniquities. [God] will cast all our sins into the depths of the sea." Micah 7:18-19 NKJV*

The forgiveness that Jesus offers us is much higher than what many suppose. Christ offers to give complete forgiveness; He can regard our sins as though they were thrown into the deepest parts of the ocean. In His forgiveness, Jesus wants to treat us as though we are innocent. As guilty as one may have been, God offers us a clean slate.

> *"If you give yourself to [Christ], and accept Him as your Saviour, then, sinful as your life may have been, for His sake you are accounted righteous. Christ's character stands in place of your character, and you are accepted before God just as if you had not sinned." Steps to Christ, p.62*

The reason God can forgive us like this is because of what Christ has done on the cross in becoming our substitute. While "the wages of sin is death" (Romans 6:23), and we are fully deserving of punishment, "the Lord has laid on [Jesus] the iniquity of us all" (Isaiah 53:6). Because Jesus has carried our guilt and taken our punishment, we can receive His innocence and all that it comes with.

> *"For [God] made [Jesus] who knew no sin to be sin for us, that we might become the righteousness of God in Him." 2 Corinthians 5:21 NKJV*

Jesus is able to take away the sins of the world because of the death He died as the Lamb of God. God the Father agreed with Jesus to "make His soul an offering for sin" (Isaiah 55:10). Consider the thought; the penalty for humanity's transgression has been paid. Thus, there is no reason why anyone should remain in a lost and guilty condition. Jesus freely offers us forgiveness.

"We have redemption through His blood, even the forgiveness of sins." Colossians 1:14

Rising From a Fall

Confess and Forsake

"If we confess our sins, He is faithful and just to forgive us our sins, and to cleanse us from all unrighteousness." 1 John 1:9

In God's plan of saving humanity, He offers His forgiveness to all who will confess their sins to Him. He has made the act of confession a necessary condition for receiving His forgiveness and experiencing His power to transform us.

Confession simply means telling God what you have done and acknowledging your sin. This is not merely to inform Him of our sins but rather to express that we acknowledge our wrong and apologise for going against His will. This is why we are to be specific and to the point whenever we confess our sins.

"True confession is always of a specific character, and acknowledges particular sins. They may be of such a nature as to be brought before God only; they may be wrongs that should be confessed to individuals who have suffered injury through them; or they may be of a public character, and should then be as publicly confessed. But all confession should be definite and to the point, acknowledging the very sins of which you are guilty." Steps to Christ p.38

"Whoever conceals his transgressions will not prosper, but he who confesses and forsakes them will obtain mercy." Proverbs 28:13 ESV

When we confess our sins, we will obtain God's mercy. Confession, however, also comes with the condition of being willing to forsake those sins. More than confessing, we are also to make the decision to separate from our transgressions of God's law.

The wise man notes an important point regarding one who "conceals his transgression." Those who cover their sins up, and make excuses for them, cannot receive God's mercy.

At times, because of the shame and guilt of sin, individuals make excuses for their sins or--like Adam and Eve--throw the blame on someone else. Some blame others for their own short tempers, or make efforts to justify their unchristlike words and acts. But such "cover ups" will not prosper. We are to acknowledge and take responsibility for our own sins and, in so doing, we are prepared to experience God's forgiveness and cleansing.

Forgiveness Comes with Power

When God forgives, He does more than clear the guilty of their charge. Not only is He faithful to forgive our sins, He also goes further to even "cleanse us from all unrighteousness." He works on the heart, the root of our actions, to bring about righteousness.

Thus, God's forgiveness is an active work. When He says "I forgive you," He not only regards you as innocent, but also makes you so.

"God's forgiveness is not merely a judicial ([or legal]) act by which He sets us free from condemnation. It is not only forgiveness for sin, but reclaiming from sin. It is the outflow of redeeming love that transforms the heart. David had the true conception of forgiveness when he prayed, "Create in me a clean heart, O God; and renew a right spirit within me." (Psalm 51:10). And again he says, "As far as the east is from the west, so far hath He removed our transgressions from us." (Psalm 103:12)." Thoughts from the Mount of Blessings p.114

God's forgiveness is often discussed in connection with the power that it comes with. This is seen in Paul's letter the Ephesians. The apostle describes those who, before conversion, used to live to fulfil the desires of the flesh. He describes them thus:

"Once you were dead because of your disobedience and your many sins. You used to live in sin, just like the rest of the world, obeying the devil--the commander of the powers in the unseen world. He is the spirit at work in the hearts of those who refuse to obey God."

218

Ephesians 2:1-2 NLT

Before coming to Christ, humanity can be said to have been "dead because of disobedience." In the letter to Timothy, it also notes that "she who lives in pleasure is dead while she lives." (1 Timothy 5:6).

In view of this description, notice how the apostle describes the change that takes place when such an individual receives forgiveness.

> *"And you, being dead in your trespasses… [God] has made alive together with [Christ], having forgiven you all trespasses." Colossians 2:13 NKJV*

God can forgive all our trespasses. When He does so, He "makes alive" those who were formerly dead in their trespasses. This means that when one truly experiences forgiveness, they are no longer dead in trespasses and sins--a transformation of the heart takes place.

The forgiveness which God promises to those who confess always includes a work of cleansing. With each sin that a person confesses, God works to remove that sin from one's heart and to empower them to live righteously.

Notice that the text also mentions that God makes us "alive together with Christ." This is a reference to Jesus' resurrection. This is important to consider. Paul mentions this point because the power that God used to resurrect Jesus from the dead is the same power that He uses to bring about a change in our hearts.

When you and I confess our sins, this is the power that God will use to remove our sins from us. This is the power of forgiveness. Hence Paul could write:

> *"I also pray that you will understand the incredible greatness of God's power for us who believe Him. This is the same mighty power that raised Christ from the dead and seated Him in the place of honour at God's right hand in the heavenly realms." Ephesians 1:19-20 NLT*

God Gives Repentance

> *"Then Peter said to them, 'Repent, and let every one of you be baptized in the name of Jesus Christ for the remission of sins; and you*

shall receive the gift of the Holy Spirit."' Acts 2:38 NKJV

"Repent therefore and be converted, that your sins may be blotted out." Acts 3:19 NKJV

Throughout the gospels, when Christ and the apostles preached the gospel, the message included a call to repentance. Repentance, together with confession, is thus made a requirement for receiving God's forgiveness (the "remission of sins") as well as a transformation of heart (being converted).

Notice the two-fold nature of repentance:

"Repentance includes sorrow for sin and a turning away from it. We shall not renounce sin unless we see its sinfulness; until we turn away from it in heart, there will be no real change in the life." Steps to Christ p.23

In the Old Testament, whenever God would call rebellious Israel to repent, He would use words such as *"turn"* or *"return."* This is because repentance is, when simply put, turning away from sin. This involves turning away from sin in the heart.

Repentance also includes a genuine remorse for sin and for the pain that it brings to God's heart. When we really see the ugliness of sin, together with what it does to us and to God, we will want nothing to do with it.

At times, however, people generally do not realise the wickedness of sin. In some instances there may even be a reluctance and unwillingness to turn away from some sins. Knowing this, God has made provision for us. Speaking to the Jewish leaders, Peter spoke these words:

"The God of our fathers raised up Jesus whom you murdered by hanging on a tree. Him God has exalted to His right hand to be Prince and Saviour, to give repentance to Israel and forgiveness of sins." Acts 5:30-31 NKJV

Jesus has been exalted in order to give us repentance; He offers it as freely as He offers forgiveness. As our Saviour, Jesus can turn us away from sin and give us a genuine sorrow for it.

It is a mistake to think that we cannot come to Jesus until we have repented or until we feel guilty enough for our sins. We are not to wait until we feel sorry enough; rather, we are to come to Jesus and receive the repentance that He offers to give.

Paul highlights that it is "the goodness of God [that] leads you to repentance." (Romans 2:5). When we understand and consider God's goodness, something about it leads to a genuine sorrow for sin and turning from it in heart.

God's goodness is most vividly seen in Him giving His Son to die in place of sinners. When we consider Jesus' death on the cross, and the fact that the He faced it all as a result of our own (personal) disobedience, it will affect our attitude to sin. Notice the effect of contemplating Christ's death:

"Then they will look on Me whom they pierced. Yes, they will mourn for Him as one mourns for his only son, and grieve for Him as one grieves for a firstborn." Zechariah 12:10 NKJV

Whenever an individual violates God's law, they "crucify…the Son of God afresh, and put Him to an open shame" (Hebrews 6:6). By disobeying God's law, we "pierce" the Saviour more painfully than the Roman soldiers did at Calvary. This is the pain that sin brings to God's heart. The fact that God loved us enough to still go through with the cross, despite the pain, is the evidence of how willing He is to redeem us. This is the evidence of His goodness.

Through Zechariah, God notes that when we realise what sin does, it will lead us to mourn. A thoughtful consideration of Jesus' sacrifice on the cross, and its personal application to oneself, will bring an individual to mourn their own sinful condition. As it reveals the ultimate cost of sin, the cross of Christ moves us to want to turn from disobedience. This is how God's goodness leads to repentance and sorrow for sin.

The mourning that comes with genuine sorrow for sin is the experience that goes before experiencing the pardon and cleansing which God has provided. Notice how this thought is elaborated on:

"The tears of the penitent ([repentant one]) are only the rain-

drops that precede the sunshine of holiness. This sorrow heralds a joy which will be a living fountain in the soul. "Only acknowledge thine iniquity, that thou hast transgressed against the Lord thy God;" "and I will not cause Mine anger to fall upon you: for I am merciful, saith the Lord." (Jeremiah 3:13, 12). "Unto them that mourn in Zion," He has appointed to give "beauty for ashes, the oil of joy for mourning, the garment of praise for the spirit of heaviness." (Isaiah 61:3)." The Desire of Ages p.300

To be turned away from our sins, and to experience God's transforming power, we may pray as David did after his adulterous affair with Bathsheba:

"Purify me from my sins, and I will be clean; wash me, and I will be whiter than snow... Create in me a clean heart, O God. Renew a loyal spirit within me. Do not banish me from your presence, and don't take your Holy Spirit from me. Restore to me the joy of your salvation, and make me willing to obey you." Psalm 51:7, 10-12 NLT

True and False Repentance

The Bible gives examples of individuals who, after their moral falls, later repented. Two cases include Judas Iscariot and Simon Peter, two of Jesus' disciples. Both individuals sinned against Jesus on the night of His crucifixion and both, following their falls, repented. The outcome of their repentance, however, was not quite the same.

When Jesus had been taken to be crucified, Peter was questioned about his association to Him. In his panic, Peter denied knowing Jesus and resorted to vulgar language to prove his point. Jesus had forewarned Peter that he would deny Him and that a rooster would crow three times once this happens. After realising what he had done, we read that:

"Peter remembered the word of Jesus who had said to him, 'Before the rooster crows you will deny Me three times.' So he went out and wept bitterly." Matthew 26:75 NKJV

That same night, Judas betrayed Jesus to the Jewish leaders. They were looking for a reason to kill Jesus and Judas accepted a bribe to betray Jesus into their hands. Judas cunningly expected Jesus to somehow free Himself miraculously, then he would still keep the money. Things did not turn out as Judas expected however.

Judas saw Jesus being taken by the Roman military and being beaten like a criminal. Seeing that his plan did not go as hoped, Judas repented:

"Then Judas… when he saw that [Jesus] was condemned, repented himself, and brought again the thirty pieces of silver to the chief priests and elders, saying, 'I have sinned in that I have betrayed the innocent blood.' And they said, 'What is that to us? See thou to that'." Matthew 27:3-5

After Peter repented, he was reconverted and later used by God as a leader of the early church. Judas, on the other hand, after he repented, "threw down the pieces of silver in the temple and departed, and went and hanged himself."(Matthew 27:5). These cases illustrate the two kinds of repentance spoken of in the Bible:

"Godly sorrow produces repentance leading to salvation, not to be regretted; but the sorrow of the world produces death." 2 Corinthians 7:10 NKJV

When Peter repented, he saw the sinfulness of his sin and mourned over it. Judas, on the other hand, repented because of the consequences of his sin and not the sin itself. He feared the judgment that would fall on him more than having a genuine sorrow for betraying Jesus.

Godly sorrow and genuine repentance mourns over the sinfulness of sin and not only its consequences. Such a genuine repentance can only come as a gift from God.

But I Knew I Should Not Do It

In briefly discussing Adam and Eve's fall, Paul writes that "Adam was not deceived, but the woman being deceived, fell into transgression." (1 Timothy 2:14). When God questioned the pair, after their act of disobedience, Eve personally acknowledged that "the serpent deceived me, and I ate." (Genesis 3:13). Adam, on the other hand, could make no such confession.

> "*Adam understood that his companion had transgressed the command of God, disregarded the only prohibition laid upon them as a test of their fidelity and love. There was a terrible struggle in his mind. He mourned that he had permitted Eve to wander from his side. But now the deed was done; he must be separated from her whose society had been his joy. How could he have it thus…? He resolved to share her fate; if she must die, he would die with her."* Patriarchs and Prophets p.56

Unlike Eve, Adam was fully aware of the fact that he was violating God's will by eating the fruit. He knew that the tree was not good for food and that he should not eat it. He was not deceived on this point, yet he chose to share the consequences with Eve.

When Adam had transgressed, and he saw the shame of his nakedness which came as the result, God still came down to the garden in an effort to save them. Though he fell as a result of his own conscious decision, Adam was still offered another chance. God made provision for Adam to be restored the moment he fell.

> "*The instant man accepted the temptations of Satan, and did the very things God had said he should not do, Christ, the Son of God, stood between the living and the dead, saying, 'Let the punishment fall on Me. I will stand in man's place. He shall have another chance.'*" S.D.A Bible Commentary, vol. 1 p.1085

Adam's case is cited because when the first man sinned, he was fully aware of what He was doing. Even though this was the case, God still came looking for Adam in order to offer him pardon. As a God of unchanging love and compassion, God offers us the same today.

At times, one of the things that make it harder for some to believe that God will forgive their sin is the fact that when they committed it they were well aware of the fact that it was wrong-- they knew that they should not do it. One may have been clearly alerted by the Spirit that they are being tempted and yet still violated their conscience. But God stands ready to forgive and remove such a sin when it is sincerely confessed.

> *"When we try to come to God, the enemy will whisper; 'it is of no use for you to pray; did not you do that evil thing? Have you not sinned against God and violated your own conscience?' But we may tell the enemy that 'the blood of Jesus Christ His Son cleanseth us from all sin.' (1 John 1:7)." Thoughts from the Mount of Blessing p.115*

When the Bible speaks about the power of Jesus' death to offer forgiveness for all oursins, it really does mean *"all* sin". God "forgives *all* your iniquity" (Psalms 103:3), even the ones committed knowingly. When confessing such sins, we must acknowledge our guilt and the fact that we knew that the sin was wrong when we committed it.

While God is able to forgive all our sins, He would not have us continue in them:

> *"For if we sin willfully after we have received the knowledge of the truth, there no longer remains a sacrifice for sin." Hebrews 10:26 NKJV*

To sin willfully means to sin deliberately and purposefully. Some consider this text to mean that if one sins after their conversion, then they are lost forever. John, in his epistle (1 John 2:1) has shown us that this is not the case. However, the text does warn us against continuing in sin, deliberately so, after we have come to know that it is sin. Unless we do confess, repent and submit, we remain on dangerous ground.

> *"Every day that you remain in sin, you are in Satan's ranks; and should you sicken and die without repentance, you would be lost." The Review and Herald, December 24, 1889*

> *"One sin unrepented of is enough to close the gates of heaven against you. It was because man could not be saved with one stain of sin upon him, that Jesus came to die on Calvary's cross." Signs of the Times, March 17, 1890*

In this instance, "there no longer remains a sacrifice for sin" because the sin is cherished and not repented of. *"Whoever makes a practice of sinning is of the devil, for the devil has been sinning from the beginning. The reason the Son of God appeared was to destroy the works of the devil.*" (1 John 3:8 ESV). Thus, it is dangerous to intentionally violate God's will.

Whenever God brings a sin to one's awareness, those sins are to be immediately confessed and forsaken. When every known sin is confessed, the blood of Christ is able to cleanse us from every one of them. Jesus is the Lamb of God that can take away our sins, even those committed knowingly. We must give Him the permission to do so.

> *"Have you fallen into sin? Then without delay seek God for mercy and pardon." Testimonies vol.5 p.277*

Will Jesus Receive Me?

In my first year of studying, I had a roommate who wanted to record his university experiences so he could look back on them later in life. He ordered a video camera online with all the money he could save on a student's budget. The delivery took about two weeks but my roommate's excitement made it seem much longer for him. When the long-awaited camera finally arrived, he couldn't wait to sign for it.

Imagine, for a moment, how my roommate would have reacted if--when the package arrived--he was asked whether he would be willing to accept it? The answer would be obvious. The fact that he had paid for the camera should be enough evidence that he really did want it. Moreover, how much he wanted the camera is seen in how much he was willing to pay for it.

With that in mind, notice how much Christ gave in order to save humanity:

> *"Grace be to you and peace from God the Father, and from our Lord Jesus Christ; who gave Himself for our sins, that He might deliver us from this present evil world, according to the will of God and our Father." Galatians 1:3-4*

In order to deliver us from our sins, Jesus gave Himself! This is what He used to "buy" us. He did not merely give what He had, as the

Creator of the universe, but He gave Himself. In another place, Paul notes that "you are bought with a price" (1 Corinthians 6:20) and the price that Christ paid was His own life.

With this thought in mind, the question may be presented as to whether Jesus would be willing to receive sinners? The same way we would figure that my roommate would obviously receive what he paid for (the camera), Jesus is more willing to receive the sinners for whom He has given His life. Hence Jesus assures us with the promise that:

> "All those the Father gives Me will come to Me, and whoever comes to Me I will never drive away." John 6:37 NIV

The invitation for us to come to Jesus to receive pardon for sin, even after we have fallen, is broad and far reaching. "All" and "whoever" comes to Him sincerely shall never be refused.

For my roommate, the camera meant much because of how much of his savings he had to use in order to buy it. For someone wealthier, it may not have been so significant. Thus we find a lesson on value--that how much something means to a person may be measured by how much they are willing to give for it. God has placed a high value on fallen humanity; hence:

> "The Lord is disappointed when His people place a low estimate upon themselves. He desires His chosen heritage to value themselves according to the price He has placed upon them. God wanted them, else He would not have sent His Son on such an expensive errand to redeem them." The Desire of Ages p.668

When, in the guilt of sin, one feels that Jesus cannot accept them --His death on cross is the strongest argument that He will. He longs to reclaim and restore the fallen. This is why "there [is] more joy in heaven over one sinner who repents than over ninety-nine just persons who need no repentance" (Luke 15:7). Jesus is excited by the idea of restoring all who come to Him, He will freely receive and restore you.

> "He will accept you just as you are; for there is no hope of your becoming better until you come to Jesus for pardon and sanctifica-

tion. Mourning and weeping will not purify you. You may mourn your life away in unbelief and in bitterness of soul; but the power to cleanse the vilest sinner is vested wholly in Him who can save unto the uttermost." Bible Echo, July 2, 1894

Surrender Again

In Chapter 1 (*Consecration*) we went through the fundamental point for abiding in Christ: surrender. Our oneness with Christ comes at the moment when we, like Paul, are "crucified with Christ." We experience Christ in us when we wholeheartedly pray the prayer "not my will by yours be done."

Should it happen that one falls into sin by taking their focus off Christ, there must be another wholehearted surrender to His will. This is essential for receiving and experiencing His forgiveness and His power to renew the heart.

"God requires the entire surrender of the heart, before justification ([forgiveness]) can take place." Selected Messages, book I, p. 366

Remember the "right action of the will" spoken of in the previous chapter. When we choose God's will, because it is His will, He enables us to carry out His will. Christ's highest purpose is to renew His image in us by removing our sins; this is why He "gave Himself for our sins."

In submitting our lives to God's will again, we are to also submit our sins to Him. Note, then, the following precious promise:

"The moment we surrender ourselves to God, believing in Him, we have His righteousness." The Review and Herald, July 25, 1899

The moment we make the choice to give ourselves to Christ, and surrender to His will, it is at that moment that Jesus gives us His righteousness! He does not delay to pardon us. When we present ourselves as offerings to God, at that moment we are "transformed by the renewing of the mind." (Romans 12:1-2). Thus, God's call to us is:

"My son, give Me your heart, and let your eyes observe My ways." Proverbs 23:26 NKJV

Moving Forward

When the apostle Paul shares his testimony with the church at Galatia, he recounts how he "persecuted the church of God beyond measure and tried to destroy it" (Galatians 1:13). Before becoming a Christian, Paul was among the worst persecutors of the early church. The Bible speaks of how Paul (previously referred to as Saul) "made havoc of the church, entering every house, and dragging off men and women, committing them to prison" (Acts 8:3). He was really bad news for the early Christians.

Although Paul hated Jesus and Christianity, even taking part in the murder of Stephen (one of the first deacons), he was still able to share this testimony:

> *"It pleased God, who separated me from my mother's womb and called me through His grace, to reveal His Son in me, that I might preach Him among the heathen." Galatians 1:15-16 NKJV*

Although Saul was the kind of man he was, hating Jesus with a fiery passion, it still pleased God to extend His grace to him. The same compassion that God showed to Paul is also available today to every individual who will accept it.

After his conversion, Paul was given the task of travelling from place to place to witness for Jesus. Even though Paul had the ugly past that he did, God still used him as fully as though he had never sinned.

> *"Even those whose course has been most offensive to Him He freely accepts. When they repent, He imparts to them His divine Spirit, and sends them forth into the camp of the disloyal to proclaim His mercy. Souls that have been degraded into instruments of Satan are still, through the power of Christ, transformed into messengers of righteousness and are sent forth to tell how great things the Lord hath done for them and hath had compassion on them." The Ministry of Healing p.99*

In his service to Christ after conversion, Paul would meet with the same Christians that he formerly tried to destroy. These encounters most likely served as constant reminders of what he had done to the

Christians before his conversion.

In a letter to the Philippians, Paul further recounts how he was zealously "persecuting the church" (Philippians 3:6) before his conversion. He had fully acknowledged his past life. Rather than mourning over his past, however, notice how he speaks of his experience afterwards:

"Brethren, I do not count myself to have apprehended; but one thing I do, forgetting those things which are behind and reaching forward to those things which are ahead, I press toward the goal for the prize of the upward call of God in Christ Jesus." Philippians 3:13-14 NKJV

When Paul writes about the "one thing" that he does in order to progress in his spiritual journey, he notes the importance of "forgetting those things which are past." This includes the guilt and the shame of past sins.

The apostle's attitude of intentionally "forgetting" was not to treat his past life as though it never happened, but rather to testify that those things were behind him. Although he could not change his past sins, he knew that Jesus had changed him; he now focussed on moving forward. Paul's experience is an example for us also. He writes:

"This is a trustworthy saying, and everyone should accept it: 'Christ Jesus came into the world to save sinners'—and I am the worst of them all. But God had mercy on me so that Christ Jesus could use me as a prime example of His great patience with even the worst sinners. Then others will realise that they, too, can believe in Him and receive eternal life." 1 Timothy 1:15-16 NLT

Although the scars and the memories of our sins may remain, like Paul, we are to "forget" the things which are past and press forward. This is especially necessary when we cannot change the past. Like the apostle Paul, we can hold on to the promise given to those who abide in Christ, that:

"If any man be in Christ, he is a new creature: old things are passed away; behold, all things are become new." 2 Corinthians 5:17

Go and Sin No More

One morning, while Jesus was teaching in the temple, the Jewish religious leaders interrupted His presentation:

> "The teachers of the law and the Pharisees brought in a woman caught in adultery. They made her stand before the group and said to Jesus, 'Teacher, this woman was caught in the act of adultery. In the Law Moses commanded us to stone such women. Now what do you say?' They were using this question as a trap, in order to have a basis for accusing Him." John 8:3-6 NLT

On that morning, the woman had been caught "in the very act" of adultery (John 8:3, KJV). Nothing is said about the man with whom she was caught, but she is taken. Perhaps with little time to fully dress up, the woman was brought into the crowd where Jesus was. With her accusers pushing her through the street and shouting accusations at her, one can only imagine her humiliation.

In bringing this woman to Jesus, these religious leaders were trying to find something against Him. They figured that Jesus would be trapped by either contradicting the Law of Moses, or by placing Himself above the Roman authorities in condemning her to death. Either way, Jesus seemed cornered. As the scenario continues:

> "Jesus bent down and started to write on the ground with his finger. When they kept on questioning Him, He straightened up and said to them, 'Let any one of you who is without sin be the first to throw a stone at her.' Again He stooped down and wrote on the ground." Verse 6-8 NLT

Jesus does not answer their request directly, but His wise response is enough to settle the matter. When the accusers looked to see what Jesus had written, they were "convicted by their conscience, [and] went out one by one, beginning with the oldest even to the last." (Verse 9)

When Jesus said "he who is without sin" should throw the first stone, the woman must have thought that her life was surely over. Whatever Jesus wrote on the ground, however, made it clear to the woman's accusers that they were not without sin. They were so ashamed of what they saw that each of them left without even saying a word.

When they were left alone, Jesus says something to the adulterous woman which would change her life forever:

"When Jesus had raised Himself up and saw no one but the woman, He said to her, "Woman, where are those accusers of yours? Has no one condemned you?" She said, "No one, Lord." And Jesus said to her, "Neither do I condemn you; go and sin no more." John 8:10-11 NKJV

Jesus speaks to her with the hope that she can live a new life. Notice that before he tells her to sin no more, he first reassures her of how He feels about her; "neither do I condemn you," He says. As immoral as this woman's life was, Jesus does not express any disapproval of her. Without lessening the wrongness of her sin in any way, Jesus reassures her of His favour towards her. He does not condemn her, He is not angry at her, her relationship with God is restored.

"In His act of pardoning this woman and encouraging her to live a better life, the character of Jesus shines forth in the beauty of perfect righteousness. While He does not palliate ([or make light of]) sin, nor lessen the sense of guilt, He seeks not to condemn, but to save." The Desire of Ages p.462

Jesus' expression of how He does not condemn the woman was very crucial for her experience. In order for her to be able to carry out the instruction to "go and sin no more," she firstly needed to be certain that Christ accepts her. The knowledge of God's love would be the fuel for her loving obedience.

It is important for us to know that Jesus loves us and does not condemn us--regardless of how fallen one may have been. When we have confidence in God's compassion towards sinners we are encouraged to depend on Him enough to receive His power for obedience.

"Though all are precious in His sight, the rough, sullen, stubborn dispositions draw most heavily upon His sympathy and love; for He traces from cause to effect. The one who is most easily tempted,

and is most inclined to err, is the special object of His solicitude ([His special care])." Education p.294

"To go forward without stumbling, we must have the assurance that... an infinite pity [will] be exercised towards us if we fall" Sons and Daughters of God p.154

Jesus specially calls to those who have fallen so that He may take away all our sins. Although one may be guilty and without an excuse (like the adulterous woman), Jesus wants us to be assured that He does not condemn us. We can boldly come to Him. When we realise how much He cares for the fallen, we can rely on Him for all the grace that we need in order to "go and sin no more."

Promises to the Fallen

"If you feel yourself to be the greatest of sinners, then Christ is just what you need; for He is the greatest of Saviours." Bible Echo, July 2, 1894

"Mercy is still extended to the sinner. The Lord is calling to us in all our wanderings: 'Return, ye backsliding children, and I will heal your backslidings' (Jeremiah 3:22). The blessing of God may be ours if we will heed the pleading voice of His Spirit." Testimonies, vol. 5 p.177

"The divine Teacher bears with the erring through all their perversity. His love does not grow cold; His efforts to win them do not cease. With outstretched arms He waits to welcome again and again the erring, the rebellious, and even the apostate." Education p.294

"Create in me a clean heart, O God, and renew a steadfast spirit within me. Do not cast me away from Your presence, and do not take Your Holy Spirit from me. Restore to me the joy of Your salvation, and uphold me by Your generous Spirit." Psalm 51:10-13 NKJV

Questions on Chapter 9

Are those who abide in Christ at risk of falling into sin? (p.208)

How does Jesus feel about me if I fall? (p.211, 226, 231)

What causes Christians to fall into sin? (p.209)

What must I do if I have fallen into sin? (p.213-214, 217, 228-231)

What if I feel like I cannot approach God because of my sin? (p.226, 214)

What steps should I take to get back up after falling? (p.217-228)

How does God work to get me back on track if I fall? (p.215, 219)

Why should I confess my sins? (p.217)

What happens when Jesus forgives me? (p.218)

How can I repent and turn from my sins? (p.219)

What is the difference between true and false repentance? (p.222)

What if I sinned knowingly, can God still forgive me? (p.223)

My sin was so bad, would Jesus still be willing to receive me? (p.223, 226)

How can I move past the guilt of past sins? (p.229-230)

Can I live a changed life? (p.231)

10

The Experience You May Have

This Experience May be Yours

God is Faithful to Keep You

Do Your Part

The Path of the Just

No Matter What

This Experience May be Yours

Abiding in Christ, being one with Him moment by moment, is the only right experience for the Christian to have. God's intention for us has never been anything less. In putting this material together the hope has been to establish that thought in the minds of all who read.

> "It is not a casual touch with Christ that is needed, but it is to abide with Him. He called you to abide with Him. He does not propose to you a short-lived blessedness that is realised occasionally through earnest seeking of the Lord and passes away as you engage in the common duties of life. Your abiding with Christ makes every necessary duty light, for He bears the weight of every burden.
>
> He has prepared for you to abide with Him. This means that you are to be conscious of an abiding Christ, that you are continually with Christ, where your mind is encouraged and strengthened." In Heavenly Places p.55

Such an experience may be ours--an intimate and continuous connection with Jesus. This experience is to be, on Earth, that which will be continued in heaven. We may have a foretaste of heaven by having a close walk with Jesus. A conscious experience of abiding in Christ is what every Christian can and must have.

This May Be Your experience, Today

Being vitally connected to Christ is not something that must be experienced only at the day of one's conversion or perhaps at some future stage in one's Christian journey. On the contrary; we are to realise that Jesus has called us to abide to Him *now*. We may have a constant communion with our Saviour today. This can be a present reality for all His true followers.

> "For God says, 'At just the right time, I heard you. On the day of salvation, I helped you.' Indeed, the 'right time' is now. Today is the day of salvation." 2 Corinthians 6:2 NLT

Today is the day of salvation; the experience of being in Christ moment by moment can and should be our experience, your experience, today. The fact that Jesus has given the invitation to abide and dwell in Him makes it a possibility. It is our privilege to enter that experience at this present moment. The deciding factor is in whether one will consecrate their life, in trust, to Christ.

> "Do not stand outside of Christ, as many professed Christians of today. To 'abide in me, and I in you' is a possible thing to do, and the invitation would not be given if you could not do this. Jesus our Saviour is constantly drawing you by His Holy Spirit, working with your mind that you will abide with Christ... The blessings He bestows are all connected with your own individual action. Shall Christ be refused? He says, 'Him that cometh to me I will in no wise cast out' (John 6:37). Of another class He says, 'Ye will not come to me, that ye might have life' (John 5:40)." In Heavenly Places p.55

> "Behold, I ([Jesus]) stand at the door, and knock: if any man hears my voice, and opens the door, I will come in to him, and will sup with him, and he with Me." Revelation 3:20

Consider this thought; Jesus constantly stands ready to give you an experience of abiding in Him. He waits patiently at the door of our hearts and there never needs to be a delay in having Him abide in us. All that He waits for is the permission to enter. With that being the case, nothing should restrict anyone from experiencing "Christ in you, the hope of glory." (Colossians 1:27)

This May Be Your Experience, Continually

> "As you therefore have received Christ Jesus the Lord, so walk in Him." Colossians 2:6 NKJV

The way in which we are to walk, to continue and advance in fellowship with Christ, is no different from how we first entered into the connection with Him; "for without Me," He says, "you can do nothing."

We enter into fellowship with Jesus by receiving Him through a total submission of all that we have and are to Him (See Chapter 1: *Consecration*). In like manner, the vital connection may be ours continually, through a *continued* submission of our lives to the will of God.

This point is important to note. As we have received Christ Jesus, through submitting wholly to His will, even so are we to walk in Him--by surrendering to Him moment by moment thereafter.

"Have you, have I, fully comprehended the gracious call, 'Come unto me'? He says, 'Abide in me,' not Abide with Me. 'Do understand My call. Come to Me to stay with Me.' He will freely bestow all blessings connected with Himself upon all who come to Him for life. He has something better for you than a short-lived blessedness that you feel when you seek the Lord in earnest prayer. That is but as a drop in the bucket, to have a word with Christ. You are privileged with His abiding presence in the place of a short-lived privilege that is not lasting as you engage in the duties of life... Will anxiety, perplexity, and cares drive you away from Christ? Are we less dependent upon God when in the workshop, in the field, in the market-place?... The Lord Jesus will abide with you and you with Him in every place." In Heavenly Places p.55

Wherever one may be, the Christian is privileged to have the abiding presence of Christ through His Holy Spirit. Through a continual dependence on Him in faith--whether at work, school or leisure--in every place, we may be conscious of abiding in Him. Jesus' desire for His earth-born children is nothing short of this.

God is Faithful to Keep You

Keep note of what Jesus has said; "I am the vine, you are the branches. He that abides in Me, and I in him, the same brings forth much fruit: for without Me you can do nothing." Apart from Jesus we can do nothing; and that includes abiding in Him. Our hope of remaining constantly connected with Him depends on our co-operation with Him.

"For by Him all things were created, that are in heaven, and that are in earth... All things were created through Him, and for Him: and He is before all things, and in Him all things consist." Colossians 1:16-17 NKJV

Jesus is the creator of all things and He faithfully upholds all that He has created. We are His by creation as well as by redemption; thus, we too--as "new creatures" in Christ--are to be "kept by the power of God through faith unto salvation" (1 Peter 1:5).

Jesus is the one that is "able to keep you from falling, and to present you faultless before the presence of his glory with exceeding joy" (Jude 1:24).

Take note of the thought that if there is one thing that Jesus is able to do, it is to keep you from falling. This is why it is important to place our full dependence on Him, and not on ourselves. "I am the vine," He says, "and you are the branches." Therefore, abide in Him.

Do Your Part

"To go forward without stumbling, we must have the assurance that a hand all-powerful will hold us up, and an infinite pity be exercised toward us if we fall." Sons and Daughters of God, p.154

To maintain a walk with Christ, without stumbling, we must have the assurance of His ability to hold us up--even with the same power that He uses to hold up the planet. This is with an all-powerful hand.

Christ's death on the cross gives the assurance that this power is available to us. By His death, Jesus provided for us a full guarantee of all the power that heaven can provide for our deliverance from sin.

"When we were yet without strength, in due time Christ died for the ungodly. (Romans 5:6). Thus it could be said in heaven that through the death of Jesus, "now is come salvation, and strength" (Revelation 12:10).

For this reason, our focus and confidence must be firmly fixed on Jesus and what He has accomplished for us by His death on the cross. Our part is to maintain a firm and constant dependence on Him, trusting Him to be the one who holds us up.

By Beholding Him, Diligently

Jesus, by His all-powerful hand, is able to hold us up and to keep us from falling into sin. How we can lay hold of His hand of strength is outlined in the Bible:

"Looking carefully [unto Jesus] lest [you] fall short of the grace of God. Hebrews 12:15 NKJV

Jesus does not intend that anyone should fall from grace. This is why He calls us to do our best to ensure that we "look diligently" (Hebrews 12:15 KJV) to Him. To "look" unto Jesus really means to *"consider* Him that endured such contradiction of sinners against Himself" (Hebrews 12:3a). This is to be done diligently, "lest you become weary and discouraged in your souls" (Hebrews 12:3b).

By "beholding as in a glass the glory of the Lord, [we] are changed into the same image, from glory to glory, even as by the Spirit of the Lord." (2 Corinthians 3:18)

Through daily communion with Christ by prayer, Bible study, meditation, faithfulness in duty and service to others, we "behold (as in a glass) the glory of the Lord." This is our part: to constantly behold Jesus in order to advance in the walk with Him. As long as one's life remains submitted to the will of Christ with each step of advance, the Christian will go from one point of glory to the next.

Surrender at Every Point

To maintain the experience of abiding in Christ, the same whole-hearted consecration we made to Christ at the beginning of our walk with Him must be made at every point of test to which He may bring us. "I die daily" says Paul (1 Corinthians 15:31), and we are to daily make the full and renewed surrender of our lives to Christ also.

"To follow Jesus requires wholehearted conversion at the start, and a repetition of this conversion every day." Christ Triumphant p.122

"I am crucified with Christ: nevertheless I live; yet not I, but Christ liveth in me: and the life which I now live in the flesh I live by the faith of the Son of God, who loved me, and gave himself for me." Galatians 2:20

Paul was able to confidently testify of his experience of having Christ live in Him. This was because Paul knew that his life was fully surrendered to the revealed will of God. With boldness he could say "I am [*presently*] crucified with Christ".

"You are to maintain this connection with Christ by faith and the continual surrender of your will to Him; and so long as you do this, He will work in you to will and to do according to His good pleasure. So you may say, 'The life which I now live in the flesh I live by the faith of the Son of God, who loved me, and gave Himself for me' (Galatians 2:20)." Steps to Christ p.62-63

The same way Jesus fully submitted to His Father's will at the cross, saying "not my will, but Yours" (Luke 22:42), even so Paul had fully submitted His will to Christ. This is what it means to be crucified with Christ and this must be a daily experience.

It is when we are thus "crucified with Christ", through the moment by moment surrender of our lives to Him, that we can also testify of abiding in Christ, and He in us.

When we choose God's way above our own, in faith, we can say with Paul, "I am fully surrendered to Christ; thus I live, yet not I but Christ lives (and abides) in me"

The Path of the Just

When we consider communion with Christ as a walk, we get to make sense of the idea of Christian growth and progress. It must ever be remembered that a relationship with Jesus is not a destination, but rather a step-by-step journey in which Jesus walks right by the believer's side at every step. Consider Solomons words:

"The path of the righteous is like the light of dawn, which shines brighter and brighter until full day." Proverbs 4:18 ESV

The path of the righteous, those who live by faith, is one where there is a daily growth in grace. The path shines brighter and brighter, while one goes forward from glory to glory.

As we daily study God's word, He may reveal things about our characters which we may have never knew were there. It may be an un-Christlike temper, or any self-centered practice. In His love for us, Jesus reveals these things to us so that we may surrender those habits and practices to Him.

As we surrender to God's will daily, He provides us with all the power that we need in order to overcome the wrong habits we have cultivated. Thus we may progress on the path of light, daily revealing more and more of His likeness.

> *"For the commandment is a lamp; and the law is light; and reproofs of instruction are the way of life." Proverbs 6:23*

The path of the just shines day by day as God reveals more of His will to us. God's will is revealed through His word and His law. This is the lamp that brightens the path of light. Each day, as we commit to the fuller revelation of His will, as we "turn at His reproof", the path continues to shine brighter and brighter.

> *"If you turn at my reproof, behold, I will pour out my spirit to you; I will make my words known to you." Proverbs 1:23 ESV*

This is how we may receive a continued supply of the Holy Spirit. As God continues to reprove and correct us in His love, and we respond positively to His reproof, He continues His work on our hearts. When we learn God's will daily, and submit our lives to it, our experience of abiding in Him will grow more and more intimate.

Complete but Continual

It is precious to note that while the path of the righteous is a journey and a walk, all along the way the path continues to remain a path of light. As we remain submitted to God's will, we remain on the righteous path with each step that we take.

The path of righteousness continues to go brighter and brighter as one continues to grow. There is continued progress, yet at every stage it is still a path of light, with no darkness at all. Thus:

> *"At every stage of development our life may be perfect; yet if God's purpose for us is fulfilled, there will be continual advancement. Sanctification is the work of a lifetime. As our opportunities multiply, our experience will enlarge, and our knowledge increase. We shall become strong to bear responsibility, and our maturity will be in proportion to our privileges." Christ's Object Lessons p.65*

To grow in grace means that your life is completely surrendered to Christ with each step of growth. While that is the case, there may be parts of one's character which they may not have considered while making the initial surrender: it may be a lifestyle practice, or how one uses their time & money for example. The closer one gets to Christ the more one sees the defectiveness of their own characters, but this is a sign of growth.

> "The closer you come to Jesus, the more faulty you will appear in your own eyes; for your vision will be clearer, and your imperfections will be seen in broad and distinct contrast to His perfect nature. This is evidence that Satan's delusions have lost their power; that the vivifying influence of the Spirit of God is arousing you." Steps to Christ p.64

Over time, as Jesus brings previously unnoticed defects to mind, it is an invitation to make a complete surrender of the life to His will again. So the surrender we make to Christ becomes a continual, daily-repeated experience.

In his book on living a life of victory over sin, Thomas Davis expresses this idea thus:

> "Genuine surrender is a complete thing, at the time it is made, as far as we know. But there are things in the life that will need to be surrendered that we do not see immediately; unrecognized habits, unconfessed or unrestituted dishonesty, forgotten transgressions, as yet unrevealed weaknesses. But when Jesus brings them to our attention we say, "Yes, Lord, I see what I must do, even though I did not know about it, or had forgotten it. I shall do what You want." How to Be a Victorious Christian [sp]

Although Jesus reveals habits and character traits that we may have never suspected we had, it is in no wise to say that one was less consecrated to Christ yesterday.

> "The Christian life is one of daily surrender, submission, and continual overcoming. Every day fresh victories will be gained. Self must be lost sight of, and the love of God must be constantly cultivated. Thus we grow up into Christ. Thus the life is fashioned according to the divine model." Lift Him Up p.65

This is why we are not to be too discouraged when we see things about our characters that we had not been aware of until now. Realising these is a sign of growth and an evidence of the Holy Spirit's working. Recommitting to a wholehearted consecration to God makes way for further growth. Thus, like David, we too can pray the prayer:

"Search me, O God, and know my heart: try me, and know my thoughts: and see if there be any wicked way in me, and lead me in the way everlasting." Psalm 139:23-24

This is how we may wholeheartedly abide in Christ, today. Our lives may be wholly in His hands and we may walk with Him, even from glory to glory. Our surrender to Him is complete and yet it is continuous as we continue to choose His will--the more He reveals it to us. As we do this, Jesus not only accepts our offering, but daily fashions and molds the character to becoming more like His own. This is what it means to grow in grace.

"Being confident of this very thing, that He who has begun a good work in you will complete it until the day of Jesus Christ." Philippians 1:6 NKJV

No Matter What

Submitting wholeheartedly to the will of God also comes with trusting Him wholeheartedly--trusting that He will take care of the life that has been submitted to Him. Such a trust is the kind that remains consistent, even through adversity.

For many individuals, circumstances often create a separation from a consistent walk with Christ. Trials experienced leave behind a burden of discouragement and doubt. While this may be the case, it is still within our reach to not be separated from Christ. As a personal God and friend, Jesus longs to be intimate with us.

I once attended the wedding of a friend who, in his wedding vows, echoed sentiments which closely relate to the commitment one should make when uniting with Jesus. The statements were made: "forsaking all others…for better or worse, for poorer or richer, in sickness and in health… 'till death do us part."

These are the expressions of a heart that has counted the cost of its commitment, and prizes the object of its love as being far more superior than any other thing. This is how Christ regards us and this is how we, in response, are to walk with Him.

When we resolve to seek Jesus above all else, with a "no matter what" attitude, circumstances will have little influence in moving us from abiding in Him. This is what commitment means. Notice the determination in the psalmist's words:

> *"I have set the Lord always before me: because He is at my right hand, I shall not be moved."* Psalms 16:8

Those who are never moved are those who have determined to set the Lord before them always. These are those who, like Enoch, walk with God. Jesus *Himself*, as a person, must be the centre of our experience, above every other earthly blessing.

At times, as a Christian, one needs to ask themselves some pointed questions: "Would I still be willing to follow God if things do not go my way?" "Would I still be faithful to Him, even in poverty, or distress?" "Will I trust God even if I were to lose out on work, or school or other earthly possessions?" These questions are raised so that we may carefully consider whether or not communion with Christ is first and foremost on the list of personal priorities.

Taking the above into consideration, we may still be certain that while we set our hearts on Christ and on abiding in Him, He will not neglect to provide for all our needs. This is because when we are willing to give ourselves wholly to Christ, whatever may come, we are placed in a position to receive from Him everything that concerns our highest good. Jesus takes care of what has been committed to Him; when we dedicate our lives to His will, we may be confident of that fact. Notice God's promise:

> *"Because he hath set his love upon Me, therefore will I deliver him: I will set him on high, because he hath known My name. He shall call upon Me, and I will answer him: I will be with him in trouble; I will deliver him, and honour him. With long life will I satisfy him, and show him My salvation."* Psalms 91:14-16

This was the experience of Enoch--He remained in Christ because he knew that "God is a rewarder of them that diligently seek *Him*" (Hebrews 11:6). Jesus Himself, and not merely the benefits that He comes with, is to be the main purpose of what we diligent seek after.

"Seek the Kingdom of God above all else, and live righteously, and He will give you everything you need." Matthew 6:33 NLT

We must honestly ask ourselves the question: "Do I really want to abide in Christ?" And "am I willing to seek Him with all my heart?" This is the decision we must make, to abide with Christ *no matter what*. Those who possess this kind of attitude who are most securely kept in Christ.

Whatever Trials May Come

It may be important to note again that a life of communion with Christ is not a life free of difficulty and trial. At times, in order to perfect the characters of those who are abiding in Him, God will allow His people to face trails; and this is how He refines us.

"For He is like a refiner's fire and like launderers' soap. He will sit as a refiner and a purifier of silver; He will purify the sons of Levi, and purge them as gold and silver, that they may offer to the Lord an offering in righteousness." Malachi 3:2-3 NKJV

Jesus, as our High Priest, is refining and purifying His people. The same way gold and silver are purified by fire in a furnace, the furnace that God uses to purify us are the difficulties that He sometimes allows us to go through. He says:

"I have refined you, but not as silver is refined. Rather, I have refined you in the furnace of suffering." Isaiah 48:10 NLT

For this reason, we must daily resolve in our hearts never to turn away from our walk with Christ, regardless of the trials that should come. Trials are, more than often, Christ's methods of making us more like Himself. Thus:

"Whatever may betide, lay hold upon Him with steady, persevering confidence." The Ministry of Healing p.513

Whatever may arise, whatever may be the opposing circumstance;

whatever feelings of unworthiness, doubt, guilt or shame; whatever disappointment you may face, you can still maintain a steady confidence in Jesus as a personal safeguard.

> *"At times a deep sense of our unworthiness will send a thrill of terror through the soul, but this is no evidence that God has changed toward us, or we toward God. No effort should be made to rein the mind up to a certain intensity of emotion. We may not feel today the peace and joy which we felt yesterday; but we should by faith grasp the hand of Christ, and trust Him as fully in the darkness as in the light."* Counsels for the Church, p.57

The difficult experiences that God allows us to go through are all designed to be a blessing to us. When we see them as such, we will thank God for them. We may remember the counsel from the apostle James:

> *"My brethren, count it all joy when you fall into various trials, knowing that the testing of your faith produces patience. But let patience have its perfect work, that you may be perfect and complete, lacking nothing."* James 1:2-4 NKJV

Commit to being Christ's follower, through whatever trial may come, and repeat this dedication of yourself to Him every day. Making such a daily commitment is an essential condition for walking with God. Choose to be wholly given to Christ today and forever, remembering that "without Me, [Jesus says] you can do nothing."

Those Who Turned Back

Most people are familiar with the pain of losing a friend. Sometimes, because of growing differences, friends may find themselves not being as close as they once were. Very few people, however, know the pain of being left by the majority their closest friends, all at once. This was the case, at some point, in Jesus' experience.

> *"From that time many of His disciples went back, and walked no more with Him."* John 6:66

While speaking in a crowded synagogue, Jesus made it plain that He had not come to offer the pleasures of an earthly kingdom. He made it clear to His audience (of Jews and disciples) that He came to offer *Himself* as the source of eternal life (John 6:22-59). He had pointed out that following Him comes with making a total commitment to Him and the sacrifice of every other selfish pleasure. This is the kind of relationship Christ offers.

> *"Christ had spoken a sacred, eternal truth regarding the relation between Himself and His followers. He knew the character of those who claimed to be His disciples, and His words tested their faith. He declared that they were to believe and act upon His teaching. All who received Him would partake of His nature, and be conformed to His character. This involved the relinquishment of their cherished ambitions. It required the complete surrender of themselves to Jesus. They were called to become self-sacrificing, meek and lowly in heart. They must walk in the narrow path travelled by the Man of Calvary, if they would share in the gift of life and the glory of heaven." The Desire of Ages p.391*

After Jesus had laid out the plain conditions of walking with Him, "many, therefore, of his disciples, when they had heard this, said, this is an hard saying; who can hear it?" (John 6:60). These are the ones who turned away from following Jesus; they left Him.

The disciples who turned their backs on Jesus were seeking Him for the benefits that they thought He came with, not because they truly wanted *Him*. This is why they were not willing to make the complete surrender of themselves to Him. So it is with many who profess Christ today. If we are to walk with Christ, and to not turn back as these disciples did, we must seek Jesus for who He is.

To Whom Shall We Go?

In contrast to those who left Jesus, there were those who still remained and chose to abide with Him. What made the difference?

Many are willing to walk with Jesus up to a certain point, until they are called to surrender some cherished object to Him. This was the case with the disciples who left. They were willing to follow Jesus as long as it was comfortable to do so.

> *"Then Jesus said to the twelve, 'Do you also want to go away?' But*

248

Simon Peter answered Him, 'Lord, to whom shall we go? You have the words of eternal life. Also we have come to believe and know that You are the Christ, the Son of the living God.'" John 6:67- 69 NKJV

The disciples who remained with Christ realised that all that they really needed could be found in Him. These disciples understood that everything else, aside from Christ, was vanity. Even after their season of failure and disappointment at Jesus' crucifixion, these same disciples still chose to follow Him. When we realise that life is meaningless apart from Christ, like Peter, we will find it pointless to turn away to any other.

Not a Joyless Service

I recall a discussion I once had with a lady at whose home I, and a few of my peers, had stayed one weekend. She asked a question that many may relate with. She asked, "Why does it seem that newly converted Christians seem to take religious things more seriously, and have more zeal in service and witnessing, than we who may have been Christian for years?"

The only thought that came to mind at the time was the simple idea that those who have had the unfortunate experience of living a worldly lifestyle, and have since come to know Christ personally, know by experience that a worldly lifestyle has nothing of real value to offer. While it is true that there are a number of additional factors, one of the greatest is the fact that the individuals described have learned, by experience, the emptiness of a life outside of Christ.

Realising the hollowness of a life without Christ, however, is not an experience that is only limited to those raised outside of good Christian homes. One of the greatest blessings is to be raised in a home where Jesus is at the center. Those raised in such a home are spared from many scars and regrets.

The point here is that true contentment is found by those who, like Peter, have realised that there is none to whom they can go to apart from Jesus. This is meant to be the experience of all who submit to Jesus--not only to those without a religious background:

"For He satisfies the longing soul, and fills the hungry soul with goodness." Psalm 107:9 NKJV

Abiding with Christ, and surrendering the life to Him, provides the highest satisfaction to the deepest longings of our hearts. This is why God calls us to wholeheartedly surrender to Him. Christ does not invite us to a life of joyless service. A life surrendered to the will of God is not one of miserable slavery; on the contrary.

"[God] satisfies the longing soul," that is to say that all that the heart most truly and deeply longs for is satisfied by a fellowship with Him. His invitation for us to abide in Him is made knowing that He is our highest source of peace, and this may be experienced when we submit wholly to the life He offers.

"Would that all who have not chosen Christ might realise that He has something vastly better to offer them than they are seeking for themselves. Man is doing the greatest injury and injustice to his own soul when he thinks and acts contrary to the will of God. No real joy can be found in the path forbidden by Him who knows what is best and who plans for the good of His creatures. The path of transgression is the path of misery and destruction." Steps to Christ p.46

"The young lions do lack and suffer hunger; but those who seek the Lord shall not lack any good thing." Psalms 34:10 NKJV

Peter's question is a question to us also; to whom shall we go? Who has offered us the peace and rest that Jesus has promised? He offers these freely and He invites us to put our trust in Him.

Without Me You Can Do Nothing

Peter had clearly understood just what it meant to have Christ as the centre of his life. Jesus is everything to the believer, and this is why Peter could later write in his epistle that:

"[God's] divine power has given to us all things that pertain unto life and godliness, through the knowledge of Him who called us by glory and virtue." 2 Peter 1:3 NKJV

Through a knowledge of Jesus--through an intimate connection with Him--we have access to all things essential for life and for godliness. Jesus not only meets our spiritual needs, but is the ultimate provider for every aspect of our lives. Hence Christ says:

> *"Abide in Me, and I in you. As the branch cannot bear fruit of itself, unless it abides in the vine; neither can you, except you abide in me. I am the vine, you are the branches: he who abides in me, and I in him, bears much fruit: for without Me you can do nothing." John 15:4-5 NKJV*

Without Jesus, we can do nothing. This is true is every sense of the phrase; in spiritual and in temporal matters. It is a great source of hope to understand this idea, because it means that the opposite is also true:

> *"I can do all things through Christ who strengthens me." Philippians 4:13 NKJV*

As much as we cannot abide in Christ apart from His aid, it is just as true that we *can* do all things through Him. In every aspect of the Christian journey, God has called us to consciously place our full dependence on Him. When we do so, we can take Him at His word that the fruits of righteousness will be seen in our lives.

> *"It is not the capabilities you now possess or ever will have that will give you success. It is that which the Lord can do for you. We need to have far less confidence in what man can do and far more confidence in what God can do for every believing soul. He longs to have you reach after Him by faith. He longs to have you expect great things from Him. He longs to give you understanding in temporal as well as in spiritual matters. He can sharpen the intellect. He can give tact and skill. Put your talents into the work, ask God for wisdom, and it will be given you." Christ's Object Lessons p.146*

Now and Forever

Communion with Christ, a present and intimate fellowship with Him, is our most essential preparation for spending eternity with Him. It is those who abide with Christ on Earth that will be translated when He comes at His second advent. Note Enoch's example:

"Enoch walked with God; and he was not, for God took him." Genesis 5:24

"By faith Enoch was translated that he should not see death; and was not found, because God had translated him: for before his translation he had this testimony, that he pleased God." Hebrews 11:5

Enoch was translated as one who walked with God. We may consider him as an example of those who will be translated at Jesus' return. Those who will be redeemed from the earth at the second coming will have had the same experience of a continual, uninterrupted communion with Jesus, as did Enoch. Hence John's words:

"And now, little children, abide in Him; that, when he shall appear, we may have confidence, and not be ashamed before Him at His coming." 1 John 2:28

Too many, who profess to be anticipating Christ's coming, look forward to the day with anxiety and worry; but this does not have be the case. It is our privilege to look forward to that day with a holy confidence because of our experience of abiding in Him.

While it is true that many will wail because of Jesus on the day of His return (Revelation 1:7), those who have walked with Him here will not be ashamed. "And *now*, little children, abide." When we have the experience of communion with Christ *today*, then the second coming will be a "blessed hope" to us. This is the experience God wants each of His followers have.

Reader, Jesus is coming soon, and we may be prepared for that day. We may have an experience of being intimately connected with Him here and now. For this reason, make a conscious choice to abide in Christ daily, moment by moment--even today.

"You must make a daily, personal consecration of all to God; you must daily renew your covenant to be His wholly and forever." Our High Calling p.124

252

Questions on Chapter 10

Is it really possible to abide in Christ? (p.236)

When can we experience the joy of abiding in Christ? (p.236)

How long am I to abide in Christ? (p.237)

Am I to abide in Christ through my own strength? (p.238, 250)

How important is it to surrender in order for me to abide in Christ? (p.240)

How often should I surrender myself to Christ? (p.240, 242)

How can I grow in my Christian journey? (p.242)

Does surrendering to Christ mean slavery and a joyless service? (p.249)

How do I maintain the experience of abiding in Christ? (p.239-240)

What is my part when it comes to communion with Christ? (p.239-240)

What if I get tired of the Christian walk? (p.244, 246-248)

What do I do when the walk gets difficult? (p.246)

Am I joyfully anticipating the second coming of Christ? (p.251)

About the Author

Simon Ngubeni is an author, speaker and architect, raised in Boksburg, South Africa. He holds a Masters in Architecture from the University of Johannesburg and, while still a student, co-founded Mission Cohort, a non-profit organization aimed at impacting communities through church planting.

While still in university, Simon authored and published *Communion with Christ - A Handbook on How to Abide in Him.*

With a passion for sharing life-transforming Biblical principles to aid others in fulfilling their God-given purpose, Simon has spoken on various subjects at conferences, training camps, churches and universities across Africa.

Simon serves as chairperson of Mission Cohort and, in his free time, enjoys reading, writing and exercise. Simon continues to share thoughts and insights in audio and blog format on his website: www.simonngubeni.co.za

www.ingramcontent.com/pod-product-compliance
Lightning Source LLC
Chambersburg PA
CBHW060232050426
42448CB00009B/1399